Business Knowledge for IT in Retail Banking

A complete handbook for IT Professionals

UK Edition

Essvale Corporation Limited
The Forward Thinking Company

bizle
PROFESSIONAL SERIES

Essvale Corporation Limited
63 Apollo Building
1 Newton Place
London E14 3TS
www.essvale.com

This is the first edition of this publication.

All rights reserved
Copyright © Essvale Corporation Ltd, 2007

Essvale Corporation Ltd is hereby identified as author
of this work in accordance with Section 77 of the
Copyright, Designs and Patents Act 1988

Requests to the authors should be addressed to:
permissions@essvale.com.

This book is sold subject to the conditions that it shall not,
by way of trade or otherwise, be lent, resold, hired out or
otherwise circulated without the author's or publisher's prior
consent in any form of binding or cover other than that in
which it is published and without a similar condition including
this condition being imposed on the subsequent purchaser.

A CIP record for this book is available from the British Library

ISBN (10-digit) 0955412420
ISBN (13-digit) 978-0955412424

This publication is designed to provide accurate and authoritative
information about the subject matter. The author makes no representation,
express or implied, with regard to the accuracy of the information
contained in the publication and cannot accept any responsibility or
liability for any errors or omissions that it may contain.

Cover design by Essvale Design Team
Design and typesetting by Boldface, London EC1
Printed by Lightning Source Ltd, Milton Keynes

Preface

This is another publication in the Business Knowledge for IT Professionals series that will include other exciting topics in the near future. The motivation for this publication is to bridge the gap in business knowledge between IT professionals and the business community. Readers will find that the topics covered in this publication will get them up to speed with the knowledge they need to work in the competitive world of Retail Banking.

This publication covers topics including an overview of Retail Banking, the major players, recent trends and so on. After reading this publication, readers will have the confidence to talk to the business users within Retail Banking, knowing that they have a firm grasp of what the business is all about.

The types of IT professional that would benefit from the knowledge in this publication include software developers, development managers, test analysts and managers already working in Retail Banking or those that would want to pursue a career in this industry. Other types are project managers, database administrators, support analysts and business analysts that are already working in Retail Banking or would like to cross over from other industries.

Undergraduates, postgraduates and those who have recently graduated can also benefit greatly from reading this publication.

Finally, readers should please note that some of the data published is not up to date. The data in this publication is meant to be a guideline to the state of the markets and not a basis for extrapolation or forecasting.

Acknowledgements

Essvale Corporation Limited would like to thank all the authors and publishers of all materials used in compiling this publication. Also thanks to all the respondents to the research carried out to justify writing this publication.

We would like to acknowledge Edward Taylor of Misys, Melinda Mattei of Chordiant, Manjinder Jaul and Catherine Atkinson of Temenos, Louise Jude of Ifex Solutions, Mark Johnson and Wesley Samways of APAK Group, Jacqueline Roose and Robert Kaar of Oracle Corporation, Mike Hutchinson of Voca, and John Randles of Polar Lake. Also Alastair Bathgate of Blue Prism, Kate Smyth of JD Marketing, Sandra Quinn and Chris Duncan of APACS, Paul Saunders, Amit Dua and Navin Rammohan of Infosys, Ramesh Ramakrishnan of Polaris Software Labs and Carol Woodcock and Roger Keel of CreditAction.

Our thanks also go to Pat Winfield of Bookworm Editorial Services, Paul Crittenden of Boldface Typesetters, Sara Fisher and Daniel Page of LightningSource, Barney Lodge of Lodge Consulting, Ruth Tellis of Palgrave Macmillan, Eric Dobby of Financial World Publishing, the staff of Amazon worldwide and the staff of City Business Library, London. Thanks for supporting Bizle Professional Series thus far.

Contents

	Preface	iv
	Acknowledgements	v
	Contents	vii
	Introduction	x

1.	**Overview of Retail Banking**	1
	Introduction	2
	Definition of a Retail Bank	2
	Types of Retail Bank	2
	Definition of Money	3
	The Banking Code	4
	Service Offerings in Retail Banking	5
	Distribution Channels in Retail Banking	5
	Banker–Customer Relationship	6
	How Banks Generate Revenue	7
	Global Retail Banking Industry	8
	Overview of the UK Retail Banking Sector	9
	Retail Banking in the UK in Recent Years	11
	Internet Banks	11
	Peer-to-Peer Banks	12
	List of Some Retail Banks	14

2.	**Product Types in Retail Banking**	15
	Introduction	16
	Accounts	16
	Investments	25
	Cards	26
	Loans	28
	Mortgages	29
	Insurance	30
	Travel Services	30
	Bank Codes	31
	Rates	34

3.	**The Business Environment in Retail Banking**	35
	Introduction	36
	Players in Retail Banking	38
	The Competitors	38
	Allied Organisations	40

4.	**Trends in Retail Banking**	52
	Introduction	53
	Introduction of SEPA	53
	Introduction of Faster Payments	54

Sarbanes-Oxley Act of 2002		56
Basel 2 Accord		56
AML/KYC		58
Growth of Social Lending		59
Emergence of Financial Supermarkets		61
Deconstruction of Banking Services		61
Remote Card Authentication		62
Use of High Technology Tools to Identify Prospects		63
Use of Customer Analytics		64
Growth of Online Banking		65
Recent Card Industry Initiatives		66
Rise of Islamic Retail Banking		69
The Introduction of SWIFT for Corporates		69
Identification of the Unbanked Retail Market		72
Onset of Banking in Virtual Worlds		73
The Growth of Buy-To-Let		73
Cheque Truncation		74
Introduction of Paperless Bank Statements		75
Popularity of Mobile Payment		76
5.	**Account Opening in Retail Banking**	78
	Introduction	79
	Background to Account Opening Systems	79
	Theoretically Underpinnings	80
	Account Opening Process	86
	Personal Banking Process	86
	Events Occurring During the Life of the Customer	92
	Account Management	93
6.	**Lending in Retail Banking**	95
	Overview of Lending	96
	Types of Lending	96
	Principles of Lending	96
	Data on Lending	98
	Collateralisation	98
	The Cost of Credit	99
	Economics of Credit	101
	Granting Credit Decisions	101
7.	**Payments in Retail Banking**	114
	Introduction	115
	Manual Payment Methods	115
	Electronic Payment Methods	119
8.	**Common Systems Used in Retail Banking**	136
	Introduction	137

	Industry Dynamics	137
	Increasing Importance of Banking Platforms	138
	Conclusion	148
9.	**IT Projects in Retail Banking**	**149**
	Introduction	150
	List of Common IT Projects	150
	Automation of Business Processes	150
	Use of Screen Scraping for Data Migration	158
	Conclusion	169
10.	**Common Terminology Used in Retail Banking**	**170**
	Introduction	171
	List of Terms	171
11.	**Methodologies, Skills and Tools**	**179**
	Introduction	180
	Overview of Mainframe Technologies	180
	Methodologies	180
	Business and Systems Analysis Methods	186
	Testing Methods	187
	Tools	187
	Common IT Skills Required	188
	Mainframe Skills	190
	Soft Skills	192
12.	**The Future**	**194**
	The Future	195
	Adopting Globalisation Strategies for Growth	195
	Introduction of a New Technology Paradigm	196
	Rethinking the Business Model	198
	Outsourcing and Offshoring	199
	Adoption of Customer Retention Strategies	200
	Growth of Bank Retailing	201
	Intensification of KYC Initiatives	202
	Conclusion	204
	Appendix	**205**
	Bizle Business Credit Card Summary Box	206
	Calculation of Simple and Compound Interest Rates	208
	Useful Websites	210
	Useful Job Boards	212
	Specialist Recruitment Agencies	213
	Bibliography	214
	Index	**218**

Introduction

Professionalism is a now a word associated with IT, but this has not always been the case. IT has traditionally been seen as a support function of many organisations, but not anymore. The strategic value of IT is underscored by the presence of IT representatives on the board of directors. Chief Information Officers are now accorded the same significance with regard to the progress of an organisation as Chief Finance Officers and Chief Operating Officers.

The British Computer Society (BCS) and other parallel societies the world over share our vision of the model IT professional who is as comfortable with technology as he/she is with business. Even governments have recognised the criticality of IT to the success of business, which leads to growth of their economies. To make this happen, the level and standard of professionalism should be raised to a parity with established professions like law, engineering and pharmacy.

Against this backdrop, the BCS launched a programme, Professionalism in IT, in 2005. The programme has had the backing of other professional institutions and trade bodies and of leading members of the IT and business communities drawn from both the public and private sectors.

The need for an IT profession with a greater emphasis on business focus cannot be overstated, especially in a constantly changing regulatory environment. Regulations like SEPA, Basel2, and Sarbanes Oxley require changes to IT systems and as such organisations require business-aligned IT staff on board to ensure timely compliance. Moreover, customer expectations are getting higher as service providers in every industry sector are facing stiff competition from existing companies as well as new entrants.

A recent global survey of senior IT and business leaders by the Economic Intelligence Unit revealed that 69% of the respondents believe that, by 2009, IT's primary role will shift from driving cost efficiency to enabling revenue growth. Interestingly, if the analysis is limited to Chief Executive Officers and Board members, the percentage increases to 83%.

Why is Business Knowledge of Retail Banking important?

IT professionals need to have knowledge of the retail banking industry for the following reasons:

- Retail banks need high-quality systems to ensure the smooth operation of the business.
- Business-critical IT projects in retail banks are executed to very aggressive deadlines and hence there is little provision for training IT professionals in the rudiments of the business justifications and implications of these projects.

- Errors in the output from IT systems can lead to fines from regulators.
- The future of IT demands that professionals have the specific industry knowledge to implement and support business-critical systems.
- The trends in the IT industry are changing the profession into a more specialised than generalised profession.
- Purely technical roles are increasingly outsourced to developing countries where labour costs are more competitive.
- To foster greater understanding between IT and the business with the benefit of creating more harmonised, multi-disciplinary project teams that will compress project timelines.

In recent years, there has been a notable transformation in retail banking; many of the retail banks are now involving themselves more and more with Investment Banking activities, which are making careers within Retail Banking IT an increasingly attractive option. What was once considered a dull and slow-paced sector of the finance world is now dynamic and diverse.

Retail banking has faced a number of challenges in recent years, such as competition from e-banking and the encroachment of other players – such as supermarket chains – on the personal finance sector.

In the face of these challenges, retail banking has modernised; there are now fewer branches and a greater number of automated services.

Despite the changing face of the sector, maintaining, managing and extending both existing and new customer relationships in a competitive market is a higher priority for retail banks than ever before.

The benefits of an IT career in retail banking are enormous. Permanently employed IT professionals in retail banking can earn an average of 10%[1] more than their counterparts in other industries. Contractors, on the other hand, can earn up to 30–40% more than their counterparts in other industries.

The topics discussed in this publication were carefully selected to ensure a wide coverage of the theoretical underpinnings of the Retail Banking discipline as well as to demonstrate the alignment with IT. Business processes and tasks in the day-to-day activities of banking are mirrored in the associated business processes in IT systems, hence the necessity for the IT professional to have a firm grasp of these activities.

This publication is targeted at the UK market and as such the practices described are primarily UK focused. However, as the financial markets are global in nature, some aspects are discussed in a global context.

---

1 Estimate based on the outcome of indpendent research.

Overview of Retail Banking

This chapter introduces the concept of retail banking, the different types of retail banks and the distribution channels.

Introduction

Retail banking is essentially mass-market banking where individual customers use high-street branches of larger commercial banks like Lloyds TSB. Retail banks offer services including savings and current accounts, mortgages, personal loans, debit cards, credit cards and so forth. Most retail banks are profit-making, private enterprises. The retail banking sector is one of the most competitive in the financial services sector.

Retail banking differs from wholesale banking, i.e. business to business banking, in that the transactions are between the customer and the bank as opposed to counterparties in wholesale banking. The relationship between the bank and the customer is usually referred to as "debtor and creditor", "principal and agent" or "mortgagor and mortgagee", depending on the services on offer by the bank to the customer.

Retail banks also offer services such as commercial lending to mid-market businesses, which is usually referred to as "business banking" as opposed to "personal banking" to individuals. Lending to organisations is an intensive activity, with banks carefully analysing the financial condition of business clients to determine the level of risk in each loan transaction.

Over the last decade, the definition of retail banking with regard to the high-street element and image has been redefined by the advent of the internet and brand stretching. The internet banks such as **Smile** are making inroads into the retail banking sector in the UK as are the big retailers like Tesco and Sainsbury's. The traditional high-street retail banks are also facing stiff competition to their product offerings such as credit cards and personal loans from the likes of MBNA.

Definition of a Retail Bank

The definition of a retail bank is relatively straightforward. The following is a definition from a financial dictionary:

"A Retail bank is a bank that caters for ordinary individuals and small businesses, as distinct from large corporations. Retail banking operations offer deposit facilities, lend money, transfer funds and are prepared to deal in relatively small amounts."

Types of Retail Bank

There are different types of retail bank and they can be categorised as:

- Commercial bank: this is a term used to describe a conventional retail bank like Barclays and Lloyds TSB.

- Postal saving bank: this type of bank is associated with the postal system. These banks have their niche market in the personal banking arena where they target people who do not pay income tax, i.e. young people, pensioners and some married women. An example in the UK is Girobank plc.
- Private bank:[2] this type of retail bank focuses solely on high net worth individuals. A well-known bank is Coutts which is the banker of the Queen of England and the Royal Family.
- Offshore banks: these are usually private banks that are located in offshore countries, i.e. outside the country of residence of the depositor, such as the Channel Islands and Bermuda, and are characterised by low taxation and regulation.
- Building societies: these are essentially retail banks that are governed by special regulations that limit their functions. Building societies are mutual organisations that traditionally lend money to customers wanting to purchase a home. The most well-known building society is the Nationwide.
- Mortgage banks: these are former building societies that converted to banks, as viewed by experts in the industry.
- Islamic banks:[3] these are banks that were formed to cater for Muslims. The concepts that govern the operations of these banks are centred on the Islamic dictates that forbid interest payment to customers.

Definition of Money

Money is something we are all used to; we refer to money in casual ways like "big money" or "silly money". Nevertheless, in order to fully understand the context in which we use the term "money", it should be accurately defined. Here are a few definitions of money:

"A generally accepted medium for the exchange of goods and services, for measuring value, or for making payments." (WallStreetwords)

"A medium of exchange that is authorised or adopted by a domestic or foreign government and includes a monetary unit of account established by an intergovernmental organisation or by agreement between two or more nations." (Investopedia.com)

Functions and Qualities of Money
In this section, functions and qualities of money will be listed. The following money functions are the most widely accepted and are usually denoted by the acronym SUMS:

---

[2] Private banking is outside the scope of this book; it is discussed in *Business Knowledge for IT in Private Wealth Management*.
[3] Islamic retail banking is discussed in detail in *Business Knowledge for IT in Islamic Finance*.

- **S**tandard of deferred payment;
- **U**nit of account;
- **M**edium of exchange;
- **S**tore of value.

The qualities of money, not be confused with functions, are those qualities that must be possessed by assets if they are to function efficiently as money. These qualities are listed below:

- **S**tability of value and scarcity;
- **P**ortability;
- **U**niformity;
- **D**ivisibility;
- **R**ecognisability;
- **A**cceptability;
- **D**urability.

The acronym SPUDRAD can be used to remember these qualities.

The Banking Code

Customers have contractual relationships with their banks, building societies and card issuers. These relationships are mainly governed by the terms and conditions for the accounts and by current legislation.

In 1991, the Banking Code was introduced to give personal banking customers added protection. It covers current accounts, personal savings (including cash ISAs) and credit cards. The Banking Code is voluntary and sets minimum standards for the manner in which banks and building societies treat their customers. There have been six revisions to the code since it was introduced, i.e. it is now in its seventh edition.

Business customers with an annual turnover of up to £1 million have been given similar added protection by the Business Banking Code since 31 March 2002. A revised edition became effective in March 2005.

The code stipulates how customers should be dealt with in such areas as:

- account opening;
- lending;
- confidentiality;
- notification of changes;
- handling financial difficulty;
- information on interest rates;
- marketing of services.

The bigger retail banks and their subsidiary/sister companies in the UK such as Lloyds TSB and Royal Bank of Scotland Group have signed up to both the banking and business banking codes. There are other banks operating in the UK, however, that have not signed up the codes and these include the Post Office and Liverpool Victoria Banking Services.[4]

Mortgages, investments, general insurance, pensions and life assurance are regulated by the Financial Services Authority.

Service Offerings in Retail Banking

Service offerings in retail banking are dependent on the type of bank and the country where it operates or originated from. Nevertheless, the following are some of the services that retail banks offer:

- opening and maintaining current accounts for individuals and businesses;
- opening and maintaining savings accounts for individuals and businesses;
- taking deposits from customers with the above accounts;
- cashing cheques;
- extending loans to individuals and businesses;
- issuing debit cards, cashpoint cards and credit cards;
- offering financial advisory services;
- effecting money transactions such has wire transfers and banker's drafts;
- selling of home insurance;
- selling of traveller's cheques.

Distribution Channels in Retail Banking

Technology is a major enabler for retail banks to create new delivery channels for services to their customers. Many banks are also looking to cut costs by offshoring, outsourcing or a combination of both.

- **Branch networks** – retail locations where retail banks provide a wide range of face-to-face services to their customers. Banks are increasingly under competitive pressure to control cost as margins on their services are getting slimmer. As a consequence, there has been a reduction in the branch network.
- **Automated teller machine** – a computer and telephony device that retail banks use to provide services such as cash withdrawal, account balance checking and even mobile phone credit top-up, usually in easily accessible public spaces without the need for human interaction. The steady increase in the importance of the ATM is in concert with the reduction of the branch network. The extension of the ATM network has helped bridge the gap created by the closure of some branches.

---

4   Source: www.bankingcode.org.uk/faq.htm.

- **Post Office banking** – banking services are offered through the national Post Office network, especially to areas that are not well served by branches. In the UK, for instance, the role of the Post Office as a banking distribution channel has been expanding as it is the largest cash handler in the country.
- **Telephone** – retail banks offer services over the phone and the range of services is called telephone banking. This entails customers calling dedicated lines that connect to call centres.
- **Internet banking** – this channel allows retail bank customers to perform transactions over the internet through a bank's secure website. Transactions performed on these websites include payments, transfers and balance requests.
- **Digital TV banking** – a channel for retail banks to offer services similar to those offered over the internet.
- **Mobile banking** – a channel that hasn't taken off as expected for offering services to customers via the mobile phone network. However, there are initiatives afoot from both retail banks and mobile phone operators to promote this medium as an alternative banking channel.
- **Corporate electronic banking** – this channel is similar to internet banking but is more demanding as it is targeted at companies. The security and performance requirements are far greater as there are more transactions and multiple users per site than in internet banking.

Banker–Customer Relationship

In order to analyse the banker–customer relationship, it is necessary to define a customer in the banking sense. A customer can be defined as a person or organisation that has a current account or similar account with a bank. It is worth noting that the customer–banker relationship starts when the application for an account is accepted by the bank.

In the retail banking world, the term customer does not apply to people who have accounts with the credit-card division of the bank but do not have a current or savings account with the bank. These people are referred to as "cardholders". For example, a customer that has an account with Barclaycard, but does not have a current or savings account with Barclays Bank, is not a customer of Barclays Bank.

From a legal standpoint, as stated above, the banker–customer relationship can assume different formats including the following:

- **Debtor and creditor** – this is the main type of relationship between banker and customer. A customer is a *creditor* when they deposit a sum of money with a bank and since they are owed the money by the bank, then the bank is the *debtor*. If the customer borrows money from the bank, they are the *debtor* and in this situation the bank is the *creditor*.

- **Principal and agent** – when a customer writes a cheque to pay a sum of money from an account held at a bank, they are the *principal*. The bank, in carrying out the instruction to pay the money to a third party (payee), is the *agent*.
- **Mortgagor and mortgagee** – a customer that mortgages their home to the bank as collateral for a loan is the *mortgagor* while the bank is the *mortgagee*.

Bank Duties to the Customer

The following are some of the key duties of banks to their customers:

- honour cheques written out by customers as long as the amount is within their credit balance or overdraft limit and there is no stop;
- provide an accurate statement within a reasonable time;
- credit customers' accounts with money and cheques received;
- exercise care when giving advice to customers;
- alert customers to any fraud involving cheque forgery;
- maintain secrecy in relation to information about a customer account;
- give adequate notice to the customer when closing an account in credit;
- pay back credit balances on demand as long as the customer has demanded this in writing at a branch during the official opening hours;
- advise customer of overseas fund transfers in their account;
- be consistent and adhere to the usual course of business.

Customers' Duties to the Bank

Customers' duties to the bank include:

- being careful when writing cheques;
- ensuring that they make out cheques only when they have sufficient funds in their accounts;
- ensuring that cheques and cash are used in accordance with their conditions of use;
- allowing banks to use deposits as they deem fit;
- paying the interest and commission that the bank stipulates;
- getting in contact with the bank in the event they discover forgery of their cheques.

How Banks Generate Revenue

The traditional business of banking involves taking in deposits, which are then packaged and offered as loans to customers. The retail aspect of banking is the large-volume, low-value end of this business activity whereby deposits taken from individuals, and small and medium-size businesses, are loaned to the same customer groups.

Retail banks generate revenue by profiting from the differential between the level of interest they pay for deposits and other sources of funds, and the level of interest they charge in their lending activities. This difference is known as the spread between the cost of funds and loan interest rate.

The needs and strength of loan customers and their cyclical nature have historically been determining factors in profitability from lending activities. However, in recent times, banks have placed more emphasis on transaction fees, primarily loan fees, and also service charges on a range of deposit activities and ancillary services including insurance, wire transfers and investments, in order to satisfy their investors' demand for a more stable revenue stream. Nevertheless, lending activities still account for the bulk of a retail bank's income.

Global Retail Banking Industry

The global retail banking landscape is shaped by important forces such as growth markets in China and the new EU member states, as well as Basel 2 and developments in mergers and acquisitions.

The global market is dominated by the retail banking arm of universal[5] banks such as Citigroup and there are also companies that offer retail banking services that are part of a diversified group of companies. As a result, it is difficult to assess the size of the global retail banking industry.

Taking a wider view of the market, some interesting statistics on the global banking industry are as follows:

- The worldwide assets of the largest 1,000 banks as at 2005 were $63.8 trillion, which represents a 10.5% growth on the previous year.
- As a result of consolidation in the banking sector, the share of the largest ten banks worldwide increased from 14% in 1994/5 to 19% in 2004/5.
- In 2004/5, Citigroup was by far the largest bank in the world for the sixth year running, both in terms of tier-one capital and assets.
- EU banks' share was 50% as of the end of 2005.
- The USA has the most banks and branches (7,540 and 75,000 respectively) as of the end of 2005.
- UK banking sector deposits, the third largest in the world, reached $4.6 trillion.

---

[5] Universal banks are financial services companies that engage in a wide range of banking services, including retail, private and investment banking.

Table 1.1 Largest banks in the world by Tier One Capital

Universal Bank	Headquarters	Tier One Capital
Citigroup	USA	74.4
JP Morgan Chase & Co.	USA	68.6
HSBC Holdings	UK	67.3
Bank of America Corp	USA	64.3
Credit Agricole Groupe	France	63.4
Royal Bank of Scotland	UK	43.8
Mitsubishi Tokyo Financial Group	Japan	39.9
Mizuho Financial Group	Japan	38.9
HBOS	UK	36.6
BNP Paribas	France	35.7
Bank of China	China	34.9
Santander Central Hispano	Spain	33.3
Barclays Bank	UK	32.2
Rabobank Group	Netherlands	30.8
Sumitomo Mitsui Financial Group	Japan	30.4

Source: The Banker

Overview of the UK Retail Banking Sector

The UK retail banking sector is dominated by a handful of players, the industry leader being Royal Bank of Scotland Group with a 20% market share in terms of total assets as of 2004. This dominance is as a result of the largest takeover in British banking history, the takeover of NatWest in 2001 in a £21 billion deal. The merger swelled the ranks of RBS, making it a bigger player than established players like Barclays.

Other major takeover deals in recent times were the takeover of Abbey National Group by Santander Central Hispano in 2004, and in the internet banking sector Egg, the largest standalone internet bank, was taken over in 2007 by Citigroup, Halifax and Bank of Scotland, merged to form HBOS.

Organisation	% Value
The Royal Bank of Scotland Group	20.0
Barclays plc	17.0
HBOS plc	14.0
HSBC Bank plc	9.0
Lloyds TSB Group plc	8.0

Source: Euromonitor

According to Euromonitor International, the market for commercial banking (including retail banking) is forecast to grow by 8% from 2007 to 2009, to reach a value of £1,915 billion (US$3,482 billion). Other interesting statistics about the UK retail banking industry include:

- The main retail banks provide over 125m accounts, clear 7bn transactions a year and facilitate 2.3bn cash withdrawals per year from their network of over 30,000 free ATMs as of 2007. [6]
- In 2005, 24 million personal customers registered to access their bank accounts online.
- 42 million are registered to access their accounts by telephone as of 2005.
- There were 11,025 bank branches as of 2004.
- There were 49,000 ATMs as of 2004.[7]
- 75% of ATMs are located at branches.
- The value of ATM cash withdrawals per inhabitant in 2004 was £2,712 (€4,000).[8]
- There were over six million cheques issued every day in 2004.[9]

In recent times, new entrants into the retail banking sector like internet banks, ING and Intelligent Finance, have been threatening the dominance of the major players. A number of non-bank firms have also made forays into retail banking and these entrants can be categorised into the following:

- **Supermarket banks**: notable examples are Tesco and Sainsbury's, already major players in the retailing business but now providing retail banking services alongside their retail product lines and doing so through a wide network. Their current business model involves partnering with existing banks but in the future it could change into more of an independent model. Tesco, for instance, offers personal loans and Sainsbury's bank is authorised to receive deposits.
- **Other non-bank firms**: these firms provide retail banking services without a branch network, unlike the traditional banks. Their services are offered via remote banking delivery channels. Virgin, a conglomerate, now offers banking services, and other examples include insurance companies Scottish Widows and Prudential.

One of the factors responsible for the increasing number of entrants into this sector is the relatively low entry and exit costs. For example, the supermarket banks like Tesco already have a branch network used for delivery of their other retail products.

---

6 Source: British Bankers' Association.
7 Source: World Retail Banking Report 2006.
8 Source: World Payments Report 2006.
9 Source APACS.

Retail Banking in the UK in Recent Years

The trend before the middle of the 1990s was for mergers involving banks and building societies to result in the loss of one or more of the brands involved. However in recent times, preservation of brand loyalties, for obvious reasons, has been the norm. An example of a merger where the brands of the banks involved have been preserved is Lloyds and TSB in forming Lloyds TSB.

A number of new entrants into the retail banking sectors in the 1990s intensified competition in the industry. As seen earlier, these new entrants included supermarkets, insurance companies and internet banks.

The 1990s also saw the introduction of internet facilities to cater for customers' banking needs. The facilities introduced initially offered basic functionality but as more customers were drawn to them, the functionality was gradually enhanced.

In 1997, a number of changes were introduced that affected the retail banking sector. These changes included:

- building societies becoming mortgage banks;
- the Bank of England being empowered with changing the interest rates with a view to achieving the Government's monetary policy;
- the announcement of the creation of the Financial Services Authority (FSA), which opened its doors in 1998.[10]

Other notable events in the British retail banking industry during the 1990s included the sensational collapse of the Bank of Credit and Commerce International (BCCI), which left 80,000 depositors out of pocket and had debts exceeding £10 billion.[11]

The retail banking landscape today is very competitive, with banks offering innovative services to retain and attract customers. The credit card and personal loan sub-sectors are also witnessing stiff competition between the established players and the emerging players, which can be anything from bookstores such as Amazon to broadcasters like Sky, backed obviously by finance houses such as MBNA.

Internet Banks

In the retail banking sector, internet banks, or online banks as they are sometimes known, can be categorised into three types: standalone; integrated and combined. Each of these three types offers different services and varied supporting channels.

---

10 http://info.worldbank.org/etools/library/229958
11 www.telegraph.co.uk/money/main.jhtml?xml=/money/2004/06/29/cnbcci29.xml

The building of a substantial customer base is paramount for the internet banks, given their lack of high-street presence. As a consequence, they have had to adopt numerous entrance strategies to establish a customer base. Standalone banks have adopted a strategy of aggressive pricing while traditional banks (integrated and combined) have been targeting their existing customers; it is becoming an important factor for them.

The market leaders in the true internet banks, i.e. the standalones, in the UK are as follows.

Internet Bank	Parent Bank
Intelligent Finance	Halifax
cahoot	Abbey
smile	Co-operative Bank
Egg	Citigroup (Prudential)
first direct	HSBC

An interesting concept by Datamonitor describes the strategies that can be employed in the online banking market:

- develop a standalone or "pure play" internet bank with a separate eBrand;
- develop internet services but integrate them with existing services;
- combine both strategies, i.e. develop a standalone internet bank as well as providing integrated internet services.

Some banks in the UK employ each of the three strategies and examples are shown below.

Standalone Internet Bank	Integrated Internet Bank	Standalone and Integrated
Egg	Barclays	Halifax
smile	NatWest	Abbey
cahoot	Woolwich	HSBC
Intelligent Finance	Nationwide	Royal Bank of Scotland
first direct	Lloyds TSB	The Co-operative Bank
Virgin One	Alliance & Leicester	Bank of Scotland

Source: Datamonitor

Peer-to-Peer Banks

What is a Peer-to-Peer Bank?
Peer-to-Peer banking is a revolutionary business model in retail banking that allows individual members to complete financial transactions on the internet with one another by using an auction-style process that lets members offer

loans for a specific amount and at a specific rate. Peer-to-Peer allows for the elimination of the middleman, i.e. the traditional retail banks, in the lending process.

Overview of Peer-to-Peer Banking
Peer-to-Peer banking seeks to combine some elements of peer-to-peer principles with social networking to allow users to be both bankers and banking customers. The internet, pioneering technologies such as Web 2.0 and the dynamic pricing technologies pioneered by eBay have been enablers for the successful adoption of this business model in the banking world.

The concept of peer-to-peer banking is viewed by industry experts as a radical shake-up of the traditional retail banking business model and is potentially a disruptive innovation in financial services. It has been suggested that the hyper-efficient operations of these banks, with few employees and no costly real estate, could force changes to established banks.

Notable examples of peer-to-peer banks are Zopa in the UK and Prosper in the USA.

How Peer-to-Peer Banks Work
The dynamics of Peer-to-Peer banking are relatively straightforward. Unlike traditional banks that take deposits and make of use of the money at their discretion, peer-to-peer banks are essentially financial exchanges that bring together borrowers and lenders of money.

Using the Zopa business model as a guideline, the following is an illustration of how peer-to-peer banks work:

- Borrowers are assigned a credit score such as A*-, A-, B- or C based on a credit scoring system.
- Lenders with money to loan out make offers to these borrowers for different tenors and at their desired interest rate.
- Borrowers assess the rates on offer and either accept them or hold out for a more favourable rate and tenor.
- The banks put risk controls in place to minimise default rates. For example, a cap may be placed on the amount of the loan extended to an individual borrower. Legally binding contracts are also required between borrowers and lenders.
- Direct debits are also mandatory to ensure the smooth paying back of loans. In the event of default, a collection agency is used for the recovery of the loan in the same way as a traditional bank.
- Borrowers are charged a transaction fee while lenders are charged an annual service fee.

Downside to Peer-to-Peer Banking
Peer-to-peer banking is a concept that has enormous potential but as it contests the conventions of mainstream banking that have been followed for eons, there are obvious downsides to it. Disadvantages of peer-to-peer banking include:

- Credit risk is borne by the lender.
- No value-added services attached to loans process are available to borrowers.
- Lender may not have instant access to their cash.
- Lenders and borrowers wanting to get the best rate can be difficult to marry up.
- Dearth of cross-selling opportunities available to a mainstream financial institution.

List of Some Retail Banks

Some financial service firms that have retail banking subsidiaries and companies that offer retail banking services in the UK include:

- HSBC
- Citigroup
- Alliance and Leicester
- Bradford and Bingley
- Northern Rock
- HBOS
- Barclays
- Lloyds TSB
- Co-operative Bank
- GE Capital Bank
- Britannia Building Society
- Marks and Spencer Financial Services plc
- Goldfish®
- Abbey
- MBNA Europe Ltd
- Capital One Bank
- American Express Bank Ltd
- Standard Life Bank Limited
- Habib Bank AG Zurich

Product Types in Retail Banking

This chapter contains a discussion of the types of products on offer at retail banks. These include current accounts, loans, insurance and investment products.

Introduction

In recent times, product types in retail banking have transcended the traditional products, i.e. loans and deposits, normally associated with the business model. Banks are extending their product range to include insurance, financial planning and even road assistance cover.

In this chapter, different product types will be discussed. However, given the wide spectrum of product types on offer and the variation in offerings from bank to bank and from country to country, this list of products is by no means exhaustive.

Accounts

Investopedia defines an account as *"an arrangement by which an organisation accepts a customer's financial assets and holds them on behalf of the customer at his or her discretion"*.

In order to understand the types of account that retail banks offer, the different types of customer and their reasons for wanting to operate an account are listed. The types of customer include:

- married couples in employment
- students
- single people in employment
- graduates
- minors
- people with Islamic religious beliefs
- pensioners.

Given the mass-market nature of retail banking, demographic changes have a direct impact on the demand for certain types of account. For example, if divorce rates are on the increase, there will be increase in demand for single accounts and less so for joint accounts. Similarly, if there are more students getting into university or it is the time universities resume a new academic year, then there will be an increase in demand for student accounts.

Specifications for accounts of fictitious retail bank BizEast will be used as illustrations throughout this chapter.

Current Accounts
A current account, as opposed to a savings account (see below), is an account that customers use for running their day-to-day finances. The accountholder is able to make cash withdrawals from the account using an Automated Teller Machine (ATM) and has access to overdraft facilities.

Payments can be made from the account through cheques, direct debits, direct credits and standing orders. It is also used for receiving payments such as wages and can be overdrawn in the event payments are made beyond the available credit in the account.

Retail banks issue statements of account periodically that detail the credits to and debits from the account. These statements are either sent to the accountholder's registered address or are viewable online.

Standard accounts

These are accounts, targeted at customers in employment, which are straightforward and usually provide benefits such as:

- free banking, i.e. no charge for everyday transactions;
- telephone banking;
- online banking;
- a debit card;
- a cheque book;
- authorised overdrafts, usually at a pre-approved AER;[12]
- offering credit interest paid at a specified AER.

The following is an example of the specification for a standard account.

BizEast standard account

Account Credit Interest Rate

Standard account   Interest paid annually

	AER%	Gross%	Net%
Above £1	0.1	0.1	0.08

Overdraft Rate

Overdraft amount	AER variable	Monthly nominal
Under £1,000	18.86%	1.45
£1,000–£4,999	17.95%	1.38
£5,000+	15.93%	1.23

Premium accounts

These are current accounts that are preferred by new and existing customers that require additional benefits to a standard account as well as savings. They usually attract annual fees and the benefits include:

---

[12] Stands for Annual Equivalent Rate and illustrates what the interest rate would be if interest was paid and compounded once a year.

- gadget insurance, i.e. MP3 players, mobile phones, PDAs;
- a credit card;
- an interest-free overdraft up to a predetermined limit;
- travel insurance;
- preferential overdraft and personal loan rates;
- identity theft protection;
- breakdown cover;
- discounts on car and home insurance;
- discounts on goods at specified retailers.

Overdrafts are usually offered at pre-approved rates and credit interest is paid at a specified AER. These accounts are tiered according to the interest-free overdraft limit and annual charges that are on offer.

The specification below is an illustration of a premium account.

BizEast Opal account
Monthly account charge: £10
Interest-free overdraft: £400

Account Credit Interest Rate
Opal account — *Interest paid annually*

	AER%	Gross%[13]	Net%[14]
Above £1	0.1	0.1	0.08
£1,500–5,000	4.25	4.17	3.34

Overdraft Rate

Overdraft amount	AER variable	Monthly nominal[15]
Under £1,000	18.86%	1.45
£1,000–£4,999	17.95%	1.38
£5,000+	15.93%	1.23

There are other premium accounts, Ruby and Topaz, with monthly account charges of £15 and £20 respectively.

---

13 The contractual rate of interest payable before deduction of income tax at the rate specified by law.
14 The rate of interest which would be payable after allowing for the deduction of income tax at the rate specified by law.
15 An unadjusted rate.

Student accounts

These current accounts are designed for students of higher education institutions such as universities and colleges. The benefits are similar to those of the standard account plus other benefits such as:

- an interest-free overdraft with a higher limit than a standard account as students are relatively poor;
- discounts on travel;
- cash gifts;
- free driving lessons;
- student advisory services.

For most student accounts, overdraft limits are increased as customers progress through their courses of study.

BizEast student account

Account Credit Interest Rate
Standard account   *Interest paid annually*

	AER%	Gross%	Net%
Above £1	0.1	0.1	0.08

Initial £200 interest-free overdraft on account opening.
 Up to £2,000 interest-free overdraft available on request depending on year of study:

- Year 1: up to £1,000
- Year 2: up to £1,250
- Year 3: up to £1,500
- Year 4: up to £1,750
- Year 5 and above: up to £2,000.

Overdrafts above the interest-free limit and up to a maximum of £3,000 will be charged interest at a rate of 1.22% per month (15.6% AER variable).

Graduate accounts

These current accounts are designed for recent graduates of higher education institutions such as universities and colleges. The benefits are usually similar to those of the student account plus other benefits such as:

- low cost loans;
- discounts on holidays and flights, plus commission-free travel money;
- the option of a further education loan.

BizEast graduate account

Account Credit Interest Rate
Standard account   *Interest paid annually*

	AER%	Gross%	Net%
Above £1	0.1	0.1	0.08

Further Education Loan Rate

Total loan amount	*£6,000*
Study period	4 years
Repayment holiday	48 months
60 monthly payments over 5 years	5 years
60 monthly payments over 5 years	£183.76
Total interest paid	£5,025.60
Total amount paid	£11,025.60
Interest rate % per month	0/79%
APR%	**9.90**

Young persons' accounts

These are accounts suited to the under-19s age group. Their features are designed to cater for the needs of this age group. The features and benefits include:

- no transaction charges;
- a debit card for over-16s;
- an ATM card for under-16s;
- a competitive interest rate.

The following is an example of the specification for a young person's account.

BizEast young persons' account

Account Credit Interest Rate
Standard account   *Interest paid annually*

	AER%	Gross%	Net%
Above £1	3.30	3.25	2.60

Cash accounts

A cash account is a basic current account that is targeted at people with no credit history and those that have been unbanked. It is usually *without* the following benefits:

- a cheque book;
- an overdraft;
- credit interest;
- loans.

International accounts

These are foreign-currency current accounts suited to applicants living and working outside their normal countries of residence. They are usually offered by offshore banks or offshore divisions of traditional high-street retail banks and the benefits on offer include:

- a selection of accounts in at least three different currencies;
- debit cards in the designated currencies;
- a cheque book in the currency of the country of residence;
- interest payments without deduction of tax;
- international private insurance.

Specialist services

Retail banks offer specialist services alongside the management of current accounts for their customers and these services include:

- stopping payment instructions, e.g. cheques;
- preparing banker's drafts;
- special cheque clearance;
- same-day transfer of funds via CHAPS;
- use of ATMs abroad;
- overseas point-of-sale transactions;
- supplying duplicate records, e.g. copy of bank statements.

These services attract fees which are extra sources of revenue for banks.

Business Accounts

Business accounts are accounts provided by banks for their business customers. They differ from personal accounts in that the transactions are of a business-to-business nature, usually more varied and involving more management effort.

Business accounts for start-ups

Banks have an appreciation of the pitfalls of starting up a business. To this end, they offer current accounts that are designed for start-up businesses to help them overcome the teething problems they might encounter in the early stages of growth of their business ventures. This type of account offers benefits including:

- waiver of charges on cash payments and deposits for a moratorium[16] up to 18 months;
- waiver of charges on inbound and outbound cheque payments over the same period;
- waiver of charges on standing orders and direct debits over the same period.

Client call account

These are business accounts targeted at professional practices such as solicitors, accountants and estate agents that hold money on behalf of their clients. They usually offer benefits including:

- tiered interest which is calculated daily, paid monthly and can be added to the firm's office account;
- no transaction charges;
- options to open accounts in different currencies;
- statements produced daily, weekly or monthly.

Below is an illustration showing specifications for a client call account.

BizEast client call account

Account Credit Interest Rate

Client call account	AER%	Gross%	Net%
£1 million+	3.66	3.60	2.88
£100,000+	3.30	3.25	2.60
£50,000+	3.09	3.05	2.44
£1+	3.04	3.00	2.40

Designated client account

This is a variant of the call account that enables the holder to hold their clients' individual funds in separate accounts. A benefit in addition to those of the call account is that interest is paid gross or net according to each client's tax status.

The example below illustrates the rate of interest that can be paid on a designated client account.

Account Credit Interest Rate

Designated client account	AER%	Gross%	Net%
£1 million+	3.66	3.60	2.88
£1+	3.04	3.00	2.40

---

16 A period of time for which there is a suspension of the charges.

Business instant access account
This account is for businesses with fast-moving cash flows that want to make the most of their day-to-day surpluses.

Account Credit Interest Rate			
Business instant access account	AER%	Gross%	Net%
£1 million+	3.45	3.40	2.72
£100,000+	3.14	3.10	2.48
£1+	3.04	3.00	2.40

Business tariffs
Banks charge fees to business account holders for the services they provide on a day-to-day basis. These charges, called tariffs, are applied to accounts by banks depending on the way the account holder (the business) operates the account.

Islamic Accounts
These are accounts that are managed according to the conventions of Shari'a, which forbids the payment of interest. They are targeted principally at the Muslim community.

Islamic current account
This is a personal account that is Shari'a-compliant and is usually designed in conjunction with eminent professionals schooled in Islamic finance law. Features and benefits include:

- no account maintenance fee;
- interest free;
- no requirement for minimum balance;
- fully Shari'a compliant;
- direct debits and standing orders.

There is no overdraft facility attached to this type of account. However, should the customer overdraw on the account, a fee is charged. Interest is not charged on the overdrawn amount in accordance with Shari'a conventions.

Islamic business account
These are business accounts that do not pay or charge interest. All deposits are managed in a Shari'a-compliant manner. Banks don't earn any interest on credit balances nor is any money deposited used for any interest-based or non-Shari'a-approved business activities. As with the personal current account, there are no overdraft facilities.

Savings Accounts

A savings account is an account for people that do not spend all their income on goods and services, i.e. under-spenders. There are various reasons why people open savings accounts and they include to:

- cater for emergencies;
- increase wealth;
- boost credit-worthiness;
- provide for future expenditure.

The following are popular types of savings account on offer at retail banks.

Online saver account

This is a type of savings account that allows the account holder to have instant access on the internet. They are usually linked to current accounts that the account holder already has at a specific bank. Most banks offer the highest interest rates on this type of account and do not have any limit on the amount that can be deposited.

Guaranteed tracker account

These are savings accounts that offer savers interest rates that track a base rate, for example the Bank of England base rate. They usually offer instant access to money deposited without any penalty charges. Features and benefits usually include:

- tiered savings rates;
- the option to have a standing order payment into the savings account;
- access to funds within a period after a change in base rate.

BizEast Guarantee Tracker

Tiers	Gross/AER%	Net%	Interest rate guarantee
£100,000+	4.15	3.32	To be no lower than 1.35% below the base rate
£50,000+	4.05	3.24	To be no lower than 1.45% below the base rate
£25,000+	3.90	3.12	To be no lower than 1.60% below the base rate
£10,000+	3.65	2.92	To be no lower than 1.85% below the base rate
£1+	3.40	2.72	To be no lower than 2.10% below the base rate

It is worth mentioning that all interest earned on all saving accounts (with the exception of ISAs) is taxed.

Children's savings accounts

With the rising cost of living and children's education, it is important for parents to start saving as soon as possible for their children. Banks offer children's savings accounts that work in a similar way to adult savings accounts.

There is no minimum age for a children's account to be opened. However most banks require a parent or guardian to open and run the account until the child is between 7 and 11 years old. Most accounts run until the child is 18 years old when, if not specified at the time, it will be transferred over into an adult savings account.

To encourage children to save their money, most banks offer incentives when an account is opened. These can range from posters and vouchers to naming the account themselves. The idea behind this is to start to persuade children to take an interest in saving money.

Investments

Guaranteed Investment Accounts

Guaranteed investment accounts are accounts that offer the option of either a guaranteed amount of interest at the end of a fixed term or a high percentage of any potential stock-market growth. This protects the account holder against adverse movements in the stock market as all the original investment plus interest will be returned at the end of the fixed term. Account holders also usually get the benefit of the flexibility to invest more money into the account until the investment date.

An illustration of a specification for a guaranteed investment account is as follows.

Bizle Guaranteed Investment Account

Investment date	24 July 2007
Maturity date	24 July 2012
Repayment date	31 July 2012
Minimum initial deposit	£500
Maximum initial deposit	£100,000
Minimum guaranteed return	15% Gross (2.83% AER)
Index participation	75%
Withdrawals	None during term
Charges	None

Individual Savings Account (ISA)

ISAs are tax-free savings accounts in the UK, which means individuals do not have to declare any income or capital gains to the tax authorities. Individuals must be UK residents for tax purposes. People working abroad or spouses and civil partners of individuals working abroad, for example civil servants or armed forces personnel who are paid by the British Government, are also entitled to open an ISA.

There are two types of ISAs – Maxi ISA and Mini ISA. An individual can only subscribe/contribute to either one Maxi ISA or up to two Mini ISAs (one for each component), each tax year. Money cannot be invested in both a Mini and Maxi ISA in the same financial year.

Maxi ISAs
Individuals can invest money in up to two different components (Cash, and Stocks and Shares) for each Maxi ISA. A Maxi ISA must have a stocks and shares component, but the life assurance and cash component is optional. A maximum of £7,000 can be invested each financial year. This can be divided between the two components in whichever way an individual wishes.

Mini ISAs
Individuals can only invest in one component of a Mini ISA each financial year. Unlike the Maxi ISA, the amount that can be invested is fixed for each component. For the risk averse or for those only wanting a cash ISA from a building society or bank, this will be the favoured option. Another advantage of a Mini ISA is that it provides greater flexibility, allowing individuals to invest in a cash ISA with, say, a building society and a Mini stocks and shares ISA with a company that specialises in equities.

Cash ISAs
Like regular savings accounts, some providers offer different types of cash ISA. Some providers will offer instant access to money with no penalty or loss of interest. Other providers have restrictions, such as a fixed term, or require notice to be given before money can be withdrawn. If a withdrawal is made within a fixed period then a penalty or loss of interest may result.

Cards

Payment cards are important products in the retail-banking product range as they offer consumers more security, convenience and control than any other payment method. Credit, debit and prepaid cards are used to purchase items in stores, on the phone or on the internet. The different types of cards are credit, debit and stored-value (prepaid) cards.

Credit Cards
This type of card offers consumers and businesses a short-term line of credit and an array of repayment options. Consumers use the line of credit to cover unforeseen or large expenses as well as to make basic routine purchases and to establish a credit history. Small businesses have been using credit cards for the same reasons as consumers in recent times. Features and benefits of credit cards usually include:

- a fixed interest-free period;
- typical variable interest;
- card protection;

- chip and pin security;
- cashback.

While credit cards are a flexible form of borrowing for the consumer, they can be a huge source of revenue for banks if they adhere to responsible lending policies.

The following is an illustration.

On January 1 2007, a cardholder makes £1,000 worth of purchases on a **BizEast Ruby Card** that charges 15.9% APR variable on purchases and does not make any additional purchases. It is assumed that:

- the monthly rate of interest on the card is 1.24%;
- the minimum payment is 2% of the balance shown on the statement;
- a statement is produced on the first day of each month;
- the cardholder makes a payment on the 15th of each month.

If the cardholder pays the minimum each month, they will be paying:

- interest of £144 in the first year;
- interest of £131 in the second year.

And it will take them 21 years and 10 months to pay off the balance.

Debit Cards

Debit cards are linked directly to consumers' current accounts, giving instant access to cash from ATMs around the world and at many retail point-of-sale outlets. Over two billion debit cards are in use worldwide, lending credence to expert opinion that debits are the fastest growing and most popular form of payment. According to Euromonitor, there were 70 billion debit transactions worldwide in 2003, with a total value of $5.5 billion dollars.[17]

Prepaid Cards

These are cards that require a set amount of money (value) to be loaded on to the card prior to use and can be reloaded over and over again. When consumers make purchases with the prepaid cards, the value of the good is subtracted from the card's value. Prepaid cards offer consumers flexibility and control and, as a result, companies are beginning to use them for employee benefits such as health savings and dependent care accounts.

The popularity of prepaid cards is gaining momentum as more and more banking giants are introducing branded prepaid cards. According to Pelorus Group, the consumer gift-card market is projected to be $95 billion strong in 2007.[18]

---

17 Euromonitor International 2003.
18 Source: http://new.greensheet.com/gs_cprofiles.php?company=datashapers.html

Merchant Services

A merchant account allows a business to accept credit cards, debit cards, gift cards and other forms of payment cards. This is also widely known as payment processing or credit-card processing. This is separate from a business account as not all banks are acquiring banks.[19]

There are various types of merchant account available depending on the method of accepting card payments. For example, retailers taking transactions in a shop using a physical terminal would need a Cardholder Present merchant account. To accept transactions over the internet, they would need an Internet merchant account, or to accept transactions via mail order or over the telephone they would need a Cardholder Not Present merchant account (this is sometimes called a Mail Order Telephone Order or MO/TO merchant account).

There are charges associated with operating a merchant account. Some fees are charged on a monthly basis but most are charged on a per-item or percentage basis. All of the monthly fees are at the discretion of the merchant-account provider but the majority of the per-item and percentage fees are passed through the merchant-account provider to the issuing bank according to a schedule of rates called Interchange fees, which are set by Visa and MasterCard.

Payment Gateways

A payment gateway is an e-commerce service that authorises payments for e-businesses and online retailers. It is the equivalent of a physical POS (point-of-sale) terminal located in most retail outlets. A merchant-account provider is typically a separate company from the payment gateway. Some merchant-account providers have their own payment gateways but the majority of companies use third-party payment gateways.

Loans

Personal Loan

A personal loan is an unsecured[20] loan that banks offer individuals for a range of different amounts. This is a simple retail banking product targeted at people that have a regular income and want to take out the loan for different purposes, although speculative purposes and business purposes are excluded. Depending on the amount and purpose of the loan, customers are able to choose from a range of repayment periods.

The amount borrowed is subject to an interest charge depending on the applied interest rate, usually quoted as an annual percentage rate (APR).

---

19 Acquiring banks provide a merchant service that allows companies to take card payments via the web or traditional PDQ machine.
20 Unsecured personal loans are offered by lending institutions such as banks and building societies and are so called because the lender requires no security for the debt.

Lenders do quote interest rates in different ways; either as fixed interest rates[21] or variable interest rates[22] and, in addition, as a typical[23] or a set interest rate.

Personal loans are repayable on a monthly basis. If there is a degree of flexibility then the lender may permit over-payments and lump-sum payments, both of which allow the customer to clear the debt over a shorter time period than first agreed.

Bridging Loan

This is a loan that is usually taken out to solve a temporary cash shortfall that might arise when buying a property or business, or perhaps paying for a renovation. There is normally a charge at a set interest rate, which is usually referred to in terms of a percentage per month.

There are two main types of bridging loan: the 'closed' bridge and the 'open' bridge. A closed bridge is only available to homebuyers who have already exchanged on the sale of their existing property. Very few sales fall through after exchange, so lenders are happy to offer closed-bridge financing.

An 'open' bridge is taken out by buyers who have found their ideal property, but may not have put their existing home on the market. A bank will ask lots of questions and want supporting information. It will also insist on the buyer having lots of equity in their existing property.

All bridging deals involve high interest rates. In the UK, it is usually the Bank of England bank rate plus 2% to 2.5%. There is also an arrangement fee ranging from 0.5% to 1.5% of the value of the loan.

Mortgages

A mortgage is a sum of money borrowed from a bank or building society in order to purchase a property. The money is then paid back to the lender over a fixed period of time, together with accrued interest.

Fixed-rate Mortgage

With a fixed-rate mortgage, the amount you repay the lender each month can be at a fixed interest rate for a specified period of time, regardless of changes to interest rates in the marketplace. It is common for lenders to offer rates fixed for a period of two to five years, but shorter and longer periods can be found in the market. At the end of the fixed-rate (or 'benefit') period, the rate will normally convert to the lender's standard variable rate (SVR).

---

21 A fixed interest rate will stay the same throughout the term of the loan, regardless of any changes in the bank base rate.
22 A variable interest rate may rise and fall in line with any changes to the bank base rate.
23 A typical interest rate is an indication of the rate applicants are offered and the rate that over two-thirds of the successful applicants are offered.

It is normal for lenders to charge up-front fees in the form of booking and/or arrangement fees. In addition, lenders frequently apply an early repayment charge (ERC) for fixed-rate mortgages. This acts as a 'lock-in', often making a heavy charge for borrowers paying off their mortgage early. Industry experts always ask consumers to be mindful, as the ERC can sometimes last longer than the fixed-rate period, e.g. a three-year fixed rate with a five-year ERC.

Tracker Mortgages

These are mortgage products that charge a variable rate linked to the movement of a prevailing rate such as the Bank of England Base Rate or London Interbank Offered Rate (LIBOR). The interest rate will be a set percentage amount above the relevant base rate for a specified period of time. For example, if the tracker mortgage is set at 1% above the Bank of England Base Rate for five years and the base rate is currently 3.75%, the pay rate will work out at 4.75%.

It can be deduced from their name that tracker mortgages change to follow or 'track' changes in the base rate to which they are linked. So if the base rate increases by 1%, the pay rate will increase accordingly. Also, if the base rate is reduced, borrowers will benefit from a lower pay rate.

Insurance

Home Insurance

Retail banks have added home insurance to their product offerings. Home insurance, or homeowners' insurance, is an insurance policy that combines insurance on the home, its contents and, often, the other personal possessions of the homeowner, as well as liability insurance for accidents such as theft, fire and windstorms. The extent of the accidents covered depends on the type of policy.

In recent times, most mortgage lenders insist that borrowers have home insurance in order to be granted a mortgage.

Car Insurance

Car insurance, i.e. insurance that consumers can purchase for cars, trucks and other vehicles, is another insurance product that is increasingly offered by retail banks. Its primary use is to provide protection against losses incurred as a result of car accidents.

Travel Services

Travel Money

Travel money is a product that encompasses transactions in different currencies and the selling of traveller's cheques. A traveller's cheque is a pre-printed, fixed-amount cheque designed to allow the person signing it to make an unconditional payment to someone else as a result of having paid the issuer (usually a bank) for that privilege. Traveller's cheques can be replaced when lost or stolen and are usually used by consumers as a substitute for cash when on holiday.

The use of traveller's cheques has been on the wane in recent times owing to the ubiquity of credit cards and their wide acceptance. American Express has been offering traveller's cheque cards, which can be used in place of traveller's cheques.

Travel Insurance
Banks are also offering travel insurance as part of their product range. Travel insurance is insurance that is intended to cover financial and other losses incurred while travelling, either within one's own country or internationally.

Travel insurance can usually be arranged at the time of booking a trip to cover exactly the duration of that trip, or a more extensive, continuous insurance can be purchased from (most often) travel agents, travel insurance companies or directly from travel suppliers such as cruise lines or tour operators.

The most common risks that are covered by travel insurance include:

- cancellation
- curtailment
- delayed departure.

Bank Codes

A bank code is a code (mostly a number) assigned by a central bank, a Bank Supervisory Body or a Bankers' Association in a country to all its licensed member banks. The rules vary to a great extent between countries. Also the name of such a code varies. In some countries the bank codes can be viewed over the internet, but mostly in the local language.

BIC
A Bank Identification Code, BIC, also known as a SWIFT code, is a universal system of identifying financial institutions in order to facilitate the automated processing of telecommunication messages in banking and related financial environments. The Society for Worldwide Interbank Financial Telecommunication (SWIFT) handles the registration of these codes, hence the name SWIFT addresses or codes.

BIC codes are required in order to effect the transfer of money across countries and can be found on account statements. They are applicable to all banks and financial institutions. All BICs are registered by SWIFT and there are two categories of BICs – those referring to financial institutions connected to SWIFT and those not connected to SWIFT.

BIC consists of 8 or 11 contiguous characters comprising the following components:

- Bank code: 4 alphanumeric characters. So far, SWIFT has only used alphabetic characters.

- Country code: 2-letter country code as specified in ISO 3166.
- Location code: 2 alphanumeric characters endorsed by SWIFT to identify the location of the institution within the specified industry.
- Branch code: 3 alphanumeric characters identifying a branch or department of the bank.

The following is an example:
Barclays bank Broadgate branch in London's BIC code is:

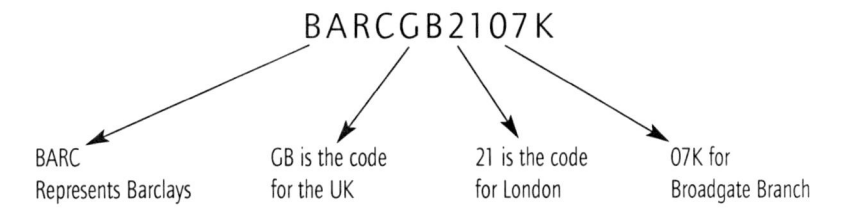

BARCGB2107K

BARC
Represents Barclays

GB is the code
for the UK

21 is the code
for London

07K for
Broadgate Branch

IBAN

The International Bank Account Number (IBAN) is an international standard for identifying bank accounts across national borders. It was developed by the International Organisation for Standardisation (ISO) and adopted by the European Committee for Banking Standards in order to encourage hassle-free cross-border transfers throughout Europe. When a cross-border payment is made in Europe, an IBAN is used to identify the account to which the payment should be made. It is always used in conjunction with a Bank Identifier Code (BIC).

An IBAN is *not* a new bank account number. It is a series of alphanumeric characters that incorporates the ISO country code, two check digits and the bank branch reference number, which precedes account numbers at that bank.

The naming convention for IBANs is:

CC NN YYYY AAAA AABB BBBB BB

Where:

C = Country code
N = Cheque number
Y = Bank code
A = Sort code
B = Account number

For example, a UK IBAN is:

GB NN YYYY AAAA AABB BBBB BB which is 22 characters long.

The Belgian IBAN is of the format:

BE NN YYYC BBBB BBBB which is 16 characters long.

IBANs in printed format (such as on an invoice) are likely to be prefaced by the word IBAN.

Sort Code

A sort code is a number which is assigned to a branch of a bank for internal purposes. Sort codes are used to inform customers about the location of branches as it is easier than writing out the full address of the branch. The convention for sort codes in the UK is six digits formatted into pairs and separated by hyphens: 91-02-88, for example, could denote a branch of a retail bank in London. Other countries have their conventions for allocating sort codes. In Canada, the bank transit number is eight digits long. This is divided into a five-digit branch number and three-digit institution code, for example 10000-200, while Austrian banks have BSB numbers which are six digits long: two groups of three numbers (e.g. 100-200). Some retail banks have sub-branches which are identified by the parent sort code rather than a unique one.

The sort code of a customer's initial branch is printed on their card or cheque book. Eighteen-digit debit-card numbers may include the six-digit sort code between the initial four-digit card type and final eight-digit account number.

Issuer Identification Number (IIN)
What is an IIN?

APACS (the UK payments association) definition of an IIN is: "*The issuer identification number (IIN) is the first six digits of the account number on a plastic card, where the card is to be used either internationally or inter-industry.*"

The national IIN is eight digits long and the fifth through to the eighth digits are assigned by APACS.

The whole number that appears embossed on a plastic card is known as the primary account number (PAN) and has a maximum length of 19 digits. There are three elements to the PAN.

The Three Elements of the Primary Account Number

	Issuer Identification Number	Account Number	Check Digit
International PANs	6 digits	Variable up to 12 digits	Last digit
National PANs	8 digits	Variable up to 10 digits	Last digit

Source: APACS

The IIN has two functions:

- identification of the card issuer;
- providing information to the acquirer and card issuer as to who to route the transaction to.

Rates

BBA LIBOR

London Interbank Offered Rate (or LIBOR) is a daily reference rate based on the interest rates at which banks offer to lend unsecured funds to other banks in the London wholesale money market (or interbank market). LIBOR is the opposite of the London Interbank Bid Rate (LIBID).

LIBOR is published by the British Bankers' Association (BBA) shortly after 11:00 each day. BBA LIBOR is the most widely used benchmark or reference rate for short-term interest rates around the world.

BBA LIBOR rates are dependent on a number of factors, including:

- local interest rates, banks;
- expectations of future rate movements;
- the profile of contributor banks (contributor panels are changed annually);
- liquidity in the London markets in the currency concerned etc.

The Business Environment in Retail Banking   3

This chapter describes the business environment in which retail banks operate and encompasses the major players, the allied industries and regulators.

Introduction

The business environment in which retail banks operate is shaped by the following key economic factors:

- government borrowing and debt repayment;
- overseas funds;
- interest rates;
- exchange rate;
- inflation;
- government fiscal policy;
- changing demographics;
- use of technology.

Government Borrowing and Debt Repayment

In any country, governments have to fund deficits that sometimes arise when expenditure exceeds income from taxation. In order to achieve this, they have to raise money through the sale of securities such as treasury bills or "gilts" in the UK. As a consequence, people buy these securities given that they are less risky than other types of securities. This reduces money supply in the relevant country.

Impact: Reduced money supply will reduce the disposable income of people in the country. This will reduce the amount of money deposited in the banks which in turn will reduce revenue from lending.

Overseas Funds

Inflow of money from overseas as a result of an increase in exports leads to an increase in money supply because exporters receive the local currency for the goods exported. Similarly, an increase in imports leads to a decrease in money supply as importers sell the local currency to foreign exporters.

Impact: Inflow and outflow of money affects lending and borrowing activity. An increase in money supply will encourage saving and a decrease will increase demand for borrowing with consequences for revenue generation.

Interest Rates

Interest rates can be considered as the price of money. Borrowers pay back an amount of money that is a percentage over and above the value of the original loan. This makes the interest rate a vital tool of economic management. A large amount of economic activity (both consumption and investment) is based on using borrowed money, and so if the interest rate is changed it will either encourage or discourage borrowing and therefore tend to increase or decrease economic growth.

Impact: Interest rate movements will impact on the revenue that banks generate from deposits and loans, especially the housing loans (mortgages).

Exchange Rates

The movements in exchange rate of currency pairs are dependent mainly on interest and inflation rates. Usually an increase in interest rates in a country results in a rise in the exchange rate of its currency. Demand and supply of currencies also dictate the exchange rate of one currency against the other.

A rise in inflation rates causes governments to increase interest rates, but if the hike in interest rate occurs too often in order to stem the sharp increases in inflation rates, foreign investors may panic and sell the local currency. As a result, the exchange rate will fall.

Impact: Exchange rate fluctuations will impact on the revenue that banks generate from travel services and wire transfers as high exchange rates for local currencies encourage foreign travel and remittance of money overseas.

Inflation Rates

Governments set the inflation targets that they are required to meet and change interest rates as they deem appropriate to achieve these targets. Inflation in a country causes people to withdraw their money from a country and invest it in assets such as real estate, equities, bonds etc.

Borrowers benefit from inflation because they can repay their loans with money that is worth less than the money they borrowed. However, lenders will be repaid the money they lent out which will have *less* purchasing power and also savers with savings that are fixed in terms of money will also have diminished purchasing power.

Impact: Banks will generate more revenue from increased borrowing in the personal loans market, but if inflation results in an increase in interest rates, revenue from mortgage borrowing could be reduced.

Government Fiscal Policy

Fiscal policy is the government spending policy that influences macroeconomic conditions. This policy affects tax rates, interest rates and government spending in an effort to control the economy. Fiscal policy in concert with monetary policy is used to control economic events.

In the case of hyperinflation,[24] the economy may need a slow down. In such a situation, governments can use fiscal policy to increase taxes in order to take money out of the economy. Fiscal policy could also dictate a decrease in government spending and thereby decrease the money in circulation.

Impact: Government fiscal policies have an influence on money and hence people's disposable income. This impacts the volume of loans and deposits, and revenue generated from these, and ancillary services.

Changing Demographics

Demographic changes (both population shifts and ageing) affect the spending patterns of people in different countries. New markets emerge as a result of fac-

---

[24] Extremely rapid or out of control inflation.

tors such as immigration and the changing membership structure of political bodies.

There are also changes in attitudes towards education, religious beliefs and ethical standing.

Impact: Demographic factors impact on revenue growth for banks as population shifts and ageing affect the demand for both current and savings accounts. Changing attitudes not only affect patterns of demand, but also the creation of new products such as Islamic accounts.

Use of Technology

Technology has altered the retail banking landscape primarily through the lowering of the barriers to entry into the market. As seen in Chapter 1, new entrants have made inroads into this market and as a result, the traditional high-street banks are seeing their dominance increasingly threatened.

Technology has also allowed the banks to expand their product offerings and introduce new payment methods.

Impact: Retail banks are able to reduce overheads by shrinking their branch networks and giving their customers the option of banking on the internet. Electronic payment methods are increasingly becoming the preferred media for transactions.

Players in Retail Banking

The business environment is made up of the following players:

- the competitors (other banks);
- allied organisations, i.e. the regulators, credit referencing agencies, card companies, and clearing organisations.

The Competitors

The retail banking industry is a fiercely competitive segment of the financial services industry. The traditional banks are competing with each other for increasingly commoditised business services and also with non-banks, such as retailers and insurance companies.

Dominant players in this industry sector are divisions of universal banking groups. This gives them a competitive edge as they benefit from consolidation and cross-subsidisation of their business by other divisions of the banking group.

Overview of the Major Players in Retail Banking

Royal Bank of Scotland Group
The Royal Bank of Scotland Group (RBSG) is one of the oldest banks in the UK. The Royal Bank of Scotland itself was founded in Edinburgh by royal charter in 1727. In 2000 the Royal Bank of Scotland acquired National Westminster Bank plc, in the biggest takeover in the history of British banking, to create a huge Group, with a highly diversified portfolio of services for personal, business and corporate customers.

National Westminster Bank, NatWest, was created through the merger of National Provincial Bank and Westminster Bank in 1968.

In August 2004, the bank expanded into China, acquiring a 10% stake in the Bank of China for £1.7 billion.[25]

Some data on RBSG:

- Revenue: £28,002 million (2006)
- Operating income: £9,186 million (2006)
- Net income: £6,497 million (2006)
- Number of employees: 137,000 (2006).

Citigroup
Citigroup Inc. is a major American financial services company based in New York City, formed by the merger of Citicorp and Travelers Group on 7 April 1998. According to Forbes Global 2000 in March 2007, it is the world's largest company, with total assets of US$2.02 trillion. It holds over 200 million customer accounts in more than 100 countries.

Citigroup's history dates back to the founding of Citibank in 1812, Bank Handlowy in 1870, Smith Barney in 1873, Banamex in 1884, and Salomon Brothers in 1910.[26]

Some data on Citigroup:

- Revenue: US$155.6 billion (2006)
- Net income: US$21.538 billion (2006)
- Number of employees: 327,000 (2006).

Barclays
Barclays is a financial services organisation which moves, lends, invests and protects money for more than 27 million customers and clients around the world – from large businesses to personal account holders.

---

25 Americans use "billion" to mean one thousand million (1,000,000,000), whereas in the UK, until the latter part of the 20th century, it was used to mean one million million (1,000,000,000,000). Billion mentioned in this section is in the UK context.
26 Source: www.citigroup.com/citigroup/about/index.htm

The history of the bank dates back to 1685 in London and the name "Barclays" became associated with the business in 1736. Recent acquisitions of Barclays include Woolwich plc in 2000, and in 2005 a £2.6bn takeover of Absa Group Limited, South Africa's largest retail bank, acquiring a 54% stake.

Global retail and commercial banking operations include UK retail and business banking, Barclaycard, and international retail and commercial banking.

Some data on Barclays:

- Revenue: £22,170 million (2006)
- Operating income: £7,136 million (2006)
- Net income: £4,571 million (2006)
- Number of employees: 118,000 (2006).

HSBC

HSBC is a banking and financial services organisation with an international network comprising around 10,000 offices in 82 countries and territories in Europe, the Asia-Pacific region, the Americas, the Middle East and Africa.

The HSBC Group is named after its founding member, the Hong Kong and Shanghai Banking Corporation Limited, which was established in 1865 to finance the growing trade between China and Europe. From 2002, the HSBC identity carried the strapline of "The world's local bank", with a view to emphasising the group's experience and understanding of a great variety of markets and cultures.

HSBC provides a comprehensive range of financial services including personal financial services and commercial banking.

Some data on HSBC:

- Revenue: US$70.1 billion (2006)
- Operating income: US$70.1 billion (2006)
- Net income: US$70.1 billion (2006)
- Number of employees: 312,000.

Allied Organisations

Allied organisations to the retail banking industry include the regulators, the news agencies, the clearing houses and credit rating agencies. The following are some of the allied organisations that service the UK retail banking industry.

The Regulators

Financial Services Authority

The Financial Services Authority (FSA) is an independent non-departmental public and quasi-judicial body that regulates the financial services industry in the United Kingdom. Its main office is based in Canary Wharf, London, with another office in Edinburgh. When acting as the competent authority for the listing of shares on a stock exchange, it is referred to as the UK Listing Authority (UKLA) and maintains the Official List.

The FSA's main role in the retail banking community is to regulate the banks as well as reduce financial crime. Investment banks have to comply with sets of regulations that govern the financial industry and have a requirement to report their activities to the FSA.

Bank of England
The Bank of England is the central bank of the United Kingdom and has two core purposes – monetary stability and financial stability. The bank has the legislative responsibility through the Monetary Policy Committee to set the UK's official interest rate and is also responsible for the issuing of banknotes. Apart from the monetary and financial stability roles, the bank works closely with financial markets and institutions to collate and publish monetary and banking statistics.

The Bank of England was established in 1694 to be the UK government's bank and since the late 18th century has been the bank to the banking system. It is based in Threadneedle Street in the heart of London's "square mile" and is sometimes referred to as the "Old Lady" of Threadneedle Street.

European Central Bank
The European Central Bank (ECB) is the central bank for Europe's single currency, the euro. The ECB's main task is to maintain the euro's purchasing power and thus price stability in the euro area. The euro area comprises the 13 European Union countries that have introduced the euro since 1999.

Since 1 January 1999, the European Central Bank (ECB) has been responsible for conducting monetary policy for the euro area – the world's largest economy after the United States.

The euro area came into being when responsibility for monetary policy was transferred from the national central banks of 11 EU Member States to the ECB in January 1999. Greece joined in 2001, followed by Slovenia, the 13th member, in 2007. The creation of the euro area and a new supranational institution, the ECB, was a milestone in a long and complex process of European integration.

The ECB headquarters is in Frankfurt am Main, Germany.

EMVCo
In February 1999, Europay International, MasterCard International and Visa International formed EMVCo LLC to manage, maintain and enhance the EMV™ Integrated Circuit Card Specifications for Payment Systems. The membership structure of the company changed in 2002 when MasterCard acquired Europay and again in 2005 when JCB International joined the organisation.

EMVCo's primary role is to manage, maintain and enhance the EMV Integrated Circuit Card Specifications to ensure interoperability and acceptance of payment system integrated circuit cards on a worldwide basis.

EMV is a standard for the interoperation of integrated circuit (IC) cards ("Chip cards") and IC-capable point-of-sale (POS) terminals, for authenticating credit and debit card payments. The name EMV comes from the initial letters of Europay, MasterCard and VISA, the three companies which originally co-operated to develop the standard. IC card systems based on EMV are being phased in across the world, under names such as "IC Credit" and "Chip and PIN".

The two most widely known implementations of the EMV standard are:

- VSDC – VISA
- MChip – MasterCard.

MasterCard has a Chip Authentication Program (CAP) for secure e-commerce. Its implementation is known as EMV-CAP and supports a number of modes.

The Card Companies

VISA

Visa is a private membership association, jointly owned by more than 20,000 member financial institutions around the world. The organisation is dedicated to serving those members, their cardholders and their merchant clients by facilitating payment as required.

The history of VISA dates back to 1968 when Dee Hock, one of the leaders of a group of BankAmericard[27] licensee banks, proposed that the banks form an association – a joint venture that would allow members to enjoy the benefits of a centralised payments system, while competing fairly for their own interests. In 1976, the BankAmericard name was changed to Visa, a simple, memorable name that is pronounced the same way in every language.

There are now 1.55 billion Visa cards in circulation that generate more than $4.6 trillion in global sales and with acceptance in more than 170 countries.

MasterCard

MasterCard was created in the USA in 1966 by a group of banks who wanted to create a member-owned association. In 1968 the company's commitment to become a global payments network led to its expansion to Mexico, Japan and Europe.

During the 1980s, MasterCard exploited the demand for electronic payments in new regions and markets around the globe. The company was the first payment card issuer in the People's Republic of China. It also launched Maestro®, a global online debit program, in partnership with Europay International.

In 2006, MasterCard introduced a new corporate name, MasterCard Worldwide, and adopted a new corporate signature and tagline "The Heart of Commerce™", to reflect the company's globally integrated structure and strategic vision of advancing commerce worldwide.

---

[27] A card programme launched in 1958 by Bank of America.

American Express

American Express, sometimes known as "AmEx" or "Amex", is a diversified global financial services company, headquartered in New York City. The company is best known for its credit card, charge card and traveller's cheque businesses.

American Express was founded in 1850 in Buffalo, New York, as a joint stock corporation that was a merger of the express companies. The company issued its first charge card in 1958. Within five years, more than one million cards were in use at approximately 85,000 establishments both inside and outside the United States. Ever since, a number of cards have been launched including the American Express Gold Card in 1966, Platinum card in 1984, Optima (the first credit-card product) in 1987 and the Centurion in 1999.

In 2006, the UK division of American Express licensed the Product Red brand and began to issue a Red Card. With each card-member purchase, the company contributes to good causes through The Global Fund.[28]

American Express operates in more than 130 countries across the globe and as of 2005, employed 65,800 people.

Diners Club

Diners Club International, originally founded as Diners Club, is a credit-card company formed in 1950 by Frank McNamara. When it first came on the scene, it became the first independent credit-card company in the world. The Diners Club Card was also the first ever charge card. As of 2002, there were eight million Diners Club card-holders in over 200 countries, and the card is accepted in six million establishments worldwide.

In 2004, Diners Club announced an agreement with MasterCard. Diners Club cards issued in the United States and Canada now feature a MasterCard logo and a 16-digit account number on the front, and can be used wherever MasterCard is accepted. Cards from other countries continue to bear a 14-digit account number on the front, with the MasterCard logo.

Japan Credit Bureau

Japan Credit Bureau (JCB) is a credit-card company that was founded in 1961 in Tokyo, Japan. Originally a player in the Japanese credit-card market, the company decided on an international development programme which led to the launch of a card issuance programme in Hong Kong in 1985; the first outside Japan.

As of March 2006, JCB had 57.7 million card members and 13.83 million merchant outlets; the JCB card is accepted in 190 countries and territories around the world.[29] In 2007, it launched a new brand slogan "Good times start here" as part of its new global branding strategy.

---

28 A fund set up to help African women and children suffering from HIV/AIDS, malaria and other diseases.
29 Source: www.jcbinternational.com/htm/about/inform.htm

The Credit Referencing Agencies

A credit reference agency is a company that provides credit information on individual borrowers. This helps lenders assess creditworthiness, the ability to pay back a loan, and can affect the interest rate applied to loans. Interest rates are not the same for everyone, but instead are based on risk-based pricing, a form of price discrimination based on the different expected costs of different borrowers, as set out in their credit rating.

Credit bureaus collect and collate personal financial data on individuals from financial institutions with which they have a relationship. The data is aggregated and the resulting information is made available on request to contributing companies for the purposes of credit assessment and credit scoring. Given the large number of consumer borrowers, these credit scores tend to be mechanistic. In other words, the different credit bureaus collect data from a variety of sources and then apply a mathematical algorithm to assess the likelihood that an individual will repay a given debt given the frequency that other individuals in similar situations have defaulted. Given the mechanical nature of this calculation, an individual's credit score is highly dependent on the information input into the algorithm. If a credit bureau has collected inaccurate or misleading data, an individual's credit score could be adversely affected as a result. Consequently, most consumer welfare advocates advise individuals to review their credit reports at least once a year, in order to ensure that the reports are accurate.

Uses of credit referencing agencies

In the United Kingdom, the three credit reference agencies are Experian, Equifax and Callcredit, which was established in 2001 and is now working closely in association with its American counterpart, TransUnion.

Most banks and other credit-granting organisations subscribe to one or more of these organisations to ensure the quality of their lending. This includes companies who sell goods or services on credit such as credit-card issuers, utility companies and store-card issuers. Subscribing organisations are expected to provide relevant data to maintain the common data pool.

Credit reference agencies are bound by the Data Protection Act, which requires that data relating to identifiable individuals must be accurate, relevant, held for a proper purpose and not out of date. Individuals have a legal right to access data held on them.

The activities of credit reference agencies are governed under UK law by the Consumer Credit Act 1974.

Equifax

Equifax, Inc. is a consumer credit reporting firm in the USA, considered one of the "big three" credit agencies along with Experian and TransUnion. Founded in 1899, Equifax is the oldest of the three agencies and gathers and maintains information on over 400 million credit holders worldwide. Based in Atlanta, Georgia, Equifax is a global service provider with over $1.5 billion in annual revenue and approximately 5,000 employees on three continents and in 14 countries.

Experian

Experian is a global information-solutions company, with operations in over 30 countries around the world, including the USA, UK, most European countries, Argentina, Brazil, South Africa, China, Japan and Australia. The largest operation, Experian North America, is a consumer credit reporting agency, considered one of the "big three" along with Equifax and TransUnion in that business in the United States.

Callcredit

Callcredit Limited is a consumer credit reference agency. Callcredit was created by Skipton Building Society and supplies information to lenders and other organisations to enable them to establish an individual's credit history, confirm application addresses and monitor significant events which may be indicators of credit risk.

Callcredit's client base includes legal firms, banks, building societies, finance houses, mail order firms, telecoms and utility companies. These typically use Callcredit's services to support applications for consumer credit, however shared financial data from consumers' credit accounts is used to underpin a variety of services including fraud and identification products, debtor tracing and over-indebtedness tracking.

Callcredit also provides credit reports directly to consumers via their consumer website MyCallcredit.

News Agencies and Trade Associations

What are news agencies?

A news agency is an organisation of journalists established to supply news reports to organisations in the news trade: newspapers, magazines, and radio and television broadcasters. They are also known as wire services or news services.

News agencies can be corporations that sell news, co-operatives composed of newspapers that share their articles with each other, or commercial newswire services which charge organisations to distribute their news. Governments may also control "news agencies", particularly in authoritarian states like China and the Soviet Union. A recent rise in internet-based alternative news agencies, as a component of the larger alternative media, has emphasised a "non-corporate view" as being largely independent of the pressures of business media.

News agencies generally prepare hard news stories and feature articles that can be used with little or no modification and then sell them to other news organisations. They provide these articles electronically in bulk through wire services (originally they used telegraphy; today they frequently use the internet). Corporations, individuals, analysts and intelligence agencies may also subscribe. The business proposition of news agencies might thus be responsible for the current trends in separation of fact-based reporting from Op-eds.[30]

---

30 Op-eds are pieces of writing expressing an opinion.

The following are notable news agencies and trade associations that service the retail banking industry.

The *Financial Times*

The *Financial Times* (FT) is an international business newspaper printed on distinctive salmon-pink broadsheet paper. The periodical is printed in 22 cities: London, Leeds, Dublin, Paris, Frankfurt, Stockholm, Milan, Madrid, New York, Chicago, LA, San Francisco, Dallas, Atlanta, Miami, Washington DC, Tokyo, Hong Kong, Singapore, Seoul, Dubai and Johannesburg.

The *FT* reports extensively on business and features extensive share and financial product listings. It also has a sizeable network of international reporters – 400 journalists in 50 editorial bureaus worldwide – covering current affairs in general. The *Financial Times* is normally seen as centre-right/liberal, although to the left of its principal competitor, *The Wall Street Journal*. It advocates free markets and is generally in favour of globalisation.

APACS

APACS, the UK payments association (formerly known as the Association for Payment Clearing Services) is the UK trade association for payment systems provided by financial institutions. It promotes standards and interoperability for systems such as Bacs, CHAPS and SWIFT, which are themselves separate companies. Additionally, APACS issues all bank branch "sort codes" used as transactional identifiers – these codes are published annually in a directory format.

APACS standards define both procedural and technical practice for:

- debits (including cheques);
- standing-order mandates;
- coin packaging and banknote wrappers;
- magnetic media interchange;
- interchange data formats.

APACS is the payments industry voice on a wide range of topics and the industry's representative in Europe. APACS forecasts payment trends, conducts market research, carries out lobbying activities, collates industry statistics, and gets involved in developing industry standards and best practices.

SWIFT

SWIFT stands for Society for Worldwide Interbank Financial Telecommunication. It is the industry-owned co-operative, headquartered in La Hulpe, Belgium, near Brussels. It supplies secure, standardised messaging services and interface software to nearly 8,100 financial institutions in 207 countries and territories. SWIFT members include banks, broker-dealers and investment managers. The broader SWIFT community also encompasses corporates as well as market infrastructures in payments, securities, treasury and trade.

In 2001 SWIFTNet[31] messaging services, saw their first fully live implementations by domestic market infrastructures: the Bundesbank's RTGSPlus system and the Bank of England's Enquiry Link. On 15 August 2002, SWIFTNet Release 4.0 went live and concurrently the first SWIFTNet FIN message was sent.

SWIFT moved to SWIFTNet in 2003, providing a total replacement of the previous X.25 infrastructure. The process involved the development of new protocols that facilitate efficient messaging, using existing and new message standards. The adopted technology chosen to develop the protocols was XML, which now provides a wrapper around all messages, legacy or contemporary. The communication protocols can be broken down into InterAct, FileAct and Browse.

Fair Isaac
Fair Isaac Corporation, founded in 1956 by engineer Bill Fair and mathematician Earl Isaac, provides consulting services and decision management systems. It developed the FICO scores, a measure of credit risk, that are the most used credit scores in the world. FICO scores are available through all of the major consumer reporting agencies in the world: Equifax, Experian and TransUnion.

Fair Isaac was founded on the premise that data, used intelligently, can improve business decisions. Retail banks and credit card issuers rely on Fair Isaac solutions to automate and improve decision strategies. These solutions include analytics such as predictive models and strategy optimisation that guide decision strategies, data management and data analysis services that bring complete customer information to every decision. Through the www.myfico.com website, consumers use the company's FICO® scores, the standard measure of credit risk, to manage their financial health.

Fair Isaac's current corporate headquarters are located in Minneapolis, Minnesota, USA with offices in North America, South America, Europe, Australia, and Asia.

Council of Mortgage Lenders
The Council of Mortgage Lenders (CML) is the trade association for the mortgage-lending industry, and its members account for around 98% of UK residential mortgage lending. Members are banks, building societies and other mortgage lenders. There are also associates, drawn from a variety of related businesses, including lawyers, conveyancers, search companies and management consultants.

As of June 2007, the CML currently has 162 members and 98 associates including notable high-street banks such as Abbey, Lloyds TSB and traditional building societies like Nationwide Building Society and Chelsea Building Society.

CIFAS
CIFAS, Credit Industry Fraud Avoidance Scheme, is an industry-funded organisation founded in 1988 that is solely dedicated to the prevention of financial

---
31 SWIFT's current IP Network infrastructure.

crime. CIFAS provides a range of fraud prevention services to its members, including a fraud avoidance system used by the UK's financial services companies, public authorities and other organisations. This system facilitates the exchange, between members, of details of suspected cases of fraud when information provided by someone applying for products or services fails verification checks. It also facilitates the exchange of information about accounts and services which are being fraudulently misused or insurance and other claims which are deemed to be fraudulent.

CIFAS members also exchange information about innocent victims of fraud to protect them from further fraud. This exchange of information is referred to in a fair processing notice, or use of personal data clause, on application/proposal/claim forms and agreements.

Building Societies Association
The Building Societies Association is the trade association for the UK's building societies. It was established in 1869 and has two principal functions – to act as the central representative body for building societies and to provide information to its members. The BSA presents the industry view to government, parliament, regulators, the media and other interested bodies. There are 60 building societies in the UK with total assets of over £305 billion. About 15 million adults have building society savings accounts and over two and a half million adults are currently buying their own homes with the help of building society loans.[32]

The BSA offers advice and assistance on a whole range of issues affecting the operation of building societies, apart from some aspects of mortgage lending which are looked after by the Council of Mortgage Lenders. It also provides information and advice to building societies on a range of relevant subjects.

British Bankers' Association
British Bankers' Association (BBA) is the UK banking and financial services trade association. It was set up in 1919, working with the Committee of London Clearing Bankers (CLCB), and the members at the time were British commercial banks. The membership structure was, however, changed in 1972 when foreign banks and British merchant banks were accepted. There are now 253 members and associate members from 60 different countries which together provide the full range of banking and financial services. They operate some 130 million personal accounts, contribute £35bn to the economy and collectively constitute the world's largest international banking centre.

The range of issues addressed by the BBA, given that it is recognised as the voice of the banking industry in the UK, includes:

- maintenance of data on bank deposits and lending as well as on such areas as credit cards and operational losses;
- guidance on money laundering;

---
32 Source: www.bsa.org.uk/aboutus/index.htm

- influencing European legislation to facilitate the provision of better financial services;
- guidance on accounting practice;
- pricing of market benchmarks such as LIBOR rates.

The BBA works with Government, the FSA and the Bank of England as well as the press, EU institutions and key opinion formers. This work extends beyond the UK and Europe to engage, where necessary, regulators and governments around the world.

LINK

LINK powers electronic real-time financial transaction processing and payments solutions for banks, retailers and mobile operators. The company enables businesses in local and global markets to deliver quality services by providing a secure processing infrastructure. The LINK infrastructure powered in excess of 2.5 billion transactions in 2005.

The company manages the ATM network for the LINK card scheme and provides the technical and commercial services, including arranging settlement, which make ATM sharing possible with over 55,000 cash machines deployed in the UK and over 101 million LINK-enabled cards in issue. It also manages transactions for the basic bank accounts that form part of the Post Office's universal banking services programmes and has implemented an ATM prepay top-up service on behalf of mobile phone operators. The company is pursuing opportunities to use its proven, secure and reliable network infrastructure to support the development and implementation of wider transaction management services and innovative payments solutions.

Clearing Organisations

What is clearing?

Clearing in retail banking involves the processing of payments made by cheque, direct debit, direct credit, or standing orders. Retail banks are members of a cheque-clearing system for the purposes of clearing cheques drawn against each others' funds. In the UK, all the major high-street commercial banks are clearing banks. Cheque clearing enables a customer of one bank to write out a cheque to a customer of another bank. The clearing system then works so that when the cheque is deposited in the system, money is transferred from one bank to the other. Direct debits, direct credits or standing orders are processed electronically. The clearing system is a very important aspect of the banking institution.

Below are examples of clearing/payments organisations.

CHAPS

CHAPS Clearing Company Limited processes and settles time-dependent payments. The CHAPS (Clearing House Automated Payment System) Sterling system started operating on the 9 February 1984 and by the end of the year the average daily volume and value transmitted was around 7,000 payments with an aggregate value of around £5 billion. By comparison, in 2004 the respective values were 130,000 payments and £300 billion.

CHAPS, used by 14 settlement banks including the Bank of England and over 400 sub-member financial institutions, continues to be one of the largest real-time gross settlement systems[33] (RTGS) in the world.

Sterling members of CHAPS include Barclays Bank Plc and Citibank N.A. while ABN Amro N.V. and Deutsche Bank AG are examples of euro members.

Cheque and Credit Clearing
The Cheque and Clearing Company is responsible for volume clearing of cheques and paper credit throughout Great Britain. Cheque and credit payments in Northern Ireland are processed locally.

Members of the Cheque and Clearing Company as of January 2006 were:

- Abbey
- Alliance and Leicester
- Bank of England
- HBOS
- Barclays
- Clydesdale
- The Co-operative Bank
- HSBC
- Lloyds TSB
- Nationwide
- Royal Bank Of Scotland Group.

Members of the Cheque and Clearing Company have the responsibility of processing cheques drawn by or credited to the accounts of their customers. Members also offer cheque-clearing facilities for their customers and negotiate agency agreements for them to enable indirect access to the cheque mechanism.

Interbank clearing in Great Britain processes 6.5 million cheques and credits each working day and operates on a three-working-day clearing cycle.

Bacs
Bacs (formerly an acronym for Bankers Automated Clearing Services) is a UK-based membership-based scheme responsible for the processing of 5.5 billion payments a year with over 80 million on a peak day.[34]

---

33 This is a system for large-value interbank funds transfers. This system lessens settlement risk because interbank settlement happens throughout the day, rather than just at the end of the day.
34 Source: www.bacs.co.uk/bacs/Corporate/Corporate+overview/?st=4hqsgdzvltmbdw45nur4zpmw&c=.

It is owned by 15 of the leading banks and building societies in the UK and Europe and is the guardian of the rules and legal structures that underpin automated payments and payment-related services in the UK.

Bacs' principal products are direct debits, direct credits and standing orders. These products have increased convenience and provided peace of mind for tens of millions of consumers through the delivery of safe and efficient payments. Almost three-quarters of British adults are positively disposed towards direct debits: 35 million adults now have at least one direct debit commitment and approximately 115,000 businesses use Bacs' services.

Voca

Voca is a provider of payments services. Responsible for the technology behind the UK's automated payments, Voca has processed 55 billion transactions in the last 37 years and during 2005 more than 5 billion financial transactions were securely processed; this accounted for 20% of all European bank-to-bank payments. In the same year, more than 100,000 businesses that connect to the Voca network, including all of the FTSE 100, transferred to a highly advanced IP-based submission channel, Bacstel-IP.[35]

Voca provides technology and services that form the core infrastructure of the UK automated payments industry, handling more than 90% of UK salaries, 70% of household bills and the majority of state benefits and pension payments.

In recent times, Voca has formed two further highly innovative joint ventures:

- OneVu (with US e-billing giant CheckFree), a service designed to revolutionise the way consumers pay bills through their online banking service;
- Digital Payments, a mobile payments venture with Retail Decisions and Mi-Pay, which will enable payments over mobile telephones, the internet and interactive TV.

---

35 Bacstel-IP is a registered trademark of Bacs Payment Scheme Limited.

4 Trends in Retail Banking

This chapter covers the trends that are shaping the retail banking industry from the regulations introduced by regulators to the product ranges that are creating markets for the banks.

Introduction

There are various regulations and technological advances that are continually creating changes in the retail banking sector. These present opportunities for relevantly skilled IT professionals to get involved with projects executed to ensure compliance and adoption of new technologies. Below are a few of the regulations and technologies that govern trends in retail banking.

Introduction of SEPA

SEPA, which stands for Single Euro Payments Area, is a new regulatory framework for payment and clearing across continental Europe. SEPA will affect banks and their customers, payment system operators and system vendors, with regulators and banks spearheading these changes.

According to the European Central Bank (ECB): *"SEPA is an area in which consumers, companies and other economic actors will be able to make and receive payments in euro, whether between or within national boundaries under the same basic conditions, rights and obligations, regardless of their location."*

Industry experts describe it as an initiative that will allow payments to be made throughout the whole SEPA area[36] from a single bank account, using a single set of payment instruments, as easily and safely as is the case in any of the individual SEPA countries today. The aim of SEPA is to achieve higher service levels, and deliver more efficient products and cheaper alternatives for making payments through the advancement of European integration of the euro area retail payments market that will be more competitive and innovative.

ECB stipulates that SEPA is made up of:

- the single currency;
- a single set of euro payment instruments – credit transfers, direct debits and card payments;
- efficient processing infrastructures for euro payments;
- common technical standards;
- common business practices;
- a harmonised legal basis;
- ongoing development of new customer-oriented services.

SEPA was introduced to allow the euro economy area to exploit fully the benefits of the single market. Traditionally, customers have faced difficulty when transacting business that involved euro retail payments to other euro area countries in the sense that their payment obligations have been time-consuming. This presents a problem that, if left unsolved, will support the perception that the euro is not a fully implemented single currency.

---

36 Twenty-nine countries.

In addition, companies operating in the eurozone, which have a substantial number of cross-border payments, have to maintain bank accounts in many of the countries in which they do business in order to allow them to manage their payments. This is the result of the slow pace of change in the number and array of payment instruments, standards and processing infrastructures for retail payments since the introduction of the euro in 1999 and despite the development of TARGET.[37] Low-value electronic payments (i.e. retail payments) are currently processed differently throughout the euro area.

This divergent payment processing also affects national euro payments, preventing innovation and competition on the eurozone stage. There are also different rules and requirements applicable to stakeholders depending on their country of origin. The promotion of innovative payment solutions by the SEPA framework will have transnational ramifications, i.e. blur national boundaries across the eurozone.

The deadline for complying with SEPA requirements for cross-border payments across the eurozone is January 2008 while compliance for local payments, i.e. on a national level, should be implemented by December 2010 unless otherwise stated.

Implications for IT Professionals

According to McKinsey[38] and the European Commission, there is considerable monetary value at stake for implementing the SEPA framework. Here are some interesting figures:

- Payment costs account for 2–3% of the EU Gross Domestic Product (GDP), 35% of bank costs.
- Cost of late payments to corporates stands at €50 billion.
- Inability to integrate payments and billing systems costs €50–100 billion.

With SEPA in place, the industry's cost base can be moved to as much as 20% above the best European performer and increase banking profit by €10 billion. In addition, the revenue pool profile[39] of the European banking industry can realise €9 billion of revenue. The above are incentives for banks to get the SEPA implementation right and as such would require appropriately skilled professionals with the required business knowledge and understanding.

Introduction of Faster Payments

In May 2005, UK banks announced plans to develop a new infrastructure to speed up internet, phone and standing order payments by the end of 2007.

---

[37] The common large-value electronic payment system.
[38] A global management consultancy firm.
[39] The profile of banks that depicts the amount of revenue they generate over a specified period.

Experts believe the massive project will revolutionise the UK's automated payments infrastructure.

The new Faster Payments clearing and settlement system is being introduced in the UK market to facilitate same-day, real-time clearing of internet and telephone banking transactions by UK bank account customers.

In the past, central banks have operated as regulators of the payment sector, and banking associations have represented the banks. Risk management has been the real concern. However, today's regulatory environment realigns the focus on customers. The aim is to reduce costs to the economy and customers, to standardise and make transparent cost and service levels and to improve service levels offered. These issues have now replaced risk management as the key driver of change.

Central to the requirements for change is the expensive method of moving money within the same day: a single CHAPS transaction for a retail customer is charged at more than £30 and banker's draft at £10 to £20.

The new system will enable standing-order payments to move more quickly so that money will move from the customer's account on the due date and arrive at the beneficiary's account on the same day.

The estimated time of delivery for this service in the UK is the end of 2007. The UK banking industry commissioned Voca and LINK to develop this payment system so that banks all over the country can offer the service. These vendors appear to be best placed to build a system of this nature, given the real-time switching capabilities of LINK and the clearing and settlement expertise of Voca. The combination provides a real-time clearing facility that already dispenses cash from ATMs in the UK and debits account-holders' bank accounts, coupled with the settlement management of Voca.

Challenges and Risks

Industry experts are of the opinion that there are some major challenges and risks presented by the Faster Payment initiative, foremost of which is its real-time nature. The almost real-time element of the service takes for granted the challenge inherent in deducting value from the payer's account and transferring it into the payee's account in near real time. In an instance where banks do not all have a facility to update their customer accounting systems in real time and, in particular, where the update to the account is reflected in customer systems in distributed databases, the management of Faster Payment processing within a bank will require more than a technical interface to manage the transaction formats and messaging between the bank and the service.

From a security risk standpoint, the current level of sophistication of criminals appears to be underestimated as the introduction of new payment services will attract criminals well-versed in the technicalities of hacking and phishing. In addition, from a fraud perspective, the absence of a delayed clearing and settlement cycle – be it one, two or three days, which gives the banks time to authenticate and validate the sources and destinations of payments and to detect patterns of payments that may indicate criminal activity before the money can leave the bank – makes the system vulnerable to perpetrators of electronic fraud.

Sarbanes-Oxley Act of 2002

The Sarbanes-Oxley Act of 2002 (known as Sox) was sponsored by US Senator Paul Sarbanes and US Representative Michael Oxley and it signifies the biggest change to federal securities laws in a long time. Large accounting scandals involving companies such as Enron, WorldCom, and Arthur Andersen, which resulted in billions of dollars in corporate and investor losses, instigated the changes to restore investor trust in the financial markets.

Since 2006, all public companies have been required to submit an annual assessment of the effectiveness of their internal financial auditing controls to the Securities and Exchange Commission (SEC). The types of companies affected include publicly traded companies in the United States, including all wholly owned subsidiaries, and all publicly traded non-US companies doing in business in the USA. Also included are private companies that are gearing up for an Initial Price Offering (IPO) that have to comply with certain aspects of the regulations.

There are 11 sections of the Sarbanes-Oxley Act including sections 302, 401, 404 and 802. Section 404 – management of internal control – requires that financial reports must include an Internal Control Report stating that management is responsible for an "adequate" internal control structure. This is the most difficult section of the Act to comply with.

Non-compliance and submission of inaccurate certification could lead to a fine of $1 million and ten years' imprisonment, even if committed in error.

Basel 2 Accord

Basel 2 is shorthand for the "New Basel Capital Accord". The original Basel Accord was agreed in 1988 by the Basel Committee on Banking Supervision. The 1988 Accord, now referred to as Basel 1, helped to strengthen the soundness and stability of the international banking system. Basel 2 is a revision of the existing framework, which aims to make the framework more risk sensitive and representative of modern banks' risk management practices.

This revised capital adequacy framework will further reduce the probability of consumer loss or market disruption as a result of prudential failure. It will do so by seeking to ensure that the financial resources held by a firm are commensurate with the risks associated with the business profile and the control environment within the firm. The new Basel Accord will be implemented in the Europe Union via the Capital Requirements Directive (CRD).

The new framework requires that the following types of risk are incorporated into banks' decision-making processes:

- Credit Risk – the possibility that a bond issuer will default by failing to repay principal and interest in a timely manner.
- Operational Risk – the risk associated with the potential for systems failure, i.e. people, technology and processes, in a given market.

- Market Risk – the risk which is common to an entire class of assets or liabilities, i.e. the economic changes that impact on a market as a whole.

Basel 2 consists of three "pillars" as follows:

- Pillar 1 of the new standards sets out the minimum capital requirements firms will be required to meet for credit, market and operational risk.
- Pillar 2 requires firms and supervisors to take a view on whether a firm should hold additional capital against risks not covered in Pillar 1 and take action accordingly.
- Pillar 3 aims to improve market discipline by requiring firms to publish certain details of their risks, capital and risk management.

Effects of Basel 2 on Retail Banks, Customers and Regulators

According to KPMG, the following are impacts of Basel 2 on banks, customers and regulators.

Constituent	Effect
Banks	• Need to implement risk management framework tying regulatory capital to economic risk • Need to choose credit and operational risk (Pillar 1) • Need to gather, store and analyse a wide array of new data • Need to embed new/enhanced practices across the organisation
Customers	• Need external/internal rating to obtain credit • Face increased transparency of account profitability • Face possibility of reduced service, standardised products, higher interest rates
Regulators	• Gain access to more and timely information through the new disclosures Basel 2 requires of banks • Gain power to set incentives, penalise wrongdoers and act (not react) – thus contributing to increased financial stability and transparency

There are quite a number of Basel 2 projects in the major retail banks.

There are systems being developed to allow for the reporting of capital adequacy and computation of the Risk Weighted Assets/Capital Requirements from the following parameters:

- PD (Probability of Default) – which measures the likelihood that the borrower will default over a given time horizon.
- LGD (Loss Given Default) – which measures the proportion of the exposure that will be lost if a default occurs.
- EAD (Exposure at Default) – which for loan commitments measures the amount of the facility that is likely to be drawn if a default occurs.

■ Maturity – which measures the remaining economic maturity at exposure.

The Future

Work is apparently already under way on Basel 3, at least in a preliminary sense. The goals of this project are to refine the definition of bank capital, quantify further classes of risk and further improve the sensitivity of the risk measures.

AML/ KYC

AML stands for "Anti Money Laundering" while KYC stands for "Know Your Customer". The laundering of money or assets to camouflage criminal activities such as global terrorism, drug trafficking or illegal tax evasion is well-known, given the high-profile political measures taken to prevent these activities. According to the International Monetary Fund (IMF), money laundering accounts for between two and five per cent of the world's GDP, with the most conservative estimates from international law enforcement agencies being in excess of a $300 billion annual ballpark figure globally.

Retail banks have to proactively manage risks associated with the menace of money laundering. These risks are illustrated in Figure 4.1.

Figure 4.1 Risks associated with AML/ KYC

Investment banks have to comply with a Financial Action Task Force (FATF) directive, which requires due diligence and maintenance of attribute records of the following:

■ counterparty IDs;
■ registered name and address;

- country of registration;
- business purpose;
- parent and trading relationships;
- information on regulator;
- exchange listing;
- list of directors;
- lists of shareholders for the business entity.

There other AML guidelines for banks to follow:

- JMLSG guidelines:
    - enhanced KYC procedures;
    - patterns of normal transactions to create profiles and monitoring;
    - abnormal transactions/activity;
    - risk-based approach for capturing additional information.

- Global AML principles for Correspondent Banking (Nov. 2002):
    - risk indicators like Correspondent Banking client's domicile, ownership and management structures, business and customer base;
    - updating the client's risk profile on a risk-assessed basis.

There are IT projects in a number of the retail banks for AML/KYC compliance.

Growth of Social Lending

Social lending is a phenomenon in retail banking that is gaining popularity as it embodies a more bona fide and transparent financial service supported by the experience of lending to and borrowing directly from people. Moreover, there is distrust among bank customers with regard to the ethical standards of mainstream financial services companies and therefore social lending symbolises a more personalised and emotional investing form of customer–financial service provider relationship, creating the perception of a real experience and essentially genuine experience as opposed to that of the mainstream financial services.

Zopa and Prosper, peer-to-peer banks mentioned in Chapter 1, are financial services providers that exemplify the concept of social lending. To substantiate the benefits of social lending, a Social Futures Observatory survey revealed that 54% of Zopa lenders and 85% of borrowers described Zopa as "exceptionally transparent" whilst 73% of respondents to a survey conducted by the organisation on general banking were of the opinion that mainstream financial services ought to be more transparent about the organisations that they invest in. Evidently, social lending transcends the transactional elements of lending and borrowing money.

The following are other factors that are enhancing the popularity of Social Lending:

- **The convergence of finance and ethicality** – the lack of information from mainstream banks about their ethical standing coupled with the transparency of a social lending scheme are attracting more people to this alternative form of banking.
- **The proliferation of online communities** – the concept of eBay, YouTube and MySpace, all burgeoning online communities, can be leveraged by social lending schemes. The peer-to-peer interactions inherent in these online communities represent a horizontal power structure as opposed to the hierarchical power structures in mainstream banking.
- **Greater financial returns** – the main motivation for users of these schemes is the perception that they offer greater financial returns given the levels of risk.
- **Negative attitudes towards mainstream financial services** – these attitudes are increasingly rampant among mainstream bank customers. According to a Social Futures Observatory survey, 76% "strongly agreed" that high-street banks were greedy, 81% felt they were self-interested and 49% felt mainstream banks did not have the customers' best interests at heart.
- **The proliferation of web technologies** – the increasing adoption of technologies such as Web 2.0, which harness the potential of the internet in a more collaborative and peer-to-peer manner, have made it easy for social lending schemes to take off. Also, according to the Social Futures Observatory report, members of online social lending schemes are amongst the most proficient internet users and exhibit a pervasive need to handle their finances on the internet.

Social Lending Market

The social lending market is expected to experience steady growth as social lending schemes embrace the trends that are defining the current age, and will continue to increase in importance in the future. Social lending schemes will carry on attracting more customers as people become more competent using the internet and more confident about the viability of the existing players. However, it is unlikely that they will replace mainstream banking institutions as they cannot rival the array of products and services on offer at these banks. Moreover, current accounts provide a means for people to create their credit ratings.

In order to have a glimpse of the future of the social lending market, the following are statistics out of Zopa as of May 2007:

- Zopa has 135,000 members.
- Zopa lenders have received on average 6.75% before-tax annual return after fees and defaults.
- Zopa borrowers have obtained loans at rates as low as 4.2% APR.
- The current default rate is only 20 basis points, 0.2%.

Emergence of Financial Supermarkets

The financial services industry landscape is currently undergoing complete redefinition. In recent times, the distinction between retail banks, investment banks and insurance companies has blurred. Against this backdrop there has been an emergence of financial supermarkets offering the entire breadth of services, from traditional retail products to investment solutions, through to insurance and retirement benefits.

Convenience banking is also a concept being offered to customers in an effort to increase the share of the wallet[40] and to alter the current practice of an average customer dealing with about four institutions to satisfy their financial requirements. Most banks are now offering an array of services including fixed income offerings, fixed annuities, variable annuities and retail investment products. As a result of this trend, some organisations are now adopting strategic initiatives involving organic growth to expand their service lines, while others use alliances to provide a wider spectrum of services. In the USA, for instance, 15% of banks use their broker-dealer subsidiary, while the majority have entered into collaborative arrangements.[41]

Deconstruction of Banking Services

In a bid to be more efficient and enhance profitability, retail banks are embarking on a strategic initiative denoted as "deconstruction". The term may give the impression of being destructive, but on the contrary it is definitely productive.

What is Deconstruction?
Deconstruction is a process which entails the decomposition of services or products into their components parts, thereby allowing the individual parts to be provided by separate firms.

An illustration[42] of deconstruction is as follows.

Recent innovation in the financial services industry allows the components of provision of a mortgage loan, for instance, to be broken into:

- Origination – brokerage of mortgage to a customer;
- Administration – processing of the paperwork;
- Risk assessment – assessment of the creditworthiness of the borrower;
- Funding – raising of finance, holding of assets on the balance sheet and allocation of capital to risk.

---

40 Share of the wallet is the proportion of one bank's services a customer uses related to their complete financial needs.
41 American Banking Association.
42 Illustration taken from *UK Financial System: Theory and Practice* by Mike Buckle.

Firms that have comparative advantage in one aspect are best placed to offer the service. One firm may have a comparative advantage in, say, risk assessment, whereas another firm may have a comparative advantage in origination. Also, owing to capital constraints, the firm that originated may not be efficient in funding the loan.

Increasing adoption of the process of deconstruction will change the market dynamics of the retail banking landscape as barriers to entry into the banking industry, as new entrants don't have to carry out the whole process. This will bring about the provision of specialist services by niche players in the part of the process in which they have a comparative advantage.

Outsourcing will be rife if this trend persists as small banks will be looking to buy into the economies of scale which would otherwise be impossible because of the limited scale of their operation.

Remote Card Authentication

Card fraud is on the rise as customers shop more online or by phone (card-not-present). Fraudsters are increasingly targeting these areas by trying to commit crime to reflect these activities. The biggest fraud type in the UK is card-not-present fraud, which cost £183.2m in 2005.

A number of organisations including APACS (the UK payments association), banks, card schemes and systems vendors are working closely together on a range of initiatives to ensure that the person making a card-not-present payment is the genuine cardholder.

One of these initiatives is Remote Card Authentication, which can be defined as the next generation of fraud prevention solutions to help tackle fraud in non face-to-face transactions. It involves the generation of a one-time-password (OTP) by a device not connected to the PC, enabling the users to authenticate themselves securely.

A long-term solution to online authentication problems seems to be pocket-sized EMV-compliant smart-card readers, incorporating a challenge/response capability. It is expected that between 1 and 1.5 million cardholders will be issued with readers for e-banking in 2007.[43]

In the past, banks depended on static passwords for remote access control to their banking applications. However, this one-factor method of authentication proved ineffective in the face of the abundance of highly sophisticated fraudulent techniques. According to APACS, online banking fraud in the UK increased from £23.2m in 2005 to £33.5m in 2006. These losses are added to by increasing customer reluctance to use online financial services, which they view as being vulnerable.

43 Source: www.remotecardauthentication.info

The emergence of phishing[44] has also been a widespread security issue in the card industry. Other weapons criminals use to compromise online security include key logging and screen-scraper programs, which capture screen shots to obtain end-user credentials.

How does Remote Card Authentication work?
There are two factor authentications that the remote card system enables and they are:

- something a cardholder has;
- something a cardholder knows.

There are a number of solutions to implement such a system; one of the solutions is described as follows:

- A cardholder making a card-not-present transaction inserts their chip and PIN card into a hand-held reader (i.e. something a cardholder has) provided by their bank.
- They enter their PIN (something a cardholder knows).
- On confirming the PIN entered, the reader generates a one-time passcode.
- The cardholder provides this passcode to the retailer for authentication with the cardholder's bank.

The card reader uses the security features built into the chip on the card and is always offline.

This solution's novelty lies in leveraging the customer's experience with chip and PIN in the normal "card present" environment. It also builds upon the current technology implemented by both the banking and retailing industries.

Use of High Technology Tools to Identify Prospects

With the advent of stiffer competition from new entrants into the retail banking marketplace, established players are looking for innovative ways of not only preventing their customers from defecting to their competitors, but also attracting new ones. They are looking to technology for the answer.

A notable example is that of Barclaycard. It was the dominant credit-card player in the British market, until American rivals emerged with cut-throat pricing and direct-mail sales tactics. The parent company of Barclaycard, Barclays, had been getting more than 80% of its customers the old-fashioned way – from

---

44 The act of sending an email to a user, falsely claiming to be an established legitimate enterprise, in an attempt to scam the user into surrendering private inforamtion that will be used for identity theft.

application forms stacked in piles at local branches. In order to recapture its market share, Barclays augmented its database of customers with demographic and behavioural data and credit reference information to reveal the details of customers who were inclined to sign up for more services. It then took advantage of the cross-selling opportunity. As a result, Barclaycard was able to attract around 500,000 to 700,000 credit-card accounts a year to more than 1.7 million a year by 2005.[45] In addition to that, it began tracking credit-card purchases and capturing what customers were looking for on its website to fine-tune promotions and spur sales in other parts of the bank.

Banks are turning the massive volume of transactions from credit-card purchases and online enquiries and call centre complaints into bits of intelligence used to piece together holistic pictures of customers' wants and needs. Most banks are also increasingly embracing data mining to uncover behavioural clues, such as when a customer is about switch banks or is searching for new services. If, for instance, a couple recently paid for flowers, an expensive cake and tropical vacation, then it is likely that they are newlyweds who might be looking to take out a mortgage in the near future.

Technology as a strategic weapon provides banks with limitless opportunities and the data captured from customers will enable these banks to develop and tailor products to offer the customers.

Use of Customer Analytics

Retail banks have had a wake-up call in recent times. Traditional strategies that the management adopted such as growth through acquisition are proving less effective and to a lesser extent have eroded performance.

Not so long ago, retail bankers had it relatively easy. They subscribed to the notion that profitability and success can be achieved by adhering to a rule of thumb: market share and location equal power. Power translated into attraction of more deposits, control over pricing and limitless opportunities to cross-sell. In the last decade, however, they have seen the power associated with market share diminish. Their dominance in, say, the credit-card market has become eroded by non-banking institutions like Capital One.

Retail bankers now seem to have found a solution in customer analytics, especially, customer value management. Customer value management is simply about extracting insights on customer profitability from the disparate systems that house product and channel data, and developing strategies and tactics to improve customer value.

Whilst this may seem straightforward on the face of it, there are unique challenges that retail bankers face. Retail banking is not like other retail businesses where the profit or losses per customer can be determined at the time of purchase of particular products. This is due to the constraints that abound in

[45] Source: www.businessweek.com/magazine/content/06_14/b3978067.htm

product pricing compounded by the minimal constraints customers face on how they use the product, what demands they place on the bank, and how long they hold the product. As a consequence, retail banking products' profitability can only be determined by how customers use the product as these products are not profitable or unprofitable in a uniform manner. Furthermore, profitability in this context is distorted because customers' usage drives cost-to-serve which in turn influences customer profitability. The consequence of this distortion is that profitable customers are used to cross-subsidise unprofitable ones.

Retail banks that are utilising customer analytics are now more knowledgeable about their profitable customers, how to better serve them (both in terms of product and price), successfully cross-sell them and ultimately retain them. In addition, they have to develop superior customer segmentation, customer relationship strategies, and sales and service tactics.

An interesting metric bankers are using in the course of analytics is lifetime value (LTV). LTV analytics offer retail bankers several advantages:

- better insight on cross-selling opportunities;
- insight on profitability based on future market conditions, for example interest rates;
- more accurate profitability calculations for customers holding products that have a negative return in the early years, e.g. mortgages;
- more refined metrics to best direct resources and efforts to maximise return.

Growth of Online Banking

The internet is increasingly seen as the future of bank delivery as transaction volumes for ATMs and the retail bank branch network are appearing to plateau. According to Tower Group, in the USA for instance, growth in internet banking is outpacing all other retail delivery channels and is rising at an annual rate of 27%. This could be attributed to the emerging customer preference for going online for the majority of their banking needs instead of waiting in line for the teller.

In the UK, the growth of internet banking has been underscored by Lloyds TSB's claim that it has four million registered internet banking customers and during a peak period had around ten customers logging on every second. APACS also claim that 16.9 million people, a third of the adult population of the UK, now use online banking services.

The first online service in the UK was launched by Nationwide Building Society, beating the other retail banks to commence operation on 27 May 1997. Ten years on, over 17 million people in the UK now get balance updates and make payments over the internet. Nationwide claims that 66 per cent of online bankers log on at least once a week, with 99 per cent of men and 6 per cent of women stating that they check their internet account every day.

Other interesting statistics that accentuate the growth of online banking include:

- Online banking among 16–24-year-olds has doubled from 13% in 2002 to 25% in 2006.
- One in five bank customers access their web accounts daily (APACS).
- The number of people using telephone banking in the first half of 2006 fell to15.4 million from 16.0 million in the same period in 2005. This may be due to the preference for banking online.
- From 2000–2007, online banking numbers have increased five-fold.

The factors responsible for the growth of online banking include:

- the advent of broadband;
- the ease of banking online compared to having to queue in a high-street branch;
- the desire to closely monitor personal finances.

Having explained the growth of internet banking, it is worth mentioning that with the rise in numbers going online to manage finances, there has inescapably been an increase in the number of fraudsters targeting internet banks. In 2006, online banking fraud cost the banking industry in the UK £33.5 million, compared with £23.3 million in 2005.

Recent Card Industry Initiatives

The card market is growing at a phenomenal rate as the general trend across most countries in the world is an obvious shift away from cheques owing to the advancement of electronic payment tools, especially payment cards, which simplify the payment process for both the consumer and the financial services provider. According to Business Insights, the US market had 842.8 million payment cards in 2003 while the European market had 542.2 million. As a result, some initiatives have recently been introduced including the following.

Chip and PIN
From 14 February 2006, Chip and PIN became the more secure way to use credit and debit cards. It was introduced to combat fraud associated with both of these types of card. According to APACS, thanks to Chip and Pin in 2005, there was a reduction of nearly £60m in counterfeit and fraud on lost and stolen cards when compared to 2004.

Chip and PIN combines two effective security features. The first is a microchip on the cards that stores card data more securely than a magnetic stripe and is therefore much harder to counterfeit (clone) or skim. The second is the four-digit PIN (personal identification number) that is much harder to use fraudulently than it is to copy a signature and proves that the user is the genuine cardholder. Instead of using signatures to verify payments, users are asked to enter a four-digit PIN known only to the bona fide cardholder.

A nationwide roll-out of Chip and PIN in the UK started in 2003 and by early 2006 the country was close to being a fully mature Chip and PIN market.

Visa has introduced V PAY, a new type of pan-European debit card, based entirely on chip and PIN. Banks across Europe will soon be issuing V PAY cards and adding the new V PAY logo to their domestic debit cards. In doing so, they will create a more open and consistent European debit card network.

Over the coming years, cardholders across Europe will carry debit cards that feature the V PAY logo. In their own countries, these new debit cards will be accepted in all the same places as they are today. The big difference is they will be increasingly accepted at merchant outlets across Europe.[46]

Industry Hot Card File (IHCF)
The IHCF is an industry database in the UK that enables retailers to electronically check every card transaction for cards being used fraudulently.

An electronic file is used to distribute data on lost and stolen cards to more than 80,000 subscribers. When a card is swiped as part of a normal transaction, it is automatically checked against the file. If the details given match those of a card on file, an alert is given to the retailer.

IHCF contains information on more than 5 million missing cards and over 440,000 cases of attempted fraud were prevented by this system in 2004.

Summary Box
A Summary Box is essentially the standard way that all credit card companies explain the main features of their cards. The Box now appears on all credit card applications and marketing materials, making it easier for applicants to compare different cards before applying.

There are lots of different credit cards around to choose from, all with different features and benefits. The summary box puts the key information in one place so that an applicant can choose the right one.

An example of a summary box is shown in the Appendix.

Remittances
Remittances come in many forms, including:

- immigrants sending money to family members in other countries;
- migrant or expatriate workers on temporary contracts in another country sending money to meet their expenses in their country;
- parents sending money to a child studying abroad;
- travellers receiving emergency funds;
- people sending money as gifts.

Remittances represent one of the most important inflows of funds for many developing economies around the world. But when wage earners live apart from their families, it can be costly and frustrating to get funds into the hands of family members back home.

---

46 Source: www.visaeurope.com/aboutvisa/products/vpay.jsp

The World Bank estimates that person-to-person cross-border remittance volumes reached more than US$232 billion in 2005. It also believes that the real volume of remittances, considering underreporting or informal channels which are not reported at all, could increase that number by 50 per cent.

Person-to-Person Payments

Facilitating person-to-person (P2P) payments is an avenue for card companies to boost transaction volumes. It also has the potential to boost card balances, as consumers using their credit cards for these transactions will substitute card borrowing for other sources, such as personal loans and overdraft.

Visa and MasterCard offer P2P transfer in the USA through VisaDirect[47] and MasterCard MoneySend respectively. These services are similar to PayPal's funds transfer services, but without the third party involved in the transaction.

P2P payments such as these offer benefits to cardholders including:

- They offer a more cost-effective and convenient method for completing cross-border fund transfers.
- They remove the risk and delay elements of sending cash gifts directly.

Contactless Payment

The latest trend in retail payments is contactless payment. This type of payment, often referred to as "wave and pay", allows people to transmit secure payment data to a point-of-sale (POS) terminal using devices such as contactless-enabled cards, key fobs and mobile devices. They are used successfully in Asia, Europe and North America.

Contactless payment systems offer a number of advantages to issuers, retailers and consumers. For issuers, they allow penetration of the cash payment market, enjoy increased customer transaction volume, and improve customer retention and loyalty. Retailers enjoy the benefits of faster transaction times, improved operational efficiency, lower operating costs coupled with increased revenue. The convenience of hands-free payment, the ability to pay for multiple services using a single device and the security of a concealed card are some the advantages of contactless cards for consumers.

Contactless cards contain a special chip that is recognised by a merchant's terminal when consumers pass the card in front of the machine. The reader beeps to signal that the transaction has been authorised. Multiple technologies including radio frequency, infrared and Bluetooth may be used to implement a contactless payment system.

The choice of the appropriate technology is driven by issues such as:

- the types of payment mechanism the technology supports;
- the commercial viability of the technology;
- security features that the technology offers for customer data;
- validation features of the technology to prevent erroneous transactions.

---

47 In Europe the service is known as Visa MoneyTransfer.

MasterCard, Visa and American Express have been releasing their own brands of contactless cards: MasterCard PayPass, Visa Contactless and Express Pay respectively. Bank of America, Chase and HSBC are already issuing MasterCard PayPass cards in the USA that are being accepted in outlets like 7-Eleven and McDonald's.

Rise of Islamic Retail Banking

Financial services firms are investing significant amounts of capital into developing products that are compliant with the principles of the Koran (i.e. Shari'a compliant) for a market estimated to be worth $500 billion and enjoying a current year-on-year growth of 15–20 per cent.

Islamic banking is a growth industry; that is without question. There are organisations outside the Islamic business sector embracing the opportunities that abound in this industry. Western banks such as HSBC and Citigroup are making swift moves to secure a place in the market with a view to capturing a substantial share. Along with the obvious benefits, there are challenges as Shari'a law forbids certain financial practices that are the cornerstone of traditional commerce, particularly the practice of lending money with a view to attracting interest.

The primary reason for the attraction to Islamic banking is that the regions in which it is growing are some of the richest and most rapidly developing parts of the world. Malaysia, a case in point, is believed to be one of the most developed Islamic finance industries in the world. And in recent times, in order to give the industry a boost, the Malaysian government has made a commitment to move 20 per cent of the national financial system to Islamic principles by 2010, a target that looks comfortably within reach. There is also the recent granting of a 10-year tax holiday for new Islamic banks with international dealings that are based in the country.

The Gulf Co-operation Council (GCC), a six-nation group that includes Saudi Arabia, Kuwait, Qatar, Oman, Bahrain and the United Arab Emirates, is of particular interest to banks that offer Islamic banking services, owing to the prosperity and financial liquidity these countries generate from record oil prices.

Apart from the predominantly Muslim countries mentioned above, banks in countries with a minority Muslim population have begun to tailor financial products for these communities. In the UK, for example, HSBC and Lloyds TSB have started to offer Shari'a-compliant current accounts, including car finance and home loans. Product development for the Islamic banking sector takes place in financial centres like London and New York for distribution through retail banks in Muslim countries.

The Introduction of SWIFT for Corporates

With increasing regulatory and audit pressure and heightened security measures in the market landscape, corporates need to reduce costs and operational risk, and centralise and automate their operations to improve efficiency and overall control.

Financial institutions are offering the panacea to address these challenges by giving corporate customers access to their services through SWIFT's secure messaging platform.

According to SWIFT: *"SWIFT for Corporates is a secure, standardised, global single window to the financial industry."*

The following are two SWIFT initiatives for corporates.

SCORE

The Standardised Corporate Environment (SCORE) is based on a closed user group, administered by SWIFT, where corporates can interact with financial institutions by using financial messaging. These are some of the challenges that corporates need to respond to that justify the adoption of SCORE:

- provision of visibility of funds;
- strengthening of security by protection against internal and external fraud;
- compliance with an increasingly restrictive framework that is designed to improve transparency towards investors.

The main initial advantage offered by SCORE is the reduction in the number of network connections and the associated hardware and mainten-

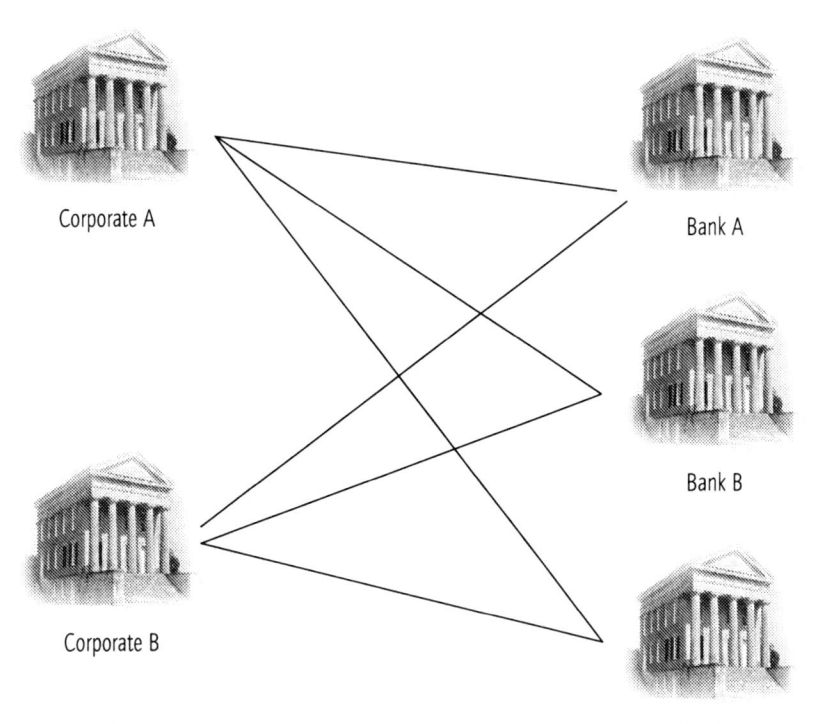

Source: SWIFT

ance costs. Many corporate to bank systems require specific network subscription, banking software, specific security devices and proprietary data standards.

According to SWIFT, SCORE can generate return on investment in the region of 400–600%. New services can also be deployed on the standard platform reducing time-to-market for the corporates who sign up.

Banks that commit to SCORE provide corporates with an access point for their services along with the traditional channels: corporate internet banking, proprietary bank software installed within the corporate or bank-specific customisations to vendor software.

Table 4.1 Swift Standard Messages Allowed in SCORE

Corporate to financial institution	Financial institution to corporate
MT 101 Request for transfer	MT 900 Confirmation of Debit
MT 104 Direct Debit	MT 910 Confirmation of Credit
MT 101 Request for cancellation	MT 940 Customer Statement
MT 101 Notice to receive	MT 942 Interim Transaction Report

Source: SWIFT

In order for corporates to be eligible for SCORE, corporates have to be listed on the regulated stock exchange of a country which is a member of the Financial Action Task Force which includes countries such as the UK, USA, Japan, Germany and Hong Kong.

With the advent of bank consolidation in the European banking market, forecast to reduce the number of banks from 7,000 banks in 2002 to 2,000 in 2015,[48] retail banks will be migrating the services of their acquisitions to a cost-effective platform like SCORE.

MA-CUG
MA-CUG stands for Member Administered Closed User Group. Companies that are ineligible for the SCORE model join SWIFT by registering in a closed user group, set up and managed by their financial institution (i.e. the financial institution chooses which customers can partake). Within the MA-CUG, a corporate can communicate only with its bank, which decides which kinds of messages and files (payments, treasury, reporting, and securities) can be exchanged. If a corporate wishes to communicate with several banks, it can register in multiple MA-CUGs, resulting in similar multi-banking capabilities as SCORE.

48 Source: www.towergroup.com

Identification of the Unbanked Retail Market

Mainstream financial institutions like retail banks all over the world have identified a large unbanked retail market as a result of advances in unmanned delivery channels and new credit-scoring models. Financial institutions have historically been wary of unbanked customers but in recent times and after intensive research there has been a paradigm shift.

Fair Isaac announced that the Expansion Credit Score[49] has proved to be both reliable and predictive of risk. Their study using aggregated outcome data from leading financial institutions showed that the credit risk of the unbanked population can be measured accurately.

Who are the Unbanked?

The types of potential customers in the market segment classed as unbanked are:

- young adults;
- recently widowed or divorced consumers;
- older people with cash predisposition;
- minorities;
- recent immigrants;
- educated immigrants;
- middle-income individuals with bad credit;
- people who once had bank accounts.

A number of financial institutions have come up with innovative products to exploit opportunities in this market space. Stored value cards, basic bank accounts, and pre-paid wireless money transfer are some of the initiatives banks are rolling out to attract the unbanked to the mainstream.

The underbanked represent large markets – more that 40 million[50] households in the United States alone – with a potential revenue of US$9 billion[51] for mainstream banks seeking to serve these markets. Extrapolation of these figures to include other developed and emerging markets presents limitless opportunities for retail banks to derive financial and social benefits.

---

49 The FICO Expansion Credit Score is a credit risk model which uses many alternative data sources, including: rental activity payment history, utility and phone bill payments, membership payment obligations and retail purchases.
50 Source: Centre for Financial Services Innovation.
51 Source: Aite Group.

Onset of Banking in Virtual Worlds

Banks are increasingly tapping into the popularity of internet-based virtual worlds. One such virtual world is Second Life[52], where banks are offering banking services such as deposit services, credit cards and corporate banking. These virtual worlds have enough members spending enough real and virtual money to have the same financial muscle as many small countries, which makes them attractive to the real-world banks.

The approach taken by the banks that have entered this market is to build a gradual presence in one or more of these virtual communities in a similar way to their approach to internet banking. This method of entry strategy appears to be the logical way as there is no tried and tested business model that can guarantee real-world profits from virtual ventures. However, estimated revenues from the virtual gaming and virtual community industry, according to experts, will be almost US$10 billion by 2009, which is only a reflection of hosting companies and not the entrepreneurs and corporations that are setting up shop in the hope of eventually turning a profit. This presents undoubted opportunities for retail banks.

One of the obvious justifications for banks to invest in the provision of virtual financial services is that even in the real world, the financial services industry already has a sizeable virtual element to it. Moreover, it is one of the most technologically advanced industries in the world, which has led industry experts to believe that the financial services industry will benefit the most from the online revolution that these three-dimensional virtual communities are spearheading.

Some of the other financial services on offer in these virtual worlds include currency exchanges, ATMs and in-world accounts for residents, which are strikingly similar to the real world. For example, Second Life has a floating currency, the Linden Dollar; and SL Bank, a model bank developed by a New York University student, offers transparent information on interest rate fluctuations.[53]

Examples of banks with communities in virtual worlds include ABN Amro and ING.

The Growth of Buy-To-Let

In the last decade, buy-to-let has been a boon to the mortgage lending aspect of the retail banking business. Buy-to-let is a mortgage scheme in the UK backed by the Association of Residential Letting Agents (ARLA) and leading mortgage lenders. The scheme has transformed mortgage lending to the private rented sector (PRS).

---

52 An internet-based virtual world that uses advanced virtual-world technology to create what is, in essence, a highly sophisticated social networking application.
53 Source: www.technewsworld.com/story/55761

Table 4.2 Size of Private Rented Sector and Buy-to-Let sub-sectors

	Number of Properties			
	PRS	Buy-to-let	PRS excluding buy-to-let	Buy-to-let as % of PRS
1998	2,452,000	28,700	2,423,300	1.2%
1999	2,433,000	73,200	2,359,800	3.0%
2000	2,419,000	120,300	2,298,700	5.0%
2001	2,419,000	185,000	2,234,000	7.6%
2002	2,496,000	275,000	2,220,500	11.0%
2003	2,518,000	417,500	2,163,500	16.2%
2004	2,626,000	526,300	2,099,700	20.0%

Source: Council of Mortgage Lenders

Prior to the 1996 launch of the buy-to-let scheme, rented property was financed mainly by finance houses and banks that treated buy-to-let like any small business start-up and generally required deposits of at least 50% of the property value, irrespective of the achievable rental income. But in recent times, only a 15% deposit has been required and buy-to-let is now treated more like a residential mortgage. This has increased the popularity of this type of mortgage finance and according to the Council for Mortgage Lenders, buy-to-let lending reached an all-time record of £94.8 billion in 2006, up from £73.4 billion in the previous year. And the number of buy-to-let mortgages reached 849,900, a rise of 21% on the 2005 figure of 701,900.[54]

One of the legislative changes that are driving the growth in buy-to-let in the UK is the 1988 Housing Act, which introduced the concept of Assured Shorthold Tenancy, which gives landlords an absolute right of possession at the end of tenancy. This gave a confidence boost to new and existing landlords and stimulated more investment in the housing sector. Other drivers include perhaps the desire for more investors to divert funds into the housing sector, the perception that property values will keep rising and there will be upward pressure on rents, and the lack of confidence in the equity markets following the technology boom that went bust in the early 2000s.

Cheque Truncation

Cheque truncation is the use of electronic (scanned) images of a cheque for processing. Cheque truncation can take place at any of the stages of processing financial paper: at the teller, in the branch back office, in the central or regional processing centre or the outsource process provider. It normally involves the

---

[54] Source: *CML News and Views* Issue 3, 20 February 2007.

capture of the cheque's code-line data and amount with an image (front and back) of the cheque. This is then electronically available for further processing and transmission whilst providing an image archive for exception and query handling.

The benefits of cheque truncation in terms of cost reduction can be huge as the processing of paper is an expensive necessity that today tends to be near the bottom of the priority list as regards a bank's investment. Banks would ideally want to focus on selling money, i.e. loans, mortgages etc., and not moving money. Therefore banks that can implement cheque truncation properly along with imaging can offer expanded services and products to their customers, both corporate and personal.

It should be noted that the use of cheques has been in decline in recent times. In the UK, figures from APACS show that the number of cheques used has halved since the peak in 1995. Nordic countries have made a concerted effort to dispense with cheques for the past two decades and they are rarely used anymore. Even in North America, where the cheque is still widely used, it is experiencing a downward spiral.

Figures in the UK show that by 2003 cheque use had fallen spectacularly by 40% from the peak of four billion in 1990 and there is further decline of 40% expected by 2013.[55] Some the factors responsible include the increasing use of debit cards, direct debits, and telephone and internet banking.

These statistics have led experts to conclude that transactions involving cheques could cease to exist in the near future, ending a method of payment that has been in existence for over 350 years.

Cheque processing will be discussed further in Chapter 7.

Introduction of Paperless Bank Statements

The banking industry is increasingly using online statement delivery as the preferred method of getting monthly statements to their customers. In fact, paperless statements are becoming the norm in the banking industry.

Retail banks brand paperless statements under various service tags including online statements, eStatements, email statements etc. Nevertheless, the aim is to adopt paperless statements to save time and reduce costs. According to a Javelin and Strategy report in 2005, in the USA printing and mailing statements can cost banks between 55 cents and 75 cents per month per customer.

Another factor responsible for choosing this method is that they look the same as paper statements and can be accessed more quickly than the paper version, which takes more time to arrive in the post. They can be made available through emails, e-banking services or over websites and are usually free of charge.

Online statement use can create greater awareness of fraud and its recognition. Customers who rely on paper statements to track their accounts detect

---

55 Source: www.onwindows.com/article.asp?id=545

fraud 114 days after it has occurred, according to Javelin. That's compared to the average 18 days it takes for online or ATM users to notice a problem. The difference in losses reported is: US$4,532 for paper users and US$551 for online users.[56]

Popularity of Mobile Payment

In recent times, a raft of new technologies is altering the payments landscape including consumers' payment/purchase behaviour. Not only are there changes in the payment channels, there are also changes in the payment instruments. One new payment technology that appears to be making waves is mobile payment.

Mobile payment (m-payment) is a point-of-sale payment or exchange of financial value between two parties made through a mobile device, such as a cellular telephone, a smartphone, or a personal digital assistant (PDA). Using m-payment, a person with a wireless device could pay for items in a store or settle a restaurant bill without interacting with any staff member. So, for example, if a restaurant patron wanted to pay quickly and leave the restaurant on time to get to an appointment, the bill could be paid directly from the table – without waiting for a server to bring the check. The patron would simply connect to the cash register with a wireless device, punch in the table number and bank personal identification number (PIN), and authorise payment.

The dependency on mobile technologies, expansion of functionality on mobile devices and increasing adoption of these technologies are the cornerstone of the m-payment industry. Mobile devices can offer a richer, more interactive payment experience that not only brings added convenience but also new capabilities such as electronic receipts, ticketing, loyalty programmes, incentives and fraud alerts. According to VISA, there are around 365 million mobile phone subscribers in Europe and according to a survey conducted by Visa USA of 800 consumers, 77 per cent of respondents admitted that they would find it difficult to get through a single day without their mobile phones and more than 50 per cent preferred to have more electronic payment options so that they could dispense with cash. According, to the study, survey respondents are twice as likely to carry mobile phones as cash, with the 18–34-year-old age group four times more likely to carry mobile phones.[57] Some industry experts are of the opinion that younger generations will play an important role in the adoption of mobile payments.

Some countries in the world, particularly in Asia, have taken to mobile payments in a big way. In Japan for instance, NTT DoCoMo implemented the largest and most sophisticated wireless system in the world. The service, known

---

56 Retail Delivery Insights, 26 October 2005, www.bai.org/n1/v1/m4/articles/1paperless.asp
57 Finance Tech., 24 August 2006, http://financetech.com/printableArticle.jhtml?articleID= 192202409

as FeliCa, was introduced in 2004 and sold five million wallet phones in its first year.[58] These phones can be used for goods at both high-value and low-value venues such as retail stores, vending machines and car parks. Telemoney is also an increasingly popular payments service in Malaysia and Singapore which consumers use to pay for concert tickets, transit fares and so on. In the UK, a mobile banking platform called MONILINK provides consumers with "on demand", 24-hour access to banking services, including mini-statements and balance enquiries, through their mobile handset. It also allows them to top up prepay mobile phones.

It is worth noting that the adoption of mobile payments is not even across the world owing to the following factors:

- Variation in laws and payment regulations across borders and industries may affect the suitability of mobile payments in some countries.
- Some countries may not feel the need for new payment types as they may already have a safe, reliable and efficient system in place.
- Attitudes of consumers in some countries towards the use of mobile devices for purchases.

---

58 The Pelorus Group, *Wireless Payments: The New Payments Paradigm 2004 to 2010*, September 2005:10-.

5 Account Opening in Retail Banking

In this chapter, the account opening process and its theoretical underpinning will be analysed. Elements of account management will also be briefly discussed.

Introduction

The account opening process is one of the most important processes in retail banking as it signifies the beginning of the customer-banker relationship. Nowadays account opening is achieved through electronic means via the internet or a web-enabled front-end on workstations in the branch of a bank. Previously account opening only entailed filling out a paper-based form, usually in the presence of a customer service representative or personal banker in the bank's branch or filled out away from the branch and sent back by post to a processing centre.

Background to Account Opening Systems

Account opening (originations) supports almost every product line and service offering in retail banking. It is also one of the first interactions that a customer has with a financial institution and greatly influences a customer's perception of the firm, its service levels, efficiency and value.

The account opening process can be a very complex process owing to multiple product lines, any supporting application tools and organisational silos. This complexity is compounded by a legacy system environment where it is not unusual to find a minimum of two or three different applications supporting the account opening process for each product. When replicated across multiple product lines, the customer service representative's (CSR) desktop becomes a blur of confusing applications.

The advantages of using account opening systems include:

- instant decision making as the electronic front-end for data entry is connected to account databases, credit decisioning systems, customer and account databases and credit reference agencies;
- cross-selling of products is made easier;
- the need for customers to manage multiple relationships with a bank is removed;
- the ease of introduction of new products that complement or replace existing ones;
- existing customer accounts can be easily upgraded;
- auditing of account opening activities is easily achieved.

In this chapter, the electronic account opening process will be discussed using pseudo cases to describe the flow of events as well as both pre- and post-conditions for each identified sub-process. Other events associated with account opening such as account closing and bankruptcy occurring during the customer's life will be discussed.

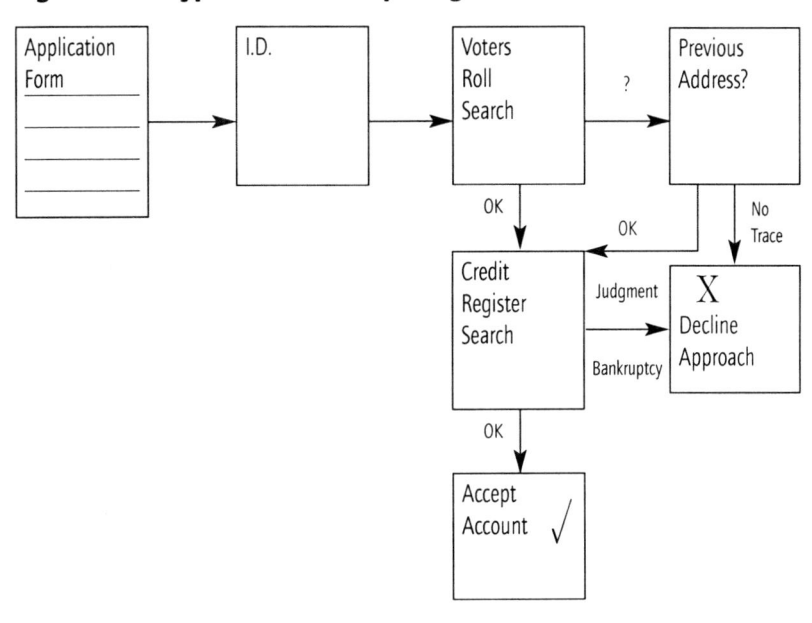

Figure 5.1 A Typical Account Opening Process

© Lipscombe, G. and Pond, K. The Business of Banking (2002). Financial World Publishing. Reproduced with permission. All rights reserved.

Theoretically Underpinnings

Theoretical concepts underpinning the account opening processes will be discussed in this section to provide the necessary background to some of the procedures described in the following sections.

Customer Due Diligence for Banks

According to the Bank for International Settlement, *"Supervisors around the world are increasingly recognising the importance of ensuring that their banks have adequate controls and procedures in place so that they know the customers with whom they are dealing. Adequate due diligence on new and existing customers is a key part of these controls. Without this due diligence, banks can become subject to reputational, operational, legal and concentration risks, which can result in significant financial cost."*

The benchmark document for supervisors to establish national practices and for banks to design their own programmes is the Basel Committee on Banking Supervision's report on Customer Due Diligence for Banks issued in October 2001 ("the Basel CDD paper").

Retail banks now have sound "Know Your Customer" (KYC) procedures in place to ensure the safety and soundness of their organisations because:

- they help to protect banks' reputations and the integrity of banking systems by reducing the likelihood of banks becoming a vehicle for, or a victim of, financial crime and suffering consequential reputational damage;
- they constitute an essential part of substantial risk management practices.

Money Laundering

Money laundering is the process by which criminals attempt to hide/disguise the true origin and ownership of the proceeds of their criminal activities – the illegally obtained money from crimes is given the appearance of having been obtained from legitimate sources.

The process can be described as turning "dirty" money into "clean" money. The need to do this is vital to the success of criminal operations. There is no one set method for laundering money and criminals are always trying to use new and more complex methods to cover their trail.

"Money laundering is called what it is because that perfectly describes what takes place – illegal, or dirty, money is put through a cycle of transactions, or washed, so that it comes out the other end as legal, or clean, money. In other words, the source of illegally obtained funds is obscured through a succession of transfers and deals in order that those same funds can eventually be made to appear as legitimate income."

Laws relating to money laundering have developed over the years in many countries of the world. In the UK, for example, the law covered terrorism and drugs, but this has now been extended to ALL crimes, including extortion, prostitution, robbery, terrorist funding etc.

Recent developments in combating money laundering:

- **Proceeds of Crime Act (POCA)** – this imposes a stricter obligation on all bank staff to report any suspicion of money laundering.
- **Corruption and Politically Exposed Persons** – recent high-profile corruption cases highlighted the need for strong anti-money-laundering controls in the UK.
- **Terrorism** – the events of 11 September 2001 resulted in new guidance for financial services firms.

Money laundering is a clandestine activity and therefore the amount of criminal money being processed either globally or locally each year is impossible to measure accurately. However, some estimates put the amount of money laundered around the world at $500 billion and criminals therefore need to target banks on a daily basis to carry out the process.

The stages of money laundering

The stages in money laundering can be described as:

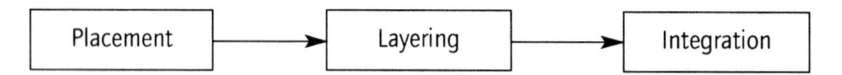

Placement → Layering → Integration

- **Placement** – cash generated from illegal activities is placed into the financial system or retail economy or smuggled out of the country. The aims of the launderer are to remove the cash from the location of acquisition so as to avoid detection by the authorities and to then transform it into other asset forms, for example: traveller's cheques, postal orders etc.
    Examples of other activities at the placement stage are as follows:
    - Depositing a lump sum into an account or investment.
    - Making part repayments in cash to pay off a mortgage or personal loan.
    - Buying assets in cash or leasing luxury items and making payments in cash.
- **Layering** – in the course of layering, there is the first attempt at concealment or disguise of the source of the ownership of the funds by creating complex layers of financial transactions designed to disguise the audit trail and provide anonymity. The purpose of layering is to disassociate the illegal monies from the source of the crime by purposely creating a complex web of financial transactions aimed at concealing any audit trail as well as the source and ownership of funds.
    Examples of other activities at the layering stage are as follows:
    - Buying of shares. The shares may be transferred to other people by gift or may be cashed in early.
    - Transferring of the illicit funds abroad.
- **Integration** – The final stage in the process. This is the stage when the money is integrated into the legitimate economic and financial system and is assimilated with all other assets in the system. Integration of the "cleaned" money into the economy is accomplished by the launderer making it appear to have been legally earned. By this stage, it is exceedingly difficult to distinguish legal and illegal wealth.
    Examples of other activities at the integration stage are as follows:
    - Buying/setting up business ventures – especially those with a high cash turnover, which may be used to help launder further illegal funds.
    - Buying investment policies/traded endowment policies. Investments can generate "clean-looking" income.

Account Opening Requirements

Retail banks recognise that in order to protect their brand reputation, procedures have to be in place to prevent money laundering. The most effective weapon against money laundering is having sufficient information about their customers and using it, as this underpins all other anti-money-laundering procedures. To this end, they stipulate requirements for account opening.

The following illustration outlines the requirements for opening a current bank account at BizEast, our fictional retail bank.

Mr Billy Bob, a UK resident,[59] wishes to open a savings account with the bank.

---

59 This is a requirement for all accounts opened by the bank. A non-UK resident cannot apply for a bank account.

In order to open the account, BizEast requires:

- a completed application form, either online or at a branch;
- an opening deposit from the customer;
- to be satisfied that a potential customer is who they claim to be. BizEast must establish that there is a real person of the name that the applicant gives and is located at the address given, and the applicant is that person.

Many financial organisations still ask the customer to provide documentary evidence in order to confirm their identity and address.

BizEast recently rolled out an initiative to make the experience of opening an account easier for the customer. In order to verify a customer's identity, the bank uses an electronic identity verification system – a web-based application, which forms the basis of the back-end processing procedures. It links into Experian and provides the customer with a score based on the information returned from the checks. If the customer meets a predefined score cut-off, and passes the bank's other validation check, then documentary confirmation of ID and address is not required.

The other validation check to fulfil is as follows:

- the account is opened with a first-party personal cheque; or
- the customer's telephone number is verified with Directory Enquiries and they can be contacted on this number.

Acceptable forms of ID

On occasions where the processing unit does require the customer to produce ID, the following rules apply.

There are a number of documents, split into two categories, which are acceptable as identification verification.

The first tier outlines the preferred forms of verification. These are:

- current full signed passport;
- current residence permit;
- current full UK driving licence (paper-based or photo card);
- current firearms certificate;
- registration cards issued by Inland Revenue;
- Benefits Agency book or letter confirming entitlement to benefits;
- Inland Revenue tax notification;
- current blue disabled-driver's pass;
- current EU member state identity card.

If the applicant does not have any of these documents available, then one of the second tier forms of verification may be used to confirm the customer's identity:

- current debit/credit card but not from the bank;

- current major employer's ID card;
- birth certificate (only acceptable for customers under the age of 18);
- current cheque guarantee card;
- current student NUS photo card;
- application registration card or immigration office document for asylum seekers;
- positive voters' roll check.

The bank would need ID from each applicant if the account applied for was a joint account.

The processing unit will complete a checklist to record details of the document inspected.

Electronic identification and verification (EID&V)

Electronic identification and verification is an electronic process for high-speed checks through ID verification and validation incorporating multiple checks on several identification types and has taken precedence as the preferred medium for undertaking these types of checks.

The popularity of this method of identification in retail banking is as a result of the falsification or counterfeiting of identity documentation, or unlawful misrepresentation of identity, which presents problems when banks want to establish the authenticity of the identity of customers. The increasingly sophisticated techniques used in falsifying identification in spite of the advances in technology have provided the banks with the momentum to circumvent these techniques by adopting more advanced identity verification techniques, particularly through biometric means.

The banks have now realised that it is essential to adopt the technology that will enable the cross-referencing of multiple databases to validate the name, address, national insurance number, passport number, utility information, driving licence, electoral roll entry and telephone number, which in turn validate each other by cross-referral. It has come to the attention of the banks that a valid passport with a fake picture can be supplied by a customer together with a valid piece of secondary identification such as a utility bill to reference the primary source. These electronic databases are, however, able to make multiple cross-references, automatically indicating any inconsistencies and providing a scoring algorithm that may be used to make an account-opening decision.

Corruption and Politically Exposed Persons

The corruption of some government leaders and public sector officials is likely to involve serious crime like theft or fraud. The illegal wealth acquired by these individuals often contrasts starkly with the relative poverty of that particular country.

Corruption can occur in any country where local council and/or government officials abuse their powers for their own financial gain.

To help address these concerns, financial services firms have to take additional steps when dealing with people who, owing to their political standing or connections, are in a position where they could benefit from corruption. These people are known as "politically exposed persons" (PEPs).

Extra care is also taken when dealing with people known to be family members or close personal or business associates of PEPs.

Some examples of a PEP are:

- a local government official;
- a national government official;
- a senior judge or other member of the judiciary;
- a senior member of the armed forces;
- an official involved in a government-owned corporation.

Given the information about these kinds of individual at the bank's disposal, their activities are closely monitored to verify the purpose of their transactions. It is therefore necessary to accurately collect the ID/Know Your Customer information.

If there are any doubts about the validity of transactions, accounts opened etc., a Suspicious Transaction Report form is submitted.

Terrorism
The tragic events of 11 September 2001 in the USA have resulted in enhanced guidance for financial services firms to ensure they do not unintentionally hide or move terrorist funds.

Under the provisions of the Anti-Terrorism, Crime & Security Act 2001, financial services organisations must report any funds which they suspect, or have reasonable grounds to suspect, are or will be associated with terrorist organisations or terrorist acts.

Funding is the collection of monies for acts of terrorism and funding of terrorism is likely to be detected from transaction activity on accounts. Examples include:

- a high volume of activity on an account;
- inconsistent deposits in comparison to income declaration/occupation;
- numerous deposits paid into an account on the same day at different branches.

Sanctions
In recent times there has been an increase in the focus on terrorist financing and as a result banks and regulators are seeking to enforce sanctions compliance. Banks in particular are putting appropriate controls in place to ensure compliance with sanctions laws at each stage of the transaction life cycle.

At account opening, banks screen clients against applicable sanctions lists before an account is opened and in the event of an upgrade, check their existing client base against new names that have been added to the sanctions lists.

Account Opening Process

The account opening process can be divided into the following sub-processes:

- customer data entry;
- address checking;
- credit checking;
- product offering and cross-selling;
- identity verification;
- account opening fulfilment.

Personal Banking Process

The electronic account opening process for personal customers to be discussed in this section will be centred on the functionality of account-opening software from vendors such as Chordiant and Infosys.

In recent times, retail banks have rolled out account-opening systems that are used by personal bankers and customer service representatives (CSR) in the presence of the applicant. The process entails a walkthrough of the process by the personal banker or CSR who captures information from the interview with the applicant, enters this into the system and is given almost real-time feedback by the system.

During the process, other players may be contacted including the following:

- call centre agents – who can interview the applicant over the phone, capture their details and enter them into the system;
- sanctions helpdesk – the staff of the bank who investigate cases where the applicant has been referred as a result of sanctions against their country of origin;
- personal lending department – the staff of the bank who make personal lending decisions when the applicant has been referred for lending or credit reasons.

Accounts offered to customers can be on a sole or joint basis; if the account to be applied for is a joint account, then both applicants have to be present at the interview.

Customer Data Entry
Preconditions
- Cost/profit centre has been recorded.
- Applicant's presence or otherwise has been noted.
- Account ownership, i.e. sole or joint, has been selected.
- Type of account, i.e. current or savings account, has been selected.
- Purpose of application, i.e. new account or upgrade, has been selected.

Flow events
Basic path
[Selection: Applicant present; Sole; Current; New Account]
1. Bank employee enters the applicant's personal details as follows:
   - Title
   - Full Name
   - Date of Birth
   - Sex
   - Address
   - Nationality
   - Home Telephone Number
   - Mobile Phone Number
2. If the applicant has lived at the address for less than three years, the previous addresses are captured (an explanation for this requirement can be found in Chapter 6).
3. Employment details of the applicant are entered. These could depend on the type of employment that the applicant is in. If the applicant is a student or a minor, the system presents fields on the screen that allow the relevant data to be captured.

Alternative path [1]
[Selection: Applicant present; Joint; Current; New Account]
1. Bank employee enters each of the applicants' personal details as follows:
   - Full Name
   - Date of Birth
   - Sex
   - Address
   - Nationality
   - Home Telephone Number
   - Mobile Phone Number
2. If either or both applicants have lived at the address for less than three years, their previous addresses are captured.
3. Employment details of each applicant are entered. This could depend on the type of employment that the applicants are in. Depending on the business rules at the bank, neither of the applicants should be a minor or a student.

Alternative path [2]
[Selection: Applicant present; Sole; Current; Upgrade]
1. Bank employee enters the applicant's full name.
2. The applicant's personal details are prefilled on the system as the applicant is already a customer of the bank.
3. Employment details are prefilled, but these details might have changed as the applicant could have changed their occupation or employer.

Alternative path [3]
[Selection: Applicant not present; Sole; Savings; New Account]
1. Bank employee enters the applicant's personal details as follows:
    - Title
    - Full Name
    - Date of Birth
    - Sex
    - Address
    - Nationality
    - Home Telephone Number
    - Mobile Phone Number
2. If the applicant has lived at the current address for less than three years, previous addresses are captured.
3. Previous address in a foreign country[60] may be captured.
4. Employment details of the applicant are entered. These could depend on the type of employment that the applicant is in. If the applicant is a student or a minor, the system presents fields on the screen that allow relevant data to be captured.

Alternative path [4]
[Selection: Present; Sole; Savings; New Account]
1. Bank employee enters the applicant's full name.
2. Based on the title supplied, the system checks that the applicant is not a politically exposed person (PEP).
3. If the applicant has lived at the address for less than three years, the previous addresses are captured.
4. Employment details of the applicant are entered. These could depend on the type of employment that the applicant is in. If the applicant is a student or a minor, the system presents fields on the screen that allow relevant data to be captured.

Post condition
The system kicks off address checking.

Address Checking
Precondition
Address has been fully captured and saved on the system.

---

[60] Some banks may decline or refer applications from applicants that previously lived in Non-Cooperative Countries and Territories (NCCT), although the last of the countries, Myanmar, was removed from the laundry blacklist in 2006. This may or may not be the case depending on the policy of the bank on account opening.

Flow events
Basic path
1. System checks on Royal Mail database to confirm that the address(es) exists.
2. In some cases, if the address is for a new area not registered in this database, depending on the system there could be an option for a manual override.
3. The electoral register is searched to confirm that the applicant is registered at the address supplied.
4. If the applicant has lived at the address for less than three years, the electoral register is searched again for the previous addresses to confirm the applicant was registered at the address supplied.

Alternative path
1. No trace of the applicant in the electoral register.
2. Application declined.

Post condition
The system kicks off a credit search on the databases of the different credit reference agencies. Anti-Money-Laundering and Know Your Customer (AML/KYC) processes also kick off.

Credit Checking
Precondition
Applicant's details exist on the electoral register.

Flow events
Basic path
1. System performs credit search.
2. Search returns a credit score that is acceptable to the bank's criteria and there is no referral against the applicant's details.

Alternative path [1]
1. Credit search returns data which requires a referral (e.g. CIFAS, Bankruptcy or CCJ).
2. System generates referral code.
3. Bank employee contacts relevant departments, quoting the referral code, to handle the referral.

Post condition
Credit decisioning process kicks off.

Product Offering
Precondition
Credit decisioning offers a product based on the bank's criteria.

Flow events
Basic path
1. Account offered to applicant.
2. Benefits attached to each product offering are displayed.
3. Bank employee selects benefits in accordance with the applicant's preference.
4. Other products such as associated savings accounts, credit cards etc. are offered to the applicant.[61]

Alternative path [1]
[Selection: Applicant present; Sole; Current; Upgrade]
1. If selection is as shown above on data entry (i.e. during the customer data entry sub-process), the applicant may not be offered an upgrade to the type of account they desire.
2. Personal Lending department will be contacted to review the product offering.
3. Personal Lending department reviews the current offering and the customer is offered the desired account.

Post condition
Product offering is accepted by applicant.

Identity Verification
This stage of the account opening process utilises the electronic identification and verification (EID&V) subsystem – if implemented as part of the system – to verify the identity of the applicant. In other cases, physical ID is required.

Precondition
The system has saved the details of the product offerings accepted by the applicant.

Flow events
Basic path
1. The applicant's personal data is processed by the EID&V subsystem.
2. Applicant's identity and address is verified.

Alternative path [1]
1. Applicant's identity and address cannot be confirmed by EID&V.
2. Applicant is required to produce the necessary physical ID for account opening purposes.

---

61 This presents cross-selling opportunities for banks.

Alternative path [2]
1. Output from EID&V shows inconsistencies in the applicant's personal data.
2. The application is referred to the relevant department within the bank for investigation.

Post condition
The application has been accepted.

Account Opening Fulfilment
Precondition
The applicant's data has been allocated a record in the customer databases.

Flow events
Basic path
1. The applicant is assigned an account number and sort code.
2. Bank employee selects other details for the account according to the applicant's requirements.
3. The terms and conditions (T&Cs) of the account are presented to the applicant for acceptance.
4. Applicant accepts T&Cs.
5. Account opening process is completed in the system.
6. Checklists are generated for audit purposes.
7. Checklists are validated by bank employee.

Alternative path [1]
1. The applicant is assigned an account number and sort code.
2. Bank employee selects other details[62] for the account according to the applicant's requirements.
3. The terms and conditions (T&Cs) of the account are presented to the applicant for acceptance.
4. Applicant rejects T&Cs.
5. Account opening process is completed in the system.
6. Applicant is not offered the account.

Post condition
The applicant is now a customer of the bank, has been assigned a customer identification number (CIN) and has a record in the customer database.

---

62 These details could include the address to send the cheque book to and how the applicant's name should appear on the cheque book, debit card and other additional products.

Events Occurring During the Life of the Customer

Mental Incapacity

If a customer is mentally incapacitated, in most cases the bank terminates their mandate to operate the customer's account.

Managing banking for mentally incapacitated customers can be a particularly confusing area of banking. Third parties looking after a mentally incapacitated customer can be an attorney, a receiver or an appointee and depending on which one they are, banking procedures will vary.

In most cases, the customer's relatives apply to the courts for the appointment of a receiver to handle the customer's affairs in accordance with the relevant laws. In the UK, the appointment of the receiver is recorded in the probate register used to maintain a record of events in the lives of customers.

Death

In the event of the death of a customer, banks terminate their mandate to operate the customer's account and cheques must be returned marked "drawer deceased" after the bank has received notice of the customer's death. The customer's relatives will need to present a valid death certificate or an official copy to the bank to carry out the necessary actions.

If the account is a sole account in the name of, say, Brad Bigfoot, then any payments into his account after the bank received the notice of death will be credited to a new account in the name of "Personal representatives of Brad Bigfoot deceased". However, if the account is a joint account in the names of Mr Brad Bigfoot and Mrs Jane Bigfoot, then the account will continue to run in the name of Mrs Jane Bigfoot.

Bankruptcy

Bankruptcy is a situation whereby a debtor, upon voluntary petition or one invoked by the debtor's creditors, is judged legally insolvent. The debtor's remaining property is then administered for the creditors or is distributed among them.

Bankruptcy is regulated by Insolvency and Bankrupt Acts that provide various ways to give legal protection to people or companies that are unable to pay their debts.

Marriage or Change of Name

When a customer changes their name on marriage or for any other reason, banks ask the customer for a marriage or deed poll certificate in order to record the event in the probate register.

Closing an Account

An account that is in credit can be closed but the bank must give reasonable notice to the customer. The notice period is dependent on the circumstances for closure of the account. The common practice is for the bank to give a month's notice but if the account has not been conducted in the proper manner, it may be closed at shorter notice. An example is where a customer draws a cheque for a large amount on their account at the bank and the account does not have sufficient cleared funds.

Account Management

Once an account is opened, details of the new account are passed to the account management system where an account record is created. In this section, a brief description of some of the elements of account management will be discussed. The diagram below shows the basic configuration of an account opening system, which can be expanded to suit any type of account on offer in retail banks.

Figure 5.2 A Typical Account Management System

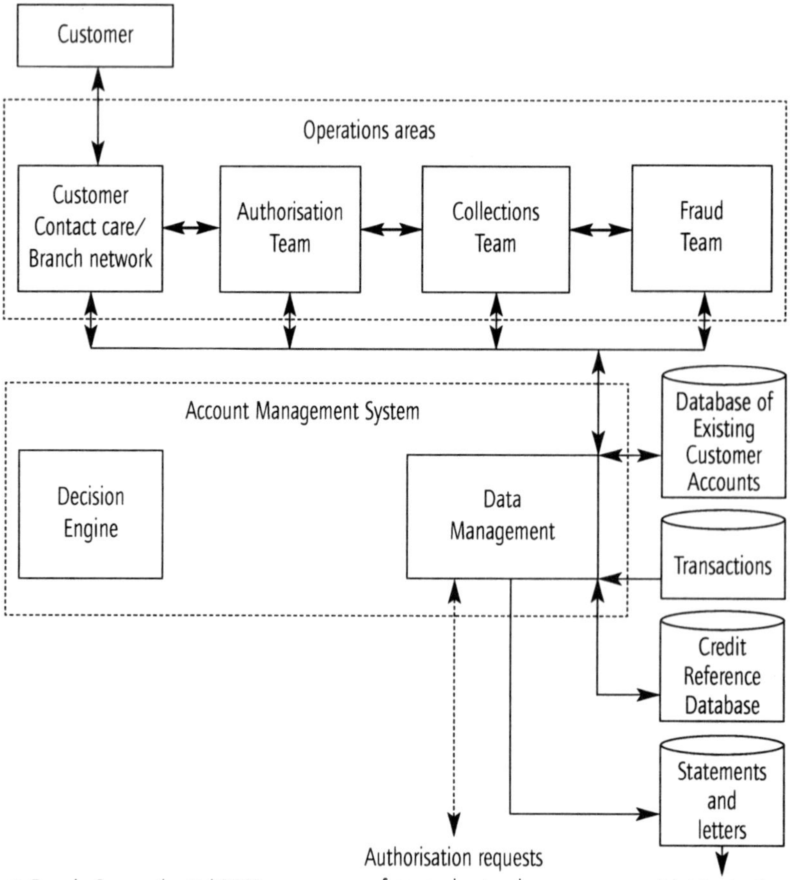

Account management systems process the large volumes of data required to maintain accounts on a daily basis. Retail banks typically have a large number of customer accounts in the customer database which need to be updated with new transactions that occur during a given business day as part of an overnight batch process. Other systems within the banks have different processing requirements. For example, mortgage systems require the processing of monthly repayments and ad hoc amendments to the terms of the agreement.

Account management also entails account cycling and statement production. Accounts are said to cycle at the end of each statement month as processing performs the calculation of interest and other charges arising and the generation of any additional information required to produce customers' statements of account. On completion of processing, statement details for all accounts for that day are produced and forwarded to the function in the bank responsible for the physical printing and posting of statements. For products such as credit cards, where credit is revolving,[63] accounts are usually passed to a decision engine where credit scoring and business rules are applied and, as a consequence, terms of business are amended.

In the course of account management, banks identify cases of suspected fraud in, say, credit card transactions, using systems-defined policy rules or a variation on credit scoring to identify transactions that reveal behavioural inconsistencies with the historical behaviour of the account.

---

[63] Revolving credit is a type of credit that does not have a fixed number of payments, as opposed to instalment credit.

Lending in Retail Banking

This chapter covers the fundamentals of lending and credit including data on lending, credit scoring and the economics of credit.

Overview of Lending

Lending is the practice of granting the use of money with the understanding that it or something else of value will be returned at a future date. Lending is a very important aspect of banking that requires dexterity and experience as bad debt can lead to the collapse of a banking institution. Furthermore, identifying and exploiting good lending opportunities can generate steady revenue for banks.

In this chapter, elementary lending principles will be mentioned as lending is a broad-based discipline and cannot be covered in just a chapter. However, one of the relationships at the core of good banking is that between credit and lending and as such the subject of credit will also be discussed.

Readers should please note the words "bank" and "lender" will be used interchangeably in some sections of this chapter.

Types of Lending

Secured Lending
Secured lending entails the pledging of assets by the borrower which the lender can use in lieu of the money borrowed. The assets, known as collateral, can be a house, car or any item of value belonging to the borrower that will be included in the terms of the loan.

Unsecured Lending
Unsecured lending is the opposite of secured lending. This type of lending does not require collateral; the security is the integrity of the borrower. An example of unsecured lending is a loan extended to individuals through credit cards or personal loans.

Principles of Lending

Two interesting acronyms, "CAMPARI "and "ICE",[64] will be used in this section to illustrate the principles of lending in retail banking. CAMPARI stands for Character, Ability, Means, Purpose, Amount, Repayment, and Insurance while ICE stands for Interest, Charges and Extras. These acronyms are suited to the principles of lending as regards the personal lending market.

CAMPARI
- **Character** – the integrity of the borrower is of the utmost importance in the lending process as the lender would like to be assured that the money from deposits is loaned to an individual of impeccable character.

---

64 Lipscombe, G. and Pond, K. (2002), *The Business of Banking*, Financial World Publishing.

- **Ability** – this is a measure of the borrower's capability of doing their job, which is important as they need future and steady cash flow to meet the repayment obligations.
- **Means/Margin** – depending on the purpose of the loan, lenders sometimes require borrowers to share in the risk of lending and as a result demand that a percentage of the value of the project/purchase is contributed by the borrower. This is so in the case of mortgage borrowing or car purchase financing.
- **Purpose** – lenders need to know the purpose of the loan being requested by the borrower to ensure that the money borrowed is not used for illegal or nefarious activities and to be sure that the borrower will be able to repay the loan, given their intentions.
- **Amount** – the amount to be borrowed is also of prime concern to the lender as they would want to know that this amount is sufficient to fulfil the purpose of the loan. For example, a mortgagee has to have accounted for legal fees, solicitors' fees and so on.
- **Repayment and term** – the borrower needs to make the repayment source of the loan known to the lender and it should be agreeable to both parties. The lender would have to be comfortable that the borrower has a history of saving to ensure monthly repayments are covered and also that the borrower has not been overstretched by the loan.
- **Insurance** – the collateral offered by the borrower should meet the requirements of the lender if the loan is secured. The lender would usually not approve a loan until the documentation of the collateral is satisfactory and it is safely deposited with them (lender). Insurance in this context also applies to payment protection for eventualities such as sickness, unemployment or death.

ICE
- **Interest** – the interest rate offered to borrowers is usually in line with their risk profiles and credit rating. In general, borrowers with high credit scores are of a low risk profile. These kinds of borrowers are able to borrow at typical interest rates offered to two thirds of the population of a given geographical area.
- **Commission** – this charge is in the form of an "arrangement fee" paid by the borrower to the lender when a loan is taken out. Lenders sometimes offer borrowers the option of adding this fee to the principal amount borrowed. Commissions (arrangement fees) compensate lenders for the effort involved in granting and monitoring the loan.
- **Extras** – there are cross-selling opportunities for lenders in the lending process given the information that they already have about their existing customers. Other products that the lenders offer, such as insurance and travel services, can be offered to existing and new borrowers and also members of their families.

Data on Lending

Borrowing is part of modern everyday life in almost every country of the world and a major source of revenue for retail banking organisations. The following are interesting statistics about debt in the UK, obtained with permission from Credit Action:[65]

- Total UK personal debt at the end of April 2007 stood at £1,325bn. The growth rate increased to 10.4% for the previous 12 months, which equates to an increase of £114bn.
- Total secured lending on homes at the end of April 2007 stood at £1,112bn. This was an increase of 11.4% over the previous 12 months.
- Total lending in April 2007 grew by £9.4bn. Secured lending grew by £8.9bn in the month. Consumer credit lending grew by £0.5bn.
- There are more credit cards in the UK than people. At the end of 2006 there were 74.4m credit and charge cards in the UK compared with around 60 million people in the country.
- The combined value of transactions made on charge, credit, debit and store cards was £511bn in 2006.
- The average interest rate on credit-card lending is currently 17.1%, around 11.5% above base rate.

Collateralisation

Collateralisation is the process whereby borrowers pledge assets like real estate (land and buildings), stocks and shares, and life assurance policies. Collateral is taken to protect the lender against risk; it screens potential borrowers and is an incentive to repay the loan. Banks usually prefer collateral where ownership is confirmed by documentation such as certificates and deeds.

There are legally binding contracts that accompany collateralisation and failure to adhere strictly to the rules of a contract can void it, leaving the bank without sufficient security for the money lent out.

Banks have to take precautionary measures to ensure that the collateral offered by the borrower is adequate for the loan requested. As with lending, an acronym "MAST"[66] will be used to illustrate the features of good collateral:

- **Marketability** – the asset should be able to be sold easily.
- **Ascertainability of Value** – valuation of the asset should be relatively easy.
- **Simplicity of Title** – legal ownership of the collateral should be easy to ascertain.

---

65 A UK-based national money education charity established in 1994.
66 Lipscombe, G. and Pond. K. (2002). *The Business of Banking*, Financial World Publishing

▓ **Transferability of Title** – the asset should be easily transferable.

Collateral-taking procedures

Procedures are in place in the banks to ensure that collateral in the form of land or shares is taken properly in order that it can be used in the event of default in payment of a loan extended to a borrower.

Below is a diagrammatic representation of the stages involved in collateral taking.

Figure 6.1 Stages in Collateral Taking

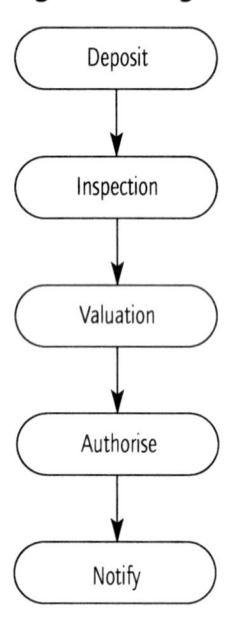

```
┌───────────┐
│  Deposit  │
└─────┬─────┘
      ↓
┌───────────┐
│ Inspection│
└─────┬─────┘
      ↓
┌───────────┐
│ Valuation │
└─────┬─────┘
      ↓
┌───────────┐
│ Authorise │
└─────┬─────┘
      ↓
┌───────────┐
│   Notify  │
└───────────┘
```

The Cost of Credit

Credit is convenient but the convenience it offers is at a cost. The cost of credit is the additional amount that a borrower pays over and above the amount borrowed. Some of the costs could be compulsory, stipulated by the lender as a fundamental part of the credit agreement, while others, such as payment cover, are discretionary depending on whether the borrower wants them included as part of the agreement. These costs include:

▓ **Interest** – interest charges, usually the major component of finance charges, are stated as a percentage of the total sum borrowed over a period. This period could be a days, months or years. For instance, if a borrower takes out a £10,000 loan for six years and then pays back this amount in full, they will have incurred interest charges at 6% per annum of £3,600 (£10,000*0.06*6).

- **Fees** – these are specific charges, which can vary widely from arrangement fees to penalty fees for late payment and annual membership charges in the case of charge cards.
- **Annual Percentage Rate of Charge** – the annual percentage rate (APR) is an expression of the effective interest rate that will be paid on a loan, taking into account one-time fees and standardising the way the rate is expressed. The goal of the APR calculation is to provide a degree of transparency and to allow a comparison to be made between competing products. The APR is a representation of interest and all mandatory charges in the form of an interest rate, and is derived from the patterns of advances and repayments made during the agreement (Finlay, 2005).

The APR is likely to differ from the "headline rate" advertised by the lender. The concept of APR can be generalised. For example, lenders use the same concept to calculate their total earnings on loans and to determine their margin on the loan. Consumers can use the APR concept to compare savings accounts and calculate the earnings on a savings account, taking transaction costs into account.

A simple illustration of the concept of APR is as follows.

Mr Bill Buzz takes out a personal loan of £6,000 from BizEast Bank for 1 year. The interest rate is 5.5 per cent and an arrangement fee of £90 is charged. Therefore the total cost of credit to Mr. Buzz is:

$(0.055*6000) + 90 = £420$

Calculating £420 as a percentage of £6,000 shows that the APR for the loan is 7 per cent, which is in contrast with the 5.5 per cent that the BizEast Bank may state as their interest per annum.

APRs can be fixed or variable. A variable APR is tied to a specific banking index (e.g. the Prime Rate index) and fluctuates in response to changes in that index. A fixed APR does not fluctuate in response to an index.

It should be noted that despite repeated attempts by regulators to establish usable and consistent standards, APR does not represent the total cost of borrowing nor does it really create a comparable standard for the following. In spite of this, it is considered a reasonable starting point for an extemporised comparison of lenders.

- **Introductory Rates** – lenders have in recent times adopted the practice of offering borrowers introductory rates over an initial period which revert to the standard rates thereafter. This is common with mortgage loans and credit cards.
- **Different Transactions, Different Rates** – this scenario is usually applicable to credit-card borrowing. It means that different types of transactions you make may have different APRs associated with them. For example, there might be one APR for purchase transactions and another for cash advances.

Economics of Credit

What is Credit?
Credit is a contractual agreement in which a borrower receives something of value now, with the agreement to repay the lender at some date in the future. It is also the borrowing capacity of an individual or company. (Investopedia.com)

Credit can also be simply defined as the granting of a loan and the creation of debt.

Five Cs of Credit[67]
The five key elements a borrower should have to obtain credit are:

- character (integrity);
- capacity (sufficient cash flow to service the obligation);
- capital (net worth);
- collateral (assets to secure the debt);
- conditions (of the borrower and the overall economy).

Granting Credit Decisions

Creditworthiness
Creditworthiness is a measure of the likelihood that a borrower will repay a loan taken out with a lender. When customers apply for credit, credit managers assess the application based on the probability of repayment. If the outcome of the assessment shows that certain applicants are too high a risk, they are declined and the application will not progress beyond this stage.

Risk associated with the credit granting process refers to the correlation between the expected return from customers who repay the credit advanced to them and losses incurred as a consequence of those that default. Banks would consider a situation whereby the expected return of those that repay their debt outweighs the losses of those that don't as *Acceptable Risk*. Banks use information that they have on applicants to guesstimate the odds that certain applicants will default on their loans. The odds of, say, 15:1 would suggest that out of 16 similar people, 15 will be expected to repay their loan and 1 will be expected to default. Therefore, on a loan of £20,000 extended to a borrower, a bank would expect to make a return on investment of 10% of the original loan, but in the event of a default the debt will be written off and the bank will incur a 100% loss. This in effect means that:

Rate of return on an individual: £20,000 * 10% = £2,000

On default, loss incurred by the bank: £20,000 * 100% = £20,000

---

[67] Source: www.investorwords.com/1/5Cs_of_credit.html

Given the odds:

> Total expected return: £2,000 * 15 = £30,000
>
> Total expected loss: £20,000 * 1 = £20,000
>
> Net expected return: = £10,000
>
> Average expected return per loan: £10,000/(15+1) = £625

From the above illustration, the average return per loan of £625 over a large number of loans, being a positive sum, will be viewed by the bank as acceptable risk. However, there has to be a cut-off value for the odds which will provide a threshold for accepting applications if the bank expects to make any return on its investment. The cut-off value, often referred to as break-even odds, is therefore the odds where the expected return will be zero. The break-even odds for the illustration above will be:

$$\text{Break-even odds}[68] = \frac{\text{Expected loss (from a customer who defaults)}}{\text{Expected return (from a customer who repays)}}$$

$$= £20,000 / £2,000$$

$$= 10:1$$

This means that the bank would ideally accept loan applications where the odds are 10:1 and reject applications where odds are below 10:1, i.e. "negative". There is no precise value for the odds used in the banking sector; different lenders use break-even odds that reflect their attitude towards risk. For example, in the sub-prime[69] lending market, odds of less than 2:1 are not uncommon, while some mainstream lenders use over 20:1.

Credit Applications

Credit applications involve applicants submitting information to prospective lenders for assessment of their risk. The types of information include basic details required to open and run an account as well as the loan amount and term of the loan. Lenders use this information and the circumstances to evaluate the risk of the applicant using two main methods: judgemental decision making and credit scoring.

Judgemental decision making

Judgemental decision making in granting credit decisions is an exercise whereby human underwriters judge credit applications on a case-by-case basis with a view to assessing the creditworthiness of the applicant. The underwriters use intuition, experience and sometimes personal knowledge of applicants

---

68 These are odds where the expected return on the loan is zero.
69 A classification for borrowers with tainted or limited credit history.

to come up with a subjective view as to the propensity of applicants to default on loans.

The five Cs of credit aid the decision making of the underwriter who seeks to establish that each of the Cs is satisfied by the information about an applicant that is at their disposal. A credit report from a credit reference agency such as Equifax, which would show the applicant's repayment history with other lenders, is also used in the decision-making process.

The approach to underwriting differs from organisation to organisation; some lenders make use of policies alongside the underwriter's judgement in making decisions. These policies are usually based on the experience of senior underwriters as to what constitutes creditworthiness. There are guidelines in these policies that underwriters follow in order to make lending decisions. For example, a policy can specify that lending is prohibited to applicants under a certain age or to people of a certain employment status.

The use of a policy helps underwriters make better decisions, but has major drawbacks including contradictions in the guidelines as the policy expands, and being inadequate to deal with every conceivable situation.

Credit scoring
Credit scoring is a statistical analysis performed by lenders and financial institutions to access a person's creditworthiness. Lenders use credit scoring, among other things, to arrive at a decision on whether to extend credit. A person's credit score is a number between 300 and 900, 900 being the highest credit rating possible.

Fair Isaac Corporation's credit scoring system, known as a FICO score, is the most widely used credit scoring system in the financial industry. Lenders use credit scoring in risk-based pricing in which the terms of a loan, including the interest rate, offered to borrowers are based on the probability of repayment. (Investopedia.com)

Credit scorecards
Credit scorecards are mathematical models which attempt to provide a quantitative measurement of the likelihood that a customer will display a defined behaviour with respect to their current or proposed credit position with a lender. In calculating the score, a range of data sources may be used, including data from an application form, from credit reference agencies or from products the customer already holds with the lender. The score is then used as an indicator of the future behaviour of the applicant, i.e. the probability that during the course of the outcome period,[70] the customer's risk profile will be in line with acceptable risk. The higher the applicant's score, the lower the risk of extending credit to them and the higher the probability of the lender profiting from the applicant.

---

70 Time between the date the sample data is extracted and the date it is classified into the principal sets in a scorecard development.

How credit scores are used for decisions making
Banks use credit scores from scorecards to categorise accounts into "good" and "bad", having observed the accounts over a period of time. The following are definitions of these categories (Guide to Credit Scoring 2000):

- **Good account** – an account where the performance is such that the credit grantor (bank) would choose to accepts the application again, all the circumstances remaining the same. "Good" will have been defined in the scorecard development. Different organisations will have different definitions of "good" depending on their business and the objective of the scorecard.
- **Bad account** – an account where the performance is such that the credit grantor[71] would decline that application in future (for example, a specified level of arrears within a given time frame). Different organisations will adopt different definitions of "bad" depending on their business and depending on the objective of the scorecards.

Good:bad odds is a measure of the ratio of good accounts to bad accounts within a population and is similar to the odds discussed earlier which measured the ratio of non-defaulters to defaulters. Credit managers in banks use good:bad odds for assessing consumer credit portfolios. The relationship between credit scores and good odds is such that the higher the credit score, the higher the odds. So a score of, say, 500 may equate to good:bad odds of 2:1 and a score of, say, 800 to good:bad odds of 10:1. When a new application is made and receives a credit score, if the good:bad odds associated with that score are below those which the lender deems creditworthy, the application will be declined (Finlay, 2005).

Technical implementation of scorecard
Scoring technology analyses historical client data, identifies links between client characteristics and behaviour, and assumes those links will persist to predict how clients will react. The technology can help a bank analyse how its clients have behaved in the past to make more reliable loan application decisions, devise more effective collection strategies, make better marketing efforts and increase client retention. Scoring technology systems can be a foundation for advanced capabilities, such as pricing loans based on individual client risks and more accurately provisioning against loan losses.

A technical solution for credit scoring using statistical techniques that identify the link between characteristics and risks is as follows.

Client data is first extracted from a bank's central database. Software packages such as SAS, S+ and SPSS then run statistical analyses using techniques such as linear and logistic regression to identify the importance of certain client variables to behaviour. The statistical scoring model generates a scorecard that indicates the probability of default, desertion or other behaviour, based on

---

71 Organisation that offers credit or credit facilities.

these unique characteristics. This can provide a foundation for more advanced credit-risk management applications.

Requirements for a technical solution for credit scoring
- Centralised database of relevant client information.
- Database dedicated to scoring information.
- Management commitment to project implementation.
- Resources from technology and credit departments in the banks to integrate, maintain and refine scoring applications.

Benefits of a technical solution for credit scoring
- Improves the efficiency of loan evaluations, recovery of arrears and customer retention.
- Frees staff to spend more time on the subjective "grey areas" of decision making.
- Offers a basis for variable pricing by including individual client risk in lending decisions.
- Lays a foundation for more sophisticated risk management and marketing applications.

Credit scoring vs judgemental decision making
Comparisons can be made between credit scoring and judgmental decision making in a number of areas.

Credit Scoring	Judgemental Decision Making
Automated processes that depend on information supplied by the applicant	Manual process that depends on skills and experience of underwriter
Consistent and repeatable	Inconsistencies abound as a result of underwriter's mood and timing of assessment
Rigidity of the criteria for making decisions as the credit scoring systems may have been developed with information that was available at the time of design	Flexibility in choosing criteria for making decisions about an applicant
Unbiased assessment of information supplied by applicants, irrespective of race, sex or religion	Biased evaluation process dependent on the underwriter's perception of the applicant

Credit Referencing
Credit referencing is the process whereby lenders perform a search with a credit reference agency on an individual that has applied for a credit facility or loan. These searches are carried out because information supplied to the lender at the time of the application is insufficient proof that the applicant will not default. Information such as details of other borrowing, previous bankruptcies, cases of

default and so on are returned from the searches giving the lender a picture of the applicant's credit history.

These credit searches involve the solicitation of information about the applicant as well as a credit report from the credit reference agencies who query their database and return information to lenders who will integrate it into their decision-making process. General types of information held by most credit reference agencies are the same all over the world, but the precise information held by credit reference agencies varies from country to country owing to the different legislation and industry agreements that dictate the uses to which information can or cannot be put (Finlay, 2005).

Information sources

In this section, the information available from each of the three UK credit reference agencies – Experian, Callcredit and Equifax – and its categorisation will be discussed.

This information can be defined as falling into one of three categories as follows.

Public information

- **County court judgments, bankruptcies and repossession** – county court judgments (CCJs) are registered against individuals that have been taken to the county court and found liable for unpaid debt. CCJs and more cases of bankruptcy are publicly available and maintained on a national register. A copy of the register is supplied to the credit reference agencies who maintain all records of bankruptcies and CCJs for a period of six years. The information on file includes:
  - the value of the judgment and bankruptcy;
  - the date on which the judgment or bankruptcy occurred;
  - the payment or repayment of the debt in line with the court's ruling.

  If a CCJ or bankruptcy is registered against an individual's credit record, it is an indication of future risk and would result in refusal of credit by mainstream credit providers like banks and credit-card companies, more so if the debt is recent or of a high value.

- **Electoral roll** – the electoral roll (or electoral register) is a listing of all those registered to vote in a particular area in the UK. The register is compiled by sending an annual canvass form to every house and updated monthly to allow people who move home to remain registered. The register has two formats: the full version and the edited version. The full version is available for credit evaluation and to verify identity. The edited version omits the details of people who have opted out and do not wish to be included for commercial purposes. This version is used primarily by commercial organisations for the production of mailing lists and can be purchased by anyone.

  Credit reference agencies use current and historical versions of the register to identify people that are registered at a previous address and whose details do not appear on the register at the current address.

Private information
- **Shared customer account information** – credit reference agencies store customer account data privately in the largest files of all the information sources. Lenders forward the following customer account details to credit reference agencies on a monthly basis:
  - personal details for identity purposes (account name, number, date of birth, current address etc.);
  - the type of product (loan, credit card, mortgage etc.);
  - start date of the credit agreement;
  - the outstanding balance;
  - the current and historic arrears status (up to date, 1/2/3 late payments etc.)
  - record of special cases or circumstances that are signified by a range of indicators. These cases include disuse of an account, situation where there is dispute with a customer, or where a lender has not provided a status of the customer's account.

  It is worth noting that the nature of the information provided to the credit reference agencies is limited. Detailed transactional information about how customers use a product, their purchases, where the transactions took place and the prices paid is not provided.
- **Credit searches** – a record of a credit search is logged by credit reference agencies any time a credit search is carried out. When subsequent searches are instigated, they will reveal any previous credit searches that have been performed. As a result, lenders' decisions are influenced by the frequency of application for credit as this is indicative of a riskier profile than average.

  The types of information about credit searches are limited to:
  - the date the search was performed;
  - the type of product applied for (for example, mortgage, personal loan or credit card);
  - the organisation that requested the search (Finlay, 2005).

  Credit reference agencies do not record the outcome, i.e. whether the application was accepted or rejected, of searches made. The usual practice for updating search information is on a daily basis and retention is for 12 months.
- **CIFAS** – this stands for Credit Industry Fraud Avoidance Scheme as discussed in Chapter 3. Credit reference agencies maintain a copy of the CIFAS database so in the event that a search carried out by a member organisation results in a CIFAS record being returned against the details of an applicant, the organisation is aware that the applicant has previously been suspected of acting fraudulently. It is worth noting that having a CIFAS record would not lead a lender to conclude that the applicant is fraudulent. It is just a sort of warning that might prompt a lender to carry out further investigations before offering credit to the applicant.
- **GAIN** – stands for Gone Away Information Network and is also managed by CIFAS. Experian, together with Equifax, processes GAIN data on behalf of those lenders that contribute records to this system. It is a network through

which the members of this closed user group share information about customers who have left the address known to the lender and, in some cases, identifies any new address to which the customer has been traced.

When a customer who has defaulted on a loan from a lender moves from their known address without informing the lender, a GAIN record will be recorded against their details on the databases of the credit reference agencies. If the defaulter's new address is known, GAIN will alert the lender in question to allow them to pursue the debtor for the outstanding debt.

- **Notice of correction** – in the UK, any individual has the right to request and receive a copy of the information held about them by credit reference agencies in accordance with the Consumer Credit Act of 1974 and Data Protection Act of 1998. If the information is evidently incorrect, then the credit reference agency is obliged to correct it. The individual in question has the right to issue a "notice of correction" to the credit reference agency. If there is a notice of correction against individual details, a lender has to review an application from the applicant manually before making a decision. The lender should, however, not allow the notice to influence their decision.

Derived information

- **Geo-demographic and socio-economic data** – credit reference agencies use credit data along with results of annual public and private surveys undertaken with a view to capturing information about individuals' and households' lifestyles, behaviours and preferences to generate demographic statistics at individual, household and postcode level.

  The surveys are carried out either for the government or on behalf of the credit reference agencies.

- **Credit scores** – credit reference agencies are able to construct generic scorecards or bureau scorecards which are indicative of the general risk profile of an individual as a result of the large and diverse information about current and historical behaviour at their disposal. The scores generated by these scorecards are called *bureau scores*. Given the volume and variety of data held by the credit reference agencies, these scores are generally of a greater accuracy than the scores generated by the bank's internal databases. Consequently, the banks combine these scores with their internally generated scores or even use them instead of their own.

- **Credit reference data and applicant matching** – credit reference agencies match credit reference data and applicants' details by using matching algorithms which are generally very reliable and are continually refined. However, given the complexity of the matching process, there can be ambiguities which result in the association of incorrect data with an individual. For example, when a search is made on a man with the following details:

Mr James Lightfast
20 Biz Vale
Ess Park
London SS1 2JJ
DOB 12/12/1962

His details are entered into the lender's application processing system, which then transmits the details above via a data link to one or more of the credit reference agencies to start the search process. One would expect that all lenders' systems will transmit the data in the same format, but that is not the case given the hundreds of millions of individual records that are involved in credit searches. This results in a mismatch of customer data and credit reference data and could lead to lack of success in obtaining credit.

Nevertheless, if the credit reference data and applicant details match, the data is fed into the bank's decision-making system.

- **No trace** – there are instances of credit searches that do not return any data for an individual at the address they supplied on the application for credit. This may be the case when the individual does not exist on the electoral register and does not have any previous credit history. This case is known in the credit world as a "No Trace" case.

  Application for credit where there is no trace of the applicant usually leads the lender to request more information about the address and identity. The applicant may also be asked to provide personal and employment references. An underwriter then assesses the application using different criteria to that of individuals with credit histories. In some instances, the lender may decline the application automatically, as they regard applicants without a credit history as high risk and not worth the time and effort required to process their applications.

- **Previous addresses, linked addresses and joint applications** – lenders usually request a single credit report for joint applicants as they could have lived at different address prior to the application for credit from a particular lender. This credit report is a combination of subsidiary searches carried out by the credit reference agencies. The reasoning behind this sort of practice is that credit reference data is matched to an individual on the strength of the person's name, address and date of birth. Therefore, if a person changes their address, ideally all existing credit data should be associated with the new address and dissociated from the old address. In some cases, individuals that have existing relationships with their lenders will inform their lenders of their recent change in address and these lenders will in turn forward the information to the credit reference agencies.

  Lenders usually require a list of addresses that an applicant has lived in for at least three years. However, not all applicants declare this information during the application process, but lenders can still have access to this information through linked addresses created by credit reference agencies. This is achieved as result of any updates in the electoral register at the applicant's new address or a request for a change of address with another lender. An address link is a connection between the old and new addresses when an address is changed. Establishing this link makes it possible to retrieve all credit data relating to both addresses even if there is no disclosure of the old address when applying for a new credit facility.

- **Third-party data** – data about individuals other than the applicant that is used to make decisions about the applicant is termed as third-party data

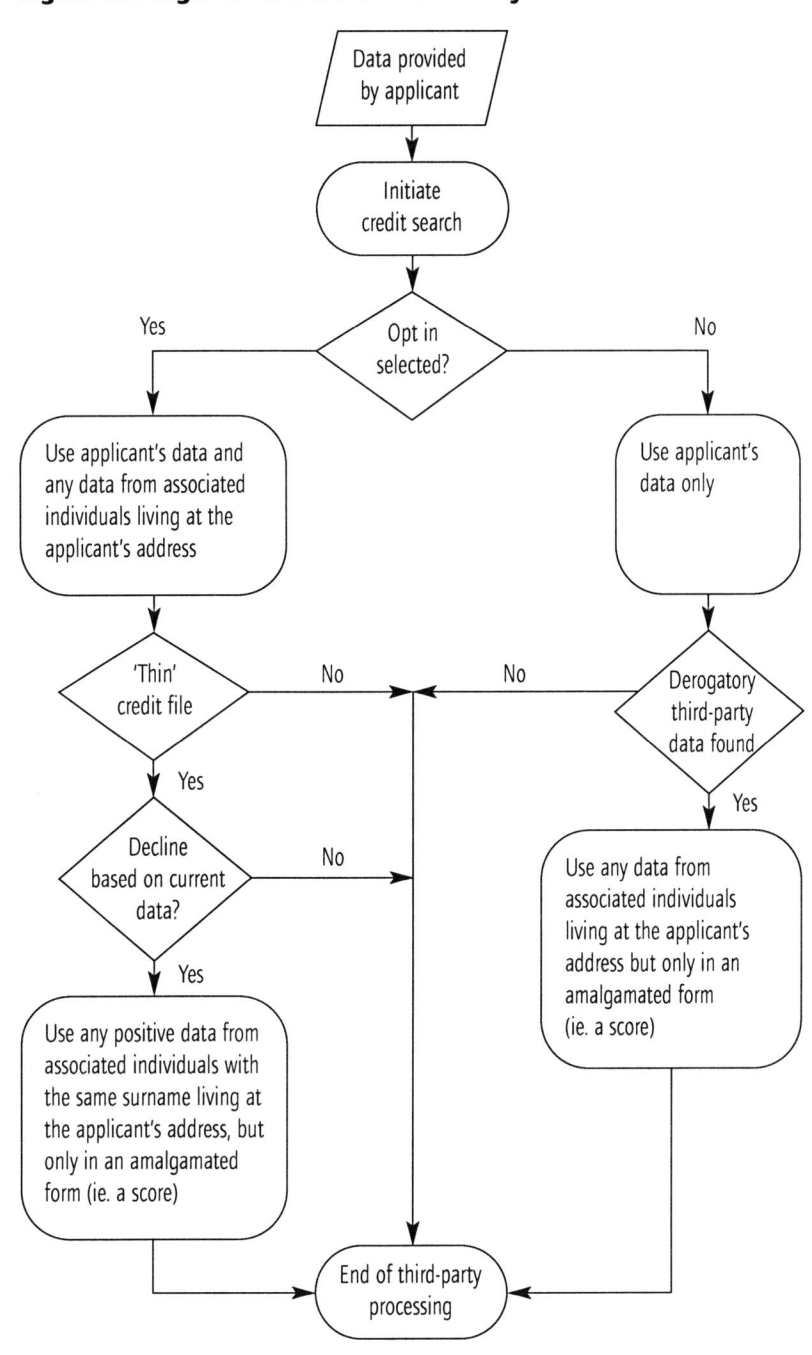

Figure 6.2 Logic for the use of Third-Party Data

© Finlay, S. Consumer Credit Fundamentals (2005), Palgrave Macmillan.
Reproduced with persmission of Palgrave Macmillan. All rights reserved.

(Finlay, 2005). Since 2004, third-party data can only be used in a limited set of circumstances, represented in the diagram in Figure 6.2.

When an applicant applies for credit they are given the option to either opt in or out. The opt-in process flow is represented by the left-hand side of the diagram in Figure 6.2, which in essence shows that the applicant has confirmed to the best of their knowledge that there is no financial association with any individual living at the stated address who has a history of default, arrears or bankruptcy and the lender should not use the information relating to this individual to make a decision.

The opt-out process flow, on the right-hand side, shows that the applicant's data returned from a credit search will include data about other individuals living at his or her address that have a financial association with the applicant. This could be some current or historic record of a joint credit agreement or a joint credit application regardless of whether the two people are related or share the same surname.

If a credit report returns only very limited data about an individual, the individual is said to have a "thin credit file". If, on the basis of this limited data, the lender would decline the application, the lender is permitted to use information about other people with the same surname living at the applicant's address, regardless of whether or not a proven financial association exists; that is, if the lender finds positive information about other family members living with the applicant, this can be used to change a preliminary decision to decline the application to one to accept it (Finlay, 2005).

Credit Management

Credit management is the organisation of the day-to-day activities of the lending and credit aspect of retail banking. The credit life cycle below shows the individual stages and credit functions of the bank involved in the life of a credit product. The stages are:

- recruitment
- account management
- collections
- debt recovery
- write off

Recruitment – this is the process whereby an applicant is converted into a new customer. The process entails gathering information about the applicant, making a lending decision, performing administrative tasks required to complete the credit agreement and opening an account.

Account management – once a credit agreement is in place, the next stage is for account management to create an account record and also to maintain the record. Maintenance tasks include the updating of transactions and applying changes to the terms of the agreement.

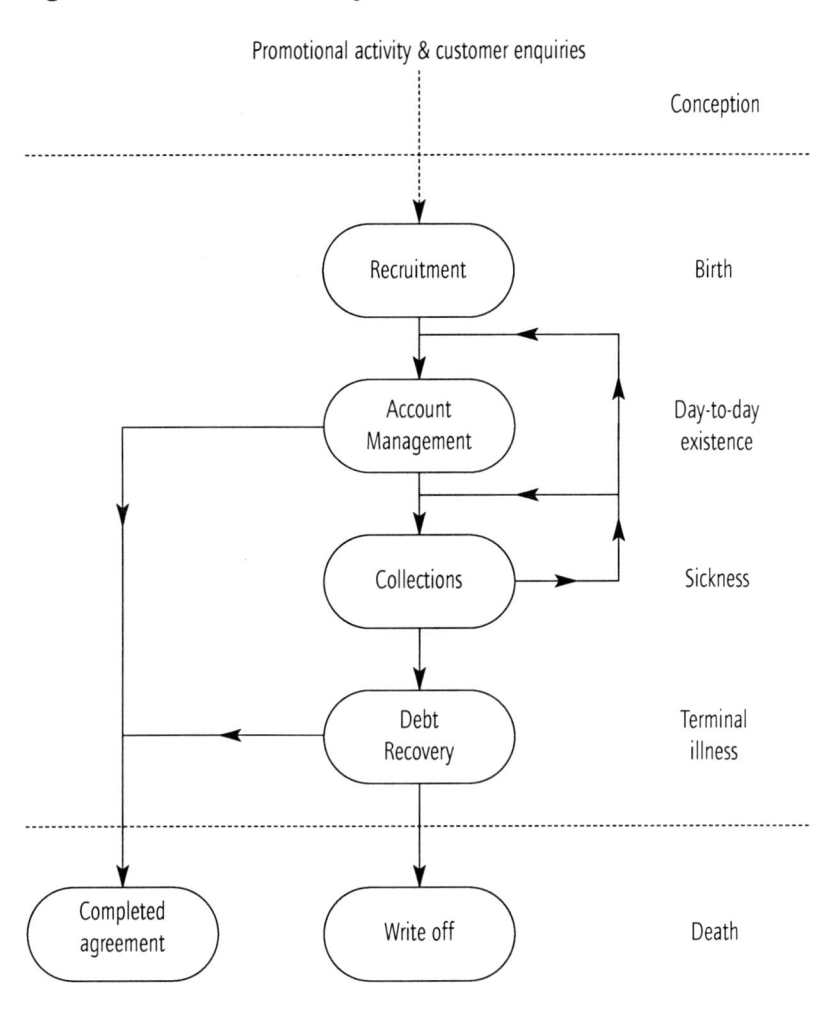

Figure 6.3 The Credit Life Cycle

```
                    Promotional activity & customer enquiries
                                                                    Conception
                                    │
- - - - - - - - - - - - - - - - - - ┼ - - - - - - - - - - - - - - - - - - - -
                                    ▼
                            ( Recruitment )                         Birth
                                    │        ◄─────────────┐
                                    ▼                      │
                         ( Account Management )            │       Day-to-day
                                    │        ◄──────────┐  │       existence
                                    ▼                   │  │
                            ( Collections ) ────────────┘──┘       Sickness
                                    │
                                    ▼
                          ( Debt Recovery )   ◄──┐                 Terminal
                                    │            │                  illness
- - - - - - - - - - - - - - - - - - ┼ - - - - - -│- - - - - - - - - - - - - -
              ┌─────────────────────┘            │
              ▼                                  ▼
    ( Completed agreement )              ( Write off )               Death
```

© Finlay, S. Consumer Credit Fundamentals (2005). Palgrave Macmillan.
Reproduced with permission of Palgrave Macmillan. All rights reserved.

Collections – when an individual's account falls into arrears, thus contravening the terms of the agreement, a lender instigates procedures to attempt to return the account to conformance with the terms of the agreement. The procedures and hence the action taken is dependent on the number of cycles (or months depending on the lender) that the account has been in arrears. If the number of cycles hasn't exceeded 3 cycles, i.e. 90 days, the action taken is a *collections action*. The lender is not looking to recover the debt and terminate the agreement at this stage; the primary objective is to get the agreement back up to date by collecting the arrears. However, if collection is unsuccessful and the situation deteriorates to the extent that the account cannot be restored to the expected paying status, it is referred to *debt recovery*, which would use specialist methods to recover as much of the debt as possible before the agreement is terminated and the credit facility rescinded.

Debt recovery – this stage involves a more determined effort from credit management to recover as much of the debt as possible as the account has probably been arrears for three to four cycles. The debtor is usually threatened with legal action and there is the possibility that the account will be frozen. Investigations are carried out by specialists in debt recovery at the bank to uncover the possibility of fraud or cases of deliberate misinformation about changes in the customer's address.

Write off – if all avenues for recovery of the debt through persuasion have been exhausted, the bank has a number of options including:

- Write off the debt and take no further action, especially if the value of the debt in question is within a range of values the lender is comfortable with.
- Negotiate with a third-party debt collector that may be interested in buying the debt.
- Pursue the debtor through the courts or lobby for bankruptcy in extreme cases.

7 Payments in Retail Banking

This chapter covers the different payment methods including cash and cheque cards, and also describes the cheque clearing process and electronic funds transfers.

Introduction

Retail banks offer their customers a wide array of payment methods. These methods can be either manual and paper-based or electronic; each method is designed to meet the requirements of customers, business and personal alike.

In recent times, new payment methods have emerged; some complement existing conventional methods and others are positioned to replace them.

Below is a discussion of some of the different payment methods.

Manual Payment Methods

Cash

Cash, the oldest and most resilient payment mechanism, is used in the majority of transactions around the world. In the UK, it was first used over 2,500 years ago in the form of payment tokens and later, over 300 years ago, as bank notes (APACS 2007). The most popular method of obtaining cash to make purchases is from automated teller machines (ATMs), sometimes called cash machines, which are available 24 hours a day, 365 days a year.

Cash as a method of payment has a distinct characteristic, which is also an advantage, in that it leaves no trace and can be passed from one person to another without the transaction being documented in any book of account. This has naturally attracted criminals such as drug traffickers and money launderers to this method of payment. There are, however, disadvantages to handling cash as it could be bulky depending on the amount and can be easily misplaced or stolen.

Cash transaction volumes are slowly in decline with the advent of payment cards, i.e. credit and debit cards. However it is projected that cash use will still account for 52% of all payments by 2017.

The cash cycle can be described as follows:

- printing and minting of notes and coins;
- supply of cash to businesses and consumers;
- payment of cash into accounts;
- processing of cash prior to reissue.

There are many players that facilitate the processes in this cycle, including cash processing centres, secure carrier centres and vehicle fleets, branches of financial institutions, retailer outlets and other service providers such as vending and transport services (APACS 2007).

Banks and building societies in the UK have arrangements in place to allow their customers access to their accounts via cash machines owned by other institutions. For example, Barclays' customers can withdraw cash from Lloyds TSB ATMs without having to pay a fee for the service. There are, however, other ATMs not provided by banks and building societies, but by independent ATM deployers (IAD).

IADs have been placing cash machines in an increasing number of locations to exploit the growing customer demand for convenient access to cash. Some of these locations include petrol stations, bars, nightclubs, restaurants and other locations that would not be deemed commercially viable by banks and building societies. In order to generate revenue, IADs charge a flat fee for the withdrawal service offered by their ATMs.

All cash machine owners in the UK are part of the LINK network that enables cardholders to use any of their machines. If a fee is charged for cash withdrawal, this will be displayed before the transaction takes place so the customer can decide whether or not to proceed.

Cheques
Cheques are written orders from account holders instructing their banks to pay specified sums of money to named beneficiaries. They are not legal tender but are legal documents and their use is governed by the Bills of Exchange Act 1882 and the Cheque Acts of 1957 and 1992.

Cheques have been a popular method of payment over the years, especially if used with a cheque guarantee card. However, there are drawbacks to using cheques for transactions and these include:

- insufficient funds in the payer's account resulting in the cheque being returned unpaid for lack of funds;
- ownership of the cheque could be in dispute resulting in the cheque being returned unpaid, marked "signature differs", "ordered not to pay" or "no account";
- incorrect drawing of the cheque by the payer which could result in it being returned.

Cheques are still a preferred payment method in business-to-business transactions as they provide evidence of payment or non-payment when returned unpaid. Other reasons include the convenience and the lag between the time the business hands over the cheque to when it clears and the amount involved is applied to the bank account.

Cheque clearing cycle
There is often confusion about how the clearing system works and the time it takes for a cheque to clear. In fact, it operates within a three-day period, illustrated as follows.

The clearing system does not operate on Saturdays, Sundays and Bank Holidays – as settlement across Bank of England accounts can only take place from Monday to Friday.

In this example Mr Smith (whose account is with the paying bank) has written a cheque payable to Miss Jones, who pays it into her account at the collecting bank on Monday. At the end of each working day, each branch sends all cheques that have been paid in to its bank's clearing centre. So the cheque paid in by Miss Jones is sent to her bank's clearing centre, arriving in the early hours of Tuesday morning. At the clearing centre, the cheques are sorted. The sort code, account number and serial number are captured from the code line at the bottom of the cheque and these, together with the amount of the cheque, are sent electronically to the bank on which the cheque is drawn (the paying bank) by 11am on Tuesday. The physical cheque is then batched up together with all other cheques drawn on accounts at the same bank and handed over to the paying bank at the exchange centre in Milton Keynes (or in Edinburgh in the case of cheques drawn on accounts held at branches in Scotland).

The paying bank debits Mr Smith's account with the amount of the cheque on Wednesday morning. At the same time, all banks calculate the amount they must pay each other on the basis of the value of all cheques exchanged on the previous day. The net balance is then settled across accounts held at the Bank of England.

If Mr Smith's bank decided that it was unable to pay the cheque owing to insufficient funds in his account or for some other reason (e.g. if Mr Smith had placed a stop on it or it had been incorrectly filled out), it would return the cheque to Miss Jones' bank on Wednesday or, in certain specific circumstances, the Thursday morning before 12 noon. Generally cheques are returned by first-class post, although it is increasingly common for them to be directly exchanged between the banks. The earliest that Miss Jones' bank could know that the cheque was not going to be paid would be Thursday or possibly Friday – the fourth or fifth day.

Banks are increasingly spotting fraudulent cheques before they enter the clearing system. Banks exchange details by phone as soon as the fraud is spotted. Individual banks set up their own competitive policies on the point at which they credit funds on cheques paid into their customers' accounts, pay interest or allow funds to be drawn against cheques. Typically, the cheque amount will be credited to Miss Jones' account on the Monday (although the funds will not normally be available to withdraw) and interest on the value is normally earned, or any overdraft interest reduced, from the third day (Wednesday in this example). This is sometimes referred to in banking as "clearing for value".

Many banks allow customers to withdraw funds against cheques from the fourth or fifth day, allowing sufficient time to ensure that the cheque has not been returned unpaid. This is sometimes referred to in banking as "cleared for withdrawal".

This illustration shows how the various stages of the clearing cycle fit together. It separates them out into fixed action, complex action and competitive action.

Banker's Draft
Banker's drafts are cheques drawn directly on the account of a bank as opposed to the account of a customer. The advantage that a banker's draft offers is that it is highly improbable that it would be returned unpaid as a result of lack of funds. It is worth noting, however, that this does not safeguard usage of this method of payment against fraud as drafts may be lost or stolen and then used fraudulently.

Figure 7.1 The Cheque Clearing Cycle[72]

If a customer pays a cheque in at their account holding branch the amount will generally appear immediately (or at least the same day) on the customer's account. If cheques are paid in at another branch or bank, the amount may not appear until day 3.	**Fixed Action** Standard for all cheques that pass through the clearing. **Complex Action** Only applicable to cheques that are returned unpaid. **Competitive Action** Subject to the policies of individual banks.
Collecting banks send all cheques received that day to their clearing centres.	
At the clearing centres cheques are mechanically read and sorted. Codeline and amount details of each cheque are sent electronically to the paying banks via the Inter-Bank Data Exchange (IBDE) network by 11am.	
Cheques are taken to the exchange centres at Milton Keynes and Edinburgh where they are handed over to paying banks. Various electronic verification checks are carried out during day 2 prior to posting to customers' accounts on day 3.	
Paying banks update their customers' accounts overnight day 2–3 and settle net amounts to one another across accounts at the Bank of England.	
If the paying bank decides not to pay a cheque, it is returned to the collecting bank by first-class post on day 3. Under certain circumstances it may not be sent until noon day 4.	
The collecting bank receives the unpaid cheque either on day 4 or day 5.	

Source: ©APACS. *Cheques and Cheque Clearing the Facts* (2007). Reproduced with permission. All rights reserved.

---

72 APACS accpets no liability that may arise from any third party's reliance on this data.

Traveller's Cheques

Traveller's cheques were briefly discussed in Chapter 2; however this method of payment is still widely used by bank customers worldwide who find them suited to their foreign travel requirements. Banks, on the hand, exploit the benefits they offer given that the buyer's money is held until the traveller's cheque is encashed and presented. The banks get free use of the customer's money for the weeks or even months that the money is in their possession.

Electronic Payment Methods

Payment Cards

Payment cards have a proven track record as a highly efficient ordering and payment mechanism for lower-value, high-volume purchases. The term payment card covers a range of different cards that can be presented by a cardholder to make a payment. Payment cards can be classified in types depending on the method of bill payment, i.e. pay now, pay later or prepaid.

Card payments differ from cash payments that involve a single step in that there are several complicated steps and a number of players. The onset of a card payment sets in motion a process with two flows:

- The information flow: information about the card and transaction has to be transmitted from the cardholder to the card issuer.
- The funds flow: the value of the transaction has to be transferred from the cardholder's account. (Business Insights, 2005)

Figure 7.2 shows the key players involved in card payments as well as the flow of transactional information and funds.

A key electronic term to be familiar with, which is usually used in conjunction with payment cards, is PDQ machine which is the generic term for the machine that is used to "swipe" a credit or debit card.

Debit Cards

A debit card is an alternative payment method to cash when making purchases. As a payment method, it is similar to a cheque as cash is withdrawn directly from the cardholder's bank account. They are issued by banks and under a card scheme such as Visa, and Maestro in the UK.

Debit card transactions involve the cardholder inserting the card into the PDQ. The transaction is authorised and processed and the customer verifies the transaction either by entering a PIN or, occasionally, by signing a sales receipt, depending on the store or merchant.

In some countries the debit card is multifunctional, including other functions such as cash machine and cheque guarantee facilities. Merchants can also offer "cashback" facilities to customers, where a customer can withdraw cash along with their purchase.

Debit cards belong to the category of "pay now" cards.

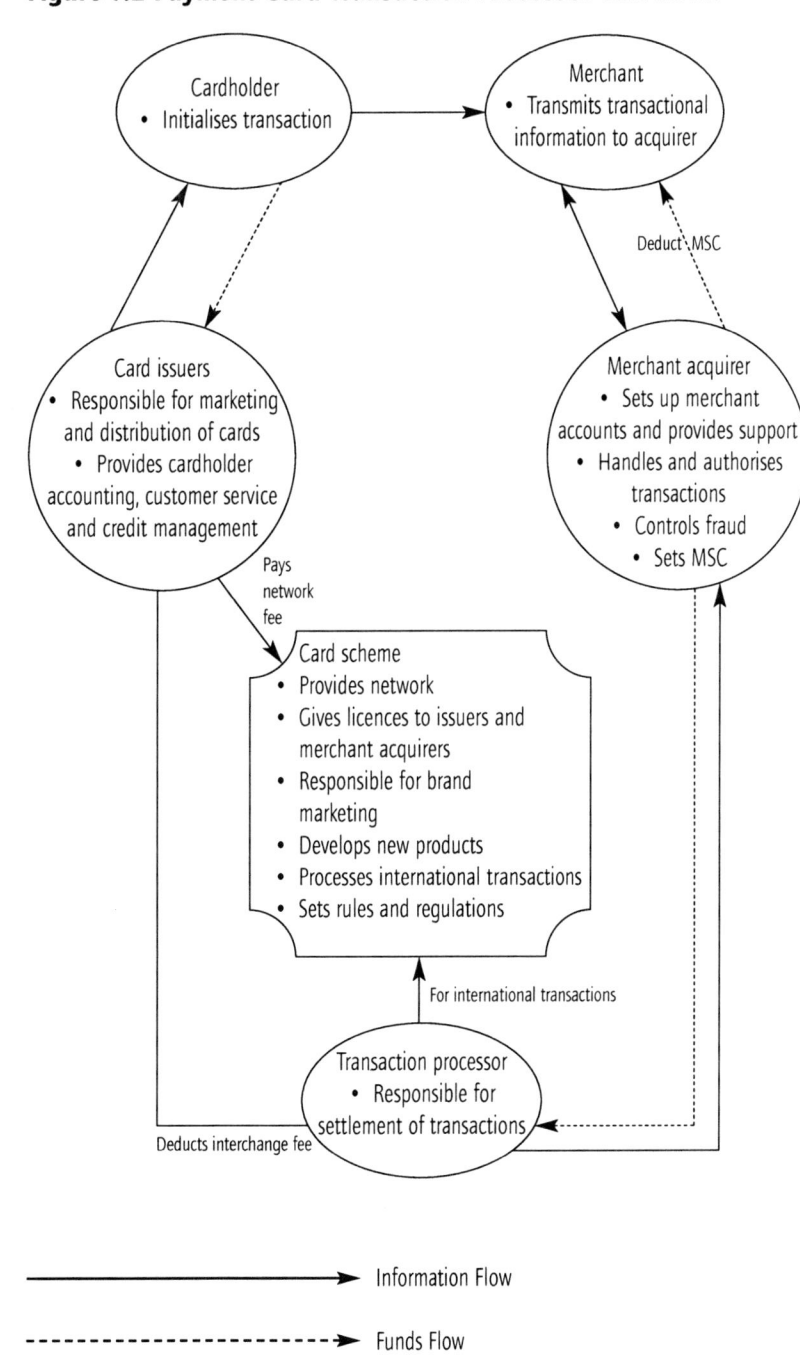

Figure 7.2 Payment Card Transaction Processes and Flows

- **Cardholder**
  - Initialises transaction

- **Merchant**
  - Transmits transactional information to acquirer

- **Card issuers**
  - Responsible for marketing and distribution of cards
  - Provides cardholder accounting, customer service and credit management

- **Merchant acquirer**
  - Sets up merchant accounts and provides support
  - Handles and authorises transactions
  - Controls fraud
  - Sets MSC

- **Card scheme**
  - Provides network
  - Gives licences to issuers and merchant acquirers
  - Responsible for brand marketing
  - Develops new products
  - Processes international transactions
  - Sets rules and regulations

- **Transaction processor**
  - Responsible for settlement of transactions

Flow labels: Deduct MSC; Pays network fee; For international transactions; Deducts interchange fee

→ Information Flow
---▶ Funds Flow

Source: Business Insights, HSBC

Credit Cards

A credit card is a method of payment allowing someone to make a purchase on borrowed money. It is different from a debit card in that it does not remove money from the user's account after every transaction.

Credit-card transactions usually involve payment for goods and services from merchants accepting that credit card up to a pre-established credit limit.

A payment made using a credit card constitutes an agreement by the credit-card user to pay the card issuer. The cardholder indicates their consent to pay by signing a receipt with a record of the card details and the amount to be paid or by entering a Personal Identification Number (PIN). Also, many merchants now accept verbal authorisations via the telephone and electronic authorisation using the internet, known as Card Not Present (CNP) transactions.

Merchants verify that a card is valid and that the customer has sufficient credit to cover purchases in a matter of seconds via electronic verification systems. The verification is performed using a PDQ system with a communications link to the merchant's acquiring bank. Data from the card is obtained from a magnetic stripe or chip on the card; in the United Kingdom the latter system is commonly known as Chip and PIN, but is more technically an EMV card.

Online merchants use other variants of verification systems to check the validity of the user's account and whether it is able to accept the charge. Additional information, such as the security code or CVS printed on the back of the card and the address of the cardholder, is usually requested.

Credit cards belong to the category of "pay later" cards.

Charge Cards

These cards are similar to credit cards. They allow the consumer to pay for goods and services on interest-free credit. However, the balance owing must be paid in full each month or additional fees may be incurred.

Most charge-card companies also offer reward systems for their customers. These can include cashback schemes, discounts, free services and point systems that the cardholder can use towards various purchases etc. In order to be able to offer this service, including benefits and interest-free credit, charge cards normally have an annual fee.

The two largest charge-card companies in the UK are American Express and Diners Club International. Some high-street retail banks also issue Visa or MasterCard charge cards.

Charge cards, also called travel and entertainment cards, have no credit limit. Cardholders usually charge as much as they want, but are required to pay off the entire balance when the bill arrives. However, if the cardholder charges airfares, cruise fees or hotel fees for a hotel room booked through a travel agent on a charge card, they can usually pay off their balance over a number of months.

Charge-card companies make their revenue by charging annual fees and by charging merchants a fee each time a customer pays using the company's charge card.

Charge cards belong to the category of "pay later" cards.

Prepaid Cards

A stored-value card or prepaid card represents money on deposit with the issuer and is similar to a debit card. One major difference between stored-value cards and debit cards is that debit cards are usually issued in the name of individual account holders, while stored-value cards are usually anonymous.

Prepaid Credit Cards

These are payment cards (usually MasterCard, Maestro, Visa Electron or Amex), preloaded with the cardholder's own money, which can then be used wherever the payment card is accepted, including on the internet and on foreign travels.

Prepaid cards have wide acceptance and can be used internationally. They are the same as credit cards but without the credit. The use of prepaid credit cards can also be a relatively cheap way of doing international money transfers.

Customers can use these cards for money transfer by adding an additional card to their prepaid account and loading it up with money in their local currency. The card is then sent to a recipient abroad who can withdraw it in their local currency.

Store Cards

Store cards are variants of credit cards issued by stores as opposed to banks. They offer a method of payment for customers of the issuing stores who receive discounts on purchases at these stores amongst other benefits. However, there are disadvantages for these customers as well as the interest rates are higher that those charged by Visa and MasterCard. This is justified by the absence of merchant commission that typical card issuers charge.

Store cards belong to the category of "pay later" cards.

Standing Orders

A standing order, a long-established banking product, is an instruction given to a bank or building society to make a payment, usually on a regular basis, to a specified third party's bank or building society account. In the UK, it is a service available to anyone with a current account.

A standing order involves a customer signing a document authorising their bank to pay a stated sum on stated days (e.g. 1st of every month, 2nd of January) to a named branch for the credit of a named customer at that branch.

The bank will, on the day specified on the order, debit the customer's account and transfer the money through the Bacs system to the bank account of the recipient.

Currently the money arrives at the recipient' account within three working days (e.g. for a standing order initiated on a Tuesday, the earliest it could arrive would be the Thursday. However, there are initiatives underway that will cut processing times considerably.

Examples of regular payments where standing orders can be used are rent and mortgage repayments, monthly gym subscriptions and magazine subscriptions.

Direct Debits

Direct debit is a payment method that allows an organisation to instruct their bank to collect varying amounts directly from customers' accounts. It differs from a standing order in that it originates from the organisation that is to be paid and does not offer the customer any control over the payments.

There are generally two ways to set up a direct debit. One method requires the customer to instruct their bank to honour debit notes from the organisation, the other one just requires the customer to give an authorisation to the organisation making the collections. The availability of these methods varies between countries and banks.

In the UK, before a company can set up direct debits from its customers (direct debits cannot be paid to individuals), it has to be vetted by its bank. This is to stop it defrauding customers. If there is considerable complaint from customers about direct debits set up by a particular company then the company may lose its ability to set up direct debits.

Banks also operate a direct debit guarantee which states that:

- If there is a change in the amount to be paid or the payment date, the person receiving the payment (the originator) must notify the customer in advance.
- If the originator or the bank/building society makes an error, the customer is guaranteed a full and immediate refund of the amount paid.

Customers can cancel a direct debit *at any time* by writing to their bank or building society.

To set up a direct debit, the customer does not need to sign any document, which is why the system is so strongly regulated. With the details needed for a direct debit, the only things that can be done are setting up that direct debit and depositing money into the account. Some types of bank account do not allow direct debits; typically all current accounts do as well as some deposit accounts. Direct debits can also be collected on credit-card accounts.

Direct Credits

A direct credit is a simple and secure service, which enables large and small organisations to make payments by electronic transfer directly into bank or building society accounts.

Direct credit is mainly used for paying wages and salaries. It can also be used for a wide variety of other applications. Over 150,000 organisations in the UK use direct credit for supplier payments, pensions, employee expenses, insurance settlements, dividends and refunds.

Bacs Payments and Collections

Bacs is a payment service that allows registered companies to make and collect payments electronically into and from customers' accounts. Banks and building societies that are members of a payment scheme such as Bacs sponsor companies to use the service.

Almost 5.5 billion payments a year are made by Bacs' principle schemes, Bacs direct debit and Bacs direct credit, equating to approximately £3.4 trillion in 2006. Almost three quarters of British adults are positively disposed towards direct debit: 35 million adults now have at least one direct debit commitment and approximately 115,000 businesses use Bacs' services.

In this section the direct debit and direct credit aspect of the electronic funds transfer service will be discussed using the Bacs[73] service as a guide. To give an illustration of how this service is provided by Bacs, a fictional company Biz Energy, a utility company that provides electricity and gas to households in the UK, will be used as the company that makes and collects payments.

Sending payment information

Biz Energy creates payment instructions to make or collect payments or set up direct debit instructions (DDIs). These payment instructions contain information about the type of transaction, the value, where the money is coming from and where it is going to.

Payment instructions are sent in payment files to the Bacs service in submissions.

Biz Energy uses Bacs-approved software that formats the payment file into APACS Standard 18 format for transmission through Bacstel-IP.[74] The standard specifies the contents and lengths of each field and record in a submission, payment file and payment instruction.

Payment instructions (items)

Payment instructions contain details of the transaction Biz Energy wants to make: paying money into customers' accounts (credits) or collecting money (debits).

The company is looking to become an AUDDIS® (automated direct debit instruction service) originator so as to be able to send payment instructions electronically to the customer's bank or building society to set up DDIs on their account and ultimately move to paperless direct debit, allowing them to set up DDIs over the phone or online.

Content	Detail
Originating account details	This is the company account. If this is a credit transaction, this is the account that the money is paid from; if this is a debit transaction, this is where the money is paid into.
Destination account details	This is the account that the transaction is directed to. For a credit, this is where the money is paid into; for a debit, this is where the money is collected from; for a DDI, this is the account that the instruction is applied on.

73 Bacs service guide reproduced with permission.
74 This is the access channel to the Bacs electronic fund transfer service.

Transaction code	A two-character code that represents the type of transaction a company is making. A list of transactions is shown below.
Value of payment	The amount in pence (for sterling) or cents (for euro) of the transaction. (The currency is set as part of the payment file). Note: DDIs have no value, therefore this is set to zero for DDIs.
Reference information	Additional reference information is held in several fields; for example, a direct debit reference.

The date a payment instruction is to be processed can be set for the whole payment file or for each payment instruction.

Transaction types

The following are the transaction types that are recognised by the Bacs service. Companies can normally only originate some of these transaction types.

Transaction type	Credit or debit
Direct credit	Credit
Debit contra[75] (a credit record to balance debit records)	Credit
Credit contra (a debit record to balance credit records)	Debit
Direct debit – first collection	Debit
Direct debit – regular collection	Debit
Direct debit – re-presentation	Debit
Direct debit – final collection	Debit
Direct debit instruction – new instruction	No value
Direct debit instruction – cancellation instruction	No value
Direct debit instruction – conversion instruction	No value
Interest payments	Credit
Dividend payments	Credit
Credit card debit	Debit
Credit card refund	Credit

Destination account details

All items contain destination accounts to identify where the payment or DDI is directed to. Destination[76] account details are made up of:

- Destination sorting code (field 1);
- Destination account number (field 2);

---

75 A contra payment is where a company invoices a customer and also receives a bill and wishes to "contra" the two transactions off against each other so only the difference is paid.
76 Destination details are usually referred to as payer's details.

- Destination account type (field 3); and
- Destination account name (field 11). The destination account name should always be quoted as it may assist a bank in applying the item.

In some cases, banks may have a redirection set up from one sorting account to another. Where the destination sorting code has a redirection on it, the Bacs service will substitute the destination sorting code with the sorting code that it is being redirected to.

Payment files
Payment files contain payment instructions. A payment file submitted over Bacstel-IP can contain a mix of credits, debits and DDIs. Nonetheless, all payment files have a processing date. The date can be up to 31 days later than the processing date. Payment files can either be:

- **Single processing date files** – All payment instructions in the payment file are processed on the file's processing date. The payment instructions in themselves do not have processing dates set against them.
- **Multiprocessing date files** – Each payment instruction has its own processing date. This can be the same as, or up to 39 days after, the processing date in the payment file.

The payment file also sets the currency of the payment instructions: sterling or euro. This means all payment instructions in a file will be the in same currency. The Bacs service currently allows sterling credit and debit transactions and euro credit transactions. (Bacs does not carry out any conversion on euro transactions. However, some banks/building societies convert euro transactions to sterling when they apply them to a person's account).

Day sections
The payment instructions in a payment file with the same processing date are known as "a day section". A single processing day is made up of one day section because all the payment instructions are processed on the same day. Biz Energy gets an input report to confirm processing of day sections; so for a multiprocessing day file, the company may get multiple input reports.

When items are submitted in advance of the processing date, the day section is stored until the processing date is reached. When the processing day is reached, the day section is processed and an input report will be produced for the company.

Account section and balancing
In each day section, the payment instructions that originate from the same account form an "account section". Details of these account sections appear on the company input report.

Each account section in a payment file must balance. This is done using contras. A contra is a type of payment instruction; the destination and originating accounts are the same (this is to identify the account section that the contra is balancing). The word "contra" is included as part of the payment instruction to identify it.

Debit and credits in an account section need separate contras. Credit contras balance credit payment instructions; the credit contra takes money from the company account. Debit contras balance debit payment instructions; the debit contra deposits money into the company account.

Adjustment items

If a payment instruction is rejected, an "adjustment" item is created. This item will be sent to the same account that the rejected item originated from. The service user's reference (field 10) from the original rejected record is included in the adjustment item; this will normally appear on the company bank statement.

Where all payment instructions in an account section are rejected, an aggregate adjustment item is created so the account section will still balance. An aggregate adjustment item will also be created where an account section does not balance. The service user's reference of an aggregate adjustment item will be ADJUSTMENT ENTRY.

Submissions

Payment files are sent in submissions. A bureau can send more than one file in a submission. A service user can only send one payment file in a submission.

Reference numbers

When a submission is received, the Bacs service assigns reference numbers to each part of the submission – the submission, the file, day sections, account sections and payment instructions (items).

These reference numbers appear on the company's processing reports, including the input report. The reference number is in the following format:

yyyymmdd99A99999999

Where:

- yyyymmdd – is the date (either the arrival or processing date);
- 99 – is the service identifier, whether it relates to payments or DDIs;
- A – identifies the component, S(ubmission), F(ile), D(ay section), A(ccount section) or I(tem);
- 99999999 – is a number to make the reference unique.

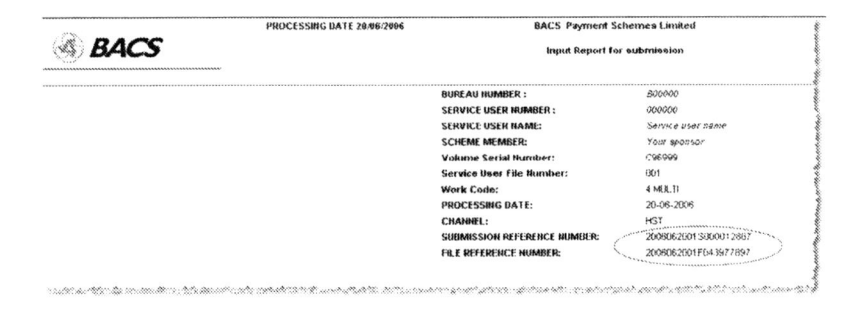

Source: Bacs. Reproduced with permission.

Processing cycle and opening times

The processing cycle is the minimum time it takes between the payment instruction being input by Bacs for validation and the payment instruction being applied to the destination account.

The processing cycle has three stages that take place on three consecutive processing days; this is the three-day cycle. In addition, "arrival" is the stage when a submission is received by the Bacs service and divided into day sections. This is often the same day as the input stage.

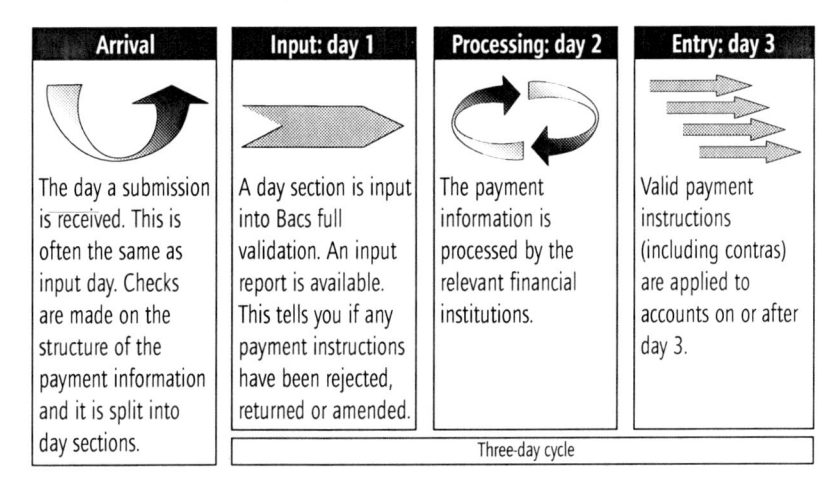

Arrival	Input: day 1	Processing: day 2	Entry: day 3
The day a submission is received. This is often the same as input day. Checks are made on the structure of the payment information and it is split into day sections.	A day section is input into Bacs full validation. An input report is available. This tells you if any payment instructions have been rejected, returned or amended.	The payment information is processed by the relevant financial institutions.	Valid payment instructions (including contras) are applied to accounts on or after day 3.
	Three-day cycle		

Source: Bacs. Reproduced with permission.

Processing and non-processing days

Input, processing and entry can only occur on processing days. Non-processing days are Saturday, Sunday and English bank/public holidays. These dates are highlighted on the processing calendar. The following is an example, showing the calendar for December 2007.

Mon	Tues	Wed	Thur	Fri	S	S
3 337	4 338	5 339	6 340	7 341	8	9
10 344	11 345	12 346	13 347	14 348	15	16
17 351	18 352	19 353	20 354	21 355	22	23
24 358	25 359	26 360	27 361	28 362	29	30
31 364						

Non-input and non-processing days

Banking holiday Northern Ireland

Source: Bacs. Reproduced with permission.

The processing calendar also highlights bank holidays in Northern Ireland that can affect entry day for accounts held in Northern Ireland. The calendar shows the Julian[77] date for each processing day. This is the date format used in submissions.

It is a major requirement that valid processing dates are used in payment files and payment instructions. If invalid processing dates are used, Bacs overrides the processing date according to certain rules. When a submission is sent using Bacstel-IP with an invalid processing date, a warning message is received saying that the date(s) has been overridden.

Processing stages and overview

DDIs and value items in files are processed separately by the Bacs service. When a submission is received, DDIs are sent to one processing engine and the value items to a separate engine. This means that if a submission or file is rejected, the company will receive a separate arrival report for DDIs and for value items. In some cases, a structural error could result in two arrival reports even if a submission does not contain both DDIs and value items.

Messaging services

Messaging services are used to support use of the Bacs service. They are used by banks to inform the company of details needed for payments, DDIs or changes to DDIs. There are three messaging services. In each service, an advice is generated (either by a bank or the Bacs systems) to provide the company with information.

The advices are produced as part of a report. The advice includes a reason as to why the change is required (for example, if an account is transferred). The company updates records as detailed in these reports.

---

[77] The Julian day or Julian day number (JDN) is the integer number of days that have elapsed since the initial era defined as non Universal Time (UT).

Stage	What can happen	How
Arrival		
When a submission is sent while the company's software is still connected to Bacstel-IP, initial checks are made on the content of the submission.	Submissions can be: • Accepted – if any processing days are invalid they may be amended during processing; the submission summary report shows how dates will be changed. • Rejected – no information is processed.	A *submission summary report* is sent to the company's Bacstel-IP software.
After submission has been accepted online.	Submissions can be: • Accepted • Rejected – no information is processed.	If the submission is rejected at this stage, the submitter receives an arrival report.
Input		
Payment instructions are validated before accepted and amended instructions are passed to the relevant banks/building societies. This occurs on day 1 of the 3-day cycle.	Payment instructions can be: • Accepted • Amended – if an incorrect date is used on a payment instruction, it will be amended. The payment will still be processed. • Returned – the payment is returned. • Rejected – the payment is not processed and an "adjustment item" is created so the day section still balances.	The originator receives an input report for each day section processed. Input reports list returned, rejected and amended payment instructions. When DDIs are submitted, the originator receives an input report and an *AUDDIS file acceptance/rejection report*. Certain amendments are not listed on input reports. These are where a bank has placed a redirection on an account or sorting code. Depending on how the bank set these redirections, the company may be notified of these changes in an *AWACS* or *ADDACS report*.
Processing and entry		
The recipient banks/building societies carry out further processing on day 2 before applying valid instructions on day 3 (or after).	Payment instructions can be: • Applied • Unapplied – the payment is returned, normally using the ARUCS or ARUDD service. If a DDI cannot be applied, notification occurs on a *bank returned AUDDIS report*.	If payments are returned using ARUCS or ARUDD, the originator receives an *ARUCS or ARUDD report*. If the account details of a payment had to be amended by the bank before they could apply the payment, an *AWACS report* will be used for notification.

Source: Bacs. Reproduced with permission.

ADDACS service

The ADDACS[78] service is used to provide companies with information of changes to DDIs that they have lodged. It includes details of DDIs that have been cancelled by a customer or have been amended, for example, because an account has been transferred. Records must be updated with this information within three working days of receipt.

Bank returned AUDDIS service

The bank returned AUDDIS[79] service allows banks to notify AUDDIS originators that a DDI has not been applied or if a DDI has been applied to a different account (because a customer has changed their account). Bank returned AUDDIS advices will be provided in a bank returned AUDDIS report.

If a DDI could not be applied by the recipient bank, necessary changes should be made and the DDI resubmitted where necessary.

Where an advice indicates that a DDI has transferred to a new account, then the new details to be used for the direct debit must be updated in the company's systems within three working days of receipt.

AWACS service

The AWACS service is used to notify the company of the correct account details to use for payments. AWACS advices are generated when:

- A bank receives a credit payment that has incorrect account details, but the payment can still be applied. The advice will detail the correct account details.
- The Bacs system redirects a credit item based on a redirection on the destination sorting code. When this happens, the Bacs system changes the destination sorting code in the item. This change is not reported on the input report but may be reported in the AWACS report[80] (depending on how the redirection was set up by the bank).
- The Bacs system redirects a credit item based on an account redirection set up by a bank. Bacs will change the destination account details. This is not reported on the input report but is normally reported in the AWACS report.

ARUCS and ARUDD services

The ARUCS and ARUDD services are used by the banks to return payments to the company when they cannot be applied. As well as the payment being returned, details of the payment and why it is being returned will be included in an ARUCS[81] (UAC) report for credit payments or an ARUDD[82] (UDD) report for debit payments.

---

78 ADDACS is derived from automated direct debit amendment and cancellation.
79 AUDDIS is derived from automated direct debit instruction service.
80 AWACS is derived from advice of wrong account for automated credit service.
81 ARUCS is derived from automated return of credits service.
82 ARUDD is derived from automated return of Direct Debit.

International Funds Transfer

International funds transfer is a banking product designed to meet the demands of the international business community, the foreign traveller, or the occasional need of one family member to send money to another. It is one of the most widely used international banking products. Money transfers can take the form of electronic transmission or written instruction and in some countries negotiable instruments such as cheques. For these reasons, international payments may take the same form as domestic payments.

In order to fully understand the concept of international funds transfer, the global market for foreign exchange will be discussed.

A global dynamic market

There are about 194 countries in the world, and most have their own currencies. A country's legal tender (or currency) is its official medium of exchange for goods and services, as well as the preferred medium of payment.

The practice of exchanging the currency of one country for that of another is called foreign exchange. Whilst this is a seemingly straightforward process, the value of one currency against another changes constantly and can have significant implications for international business and the traveller.

Foreign currencies

Despite the number of countries in the world, and given that almost all countries have their own currencies; there are only six currencies that are considered to be major. This is as a result of the ready market available for these currencies and the competitive trading of the currencies on major exchanges. The following is a list of the majors:

- US dollar
- the euro
- Canadian dollar
- Swiss franc
- Japanese yen
- British pound (sterling).

In addition, there is another group of currencies that are considered to be minor. The foreign exchange market arbitrarily assigns the currencies of countries to this group. While the number of minor currencies fluctuates, they could at one time or another include the Swedish krona, the Danish kronor and the Australian dollar.

There is generally less demand for these minor currencies in the spot and forward markets; their value is more volatile than the major currencies. They also have an increased likelihood of artificial controls on their exchange rate, and tend to follow a major currency in value fluctuation, often because of close economic ties to the country.

The remaining currencies of the world are known as exotics. These exotics are mostly currencies of small countries or those that impose controls on currency conversions.

Foreign exchange rates

Base foreign exchange rates are not absolute values, but comparative values of one currency against that of another. In the UK, exchange rates are typically expressed as a foreign currency's value against the pound. For instance, one British pound will buy 2.02 US dollars, which is expressed as 2.02 dollar/pound, therefore:

- the exchange value of the dollar in terms of British pounds for say $1,000 will be $1,000/2.02;
- the exchange value of the British pound in terms of the US dollar for £1,000 will be £1,000 * 2.02.

The exchange rate of some currencies, known as direct currencies, is expressed as a percentage of the US dollar. These currencies can be from any of the major or minor currencies mentioned above, including the British pound, New Zealand dollar, the Australian dollar and the euro. For example, if the euro is valued at, say, 1.680, it means you can buy one euro for US$1.68.

Overview of international fund transfers

Fund transfers in every country of the world occur through their respective central banks and local clearing organisations. However, an international system for payments does not exist between countries except for the euro clearing system used in the European monetary union. Banks, therefore, rely on their correspondents to obtain these services.

All payment requests consist of two parts: a message which contains the payment instructions, and the settlement information.

- **Payment instructions**. These include the name and address of the payee, the name of the bank to which the payment is destined, and other pertinent facts that will allow the payee to apply the funds.
- **Settlement information**. This information identifies the account to be debited or one that will be credited to cover the amount of the transfer and any applicable fee.

Correspondent banks do not require reciprocal accounts in order to process a request for a funds transfer, but each payment message contains information for the receiving bank which details the means by which the bank is reimbursed. Most banks routinely exchange standard settlement instructions when their correspondent relationship is established and/or reviewed.

Settlement usually occurs in the country of the currency named in the payment order. For example, if a fictional bank BizEast in New York were to send a wire transfer denominated in British pounds to another fictional bank Banklaze Bank PLC, London, settlement instructions would include authorisation to debit BizEast's account.

However, if a wire transfer request denominated in US dollars were sent to Banklaze, settlement would occur by a credit to Banklaze's account with their

New York branch or some other named correspondent in the United States. This is usually accomplished by wire transfer through the Federal Reserve system in the USA.

Forms of payment

International fund transfers can take various forms. The most common are cheques, drafts and international wire transfers.

- **Cheques and drafts** – the oldest and simplest payment method is by cheque, money order or draft and they all exist in paper form. There are limitations with this kind of payment as the authenticity may be questionable given the presence of third parties in the transactions.

    The mail payment order, however, is a reliable method of effecting payment because it is initiated by a bank and is sent directly to another bank. It bears a signature that can be verified, so its authenticity can be assured.

    Mail payment orders are typically slow because international postal procedures and schedules differ from country to country. Moreover, mail destined for remote locations may be delayed for weeks in places.

    The use of mail payment order has been in steady decline in recent times owing to the delay inherent in its delivery and the attendant expense of handling paper requests when superior electronic methods of delivery are more reliable and less costly to process. The draft, however, is still in use and usually denominated in the currency of the country in which it is issued.

    Remitters obtain mail payment orders or bank drafts by contacting their banks, stating their requests and making the necessary payments.

- **International wire transfers** – the most convenient method for transferring funds between bank accounts is bank wire transfer. It is a secure message (via a secure system such as SWIFT) to the receiving bank, requesting that they effect payment in accordance with the instructions given. The message also includes settlement instructions. The actual wire transfer itself is virtually instantaneous, requiring no longer for transmission than a telephone call. Most international, country-to-country transfers are executed using SWIFT messages. Banks use these messages to exchange data for the transfer of funds between different financial institutions.

Directing fund remittance

Most bank customers use international wire transfers to receive funds from individuals and businesses in foreign locations, hence the importance of providing the remitter with adequate information about their bank (receiving bank) and the routing required to prevent delay. For example, if John Bigfoot, a UK resident, is expecting money from his friend Paul Lightfoot, resident in Switzerland, he would need to provide Paul Lightfoot with the following details:

Account name: John Bigfoot
Account number: 00123456
Bank name and address: BizEast Bank
                                     1 Ess Street
                                     London S1 5XX
                                     UK
SWIFT Code: BZETGB2L555
IBAN: GB77 BZET 2222 2200 1234 56

Paul Lightfoot will need to present these details to his bank to ensure the remittance to John Bigfoot's BizEast account.

Common Systems Used in Retail Banking

This chapter contains an overview of the state of the retail banking technology market and a description of a number of systems from notable vendors used in retail banking.

Introduction

Retail banking customers' needs have grown increasingly sophisticated and competition in the industry is intensifying. The constraints that legacy systems and outdated technologies place on business are some of the most pressing issues that decision makers in the banks are facing up to. In fact, industry experts are of the opinion that these issues have moved to mission-critical problems that could undermine a bank's competitive edge.

Retail banks have long been some of the biggest investors in technology, and today a large bank's list of installed IT systems runs to hundreds if not thousands of entries. However, one problem area for banks in terms of installed technology is their portfolios of legacy systems, often installed during the 1960s and 1970s. They have proven extremely inefficient, costly to maintain, and no longer flexible enough to handle system changes and the new applications necessary to meet the growing needs and requirements of the marketplace.

Global IT Spend by Financial Services Firms

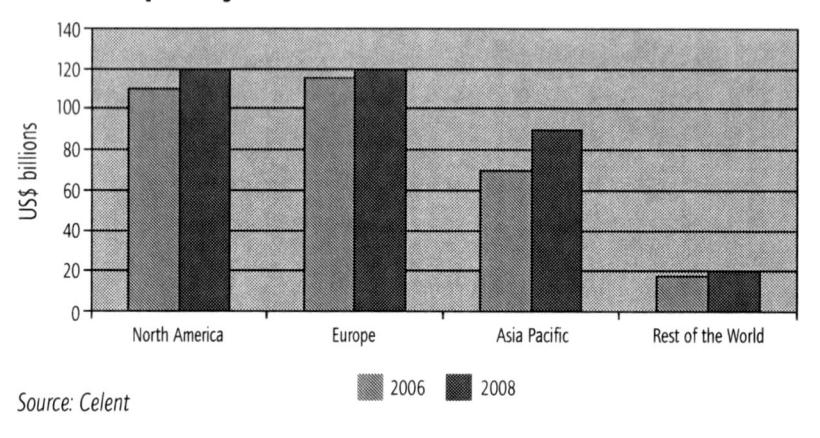

Source: Celent

Industry Dynamics

The abolition of the Gold Standard in most countries in the middle of the last century is a milestone that represented the morphing of paper money from being a proxy for gold to carrying value in its own right. Ever since then, banking has been concerned with tracking information about money through a complex web of transactions, with paper simply acting as one of the possible tokens of evidence of an exchange completed. As an industry founded entirely on information flow, it is therefore no surprise that even today, the banking industry spends more on technology than any other sector of the global economy.

Initially, technology was used to treat information in the same way as previous manual processes – only quicker and more efficiently. In this respect, the integration of IT into banking has been a remarkable success. For banks to deliver the kind of service that they do today without IT would require vast armies of staff.

As the technology industry has matured, however, there has been a shift towards using technology to do things not just faster, but better. Some of these initiatives have been strikingly successful with centralisation, outsourcing and electronic sales channels standing out as particularly effective drivers of efficiency. Others, including customer relationship management (CRM) and branch reduction, have proven rather less so.

Post 9/11 and the dot.com boom, enthusiasm for technology as an opportunity for business growth has been replaced by a more cautious, even sceptical view of IT and a sharper eye on the returns that banks can really expect from their investments. This is underscored by the fact that financial services institutions, in general, continue to invest briskly in maintenance rather than in new investments. According to Celent (2006), 74.5% of the total IT investments are in maintenance, with only 25.5% available for new projects that deliver sustainable competitive advantage.

At the same time, however, competitive pressures have grown. The global players have started to move into almost every market, with big marketing budgets and wide services portfolios, whilst new market entrants have been able to capitalise on their lack of out-dated cumbersome infrastructure and on their entrepreneurial cultures necessary to become nimble exploiters of profitable market niches.

This now leaves the banks facing a dilemma. They must address the deep limitations of their infrastructure in the face of significant competitive threat. At the same time, they must find a way out of the good-money-after-bad cycle of IT investment.

Increasing Importance of Banking Platforms

Industry experts are in agreement that today's banking industry enjoys a highly dynamic environment – with mergers, acquisitions, divestitures, outsourcing initiatives, and branches closing and reopening – characterised by a fast-changing set of business, regulatory, and IT requirements. It is imperative for banks to gain market share while increasing operational efficiency. As stated above, customers have grown increasingly sophisticated, demanding new products in shorter cycles as well as more compelling, customisable, and innovative product offerings. Consequently, banks are creating products across lines of business, based on analytics and a 360-degree view of the customer.

An interesting view from Forrester Research is that on the IT side, existing banking platforms can be compared with baroque castles. These ancient constructs are not up to the quality, cost and time-to-delivery requirements of modern banks.

The emphasis for banks in most parts of the world is now on replacement of core banking systems despite the high risks and costs involved. Slowly but surely, many retail banks, which often are relying on technologies that are nearly thirty years old, are realising the competitive advantage of modernising their antiquated core systems. To this end, they have been choosing systems from a host of the major software vendors.

Figure 8.1 Typical Core Banking Functional Architecture

FLEXCUBE, i-flex's core banking solution

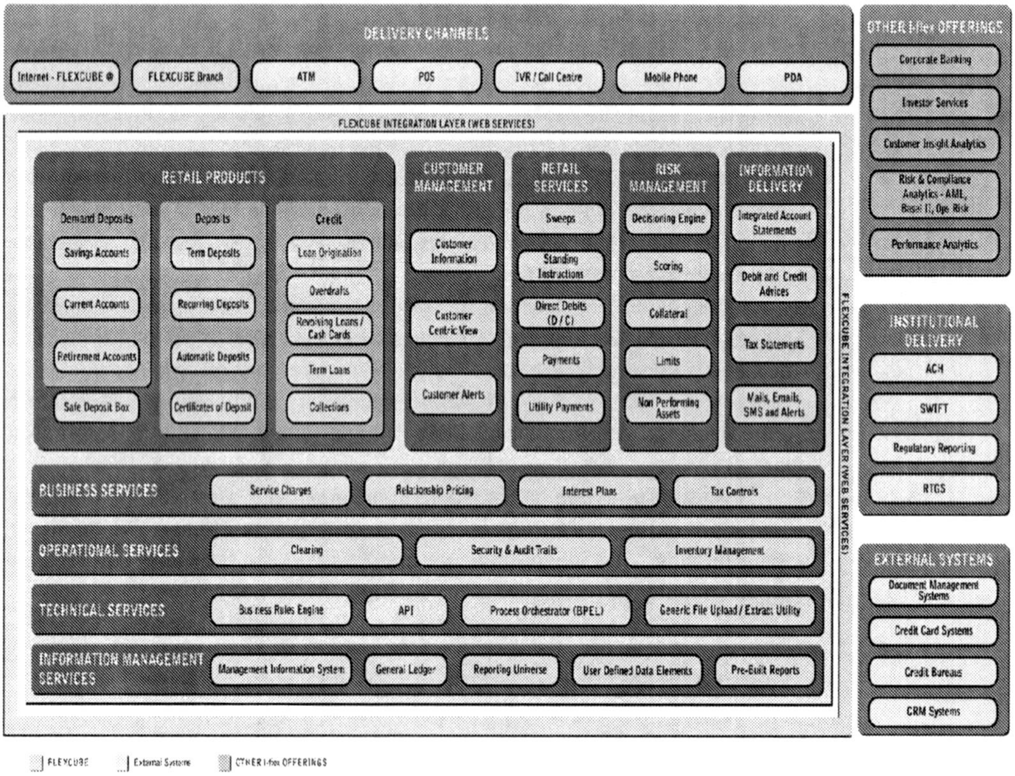

The following are some of the retail banking systems from a few of the notable vendors in the retail banking technology marketplace.

Misys Equation

Equation™ is an integrated, real-time, multi-currency retail banking system that helps organisations deliver products and services to customers. It supports consumer and corporate banking as well as treasury operations within a single platform.

Equation is customer-centric rather than account-centric and thus ensures that tellers have the total view they need to deliver services, and managers have access to consolidated limit exposures and customer worth indicators. And since all information is centrally held, it is available to all channels and all areas of the business.

The system is modular, containing modules such as:

- **Core Management** – this module provides services such as interest, tax and service fee calculation and correspondence production to the other modules.
- **Retail Services** – provides full support for the services required for retail products. Standing orders – automatic or manual, cheque management and cheque book issue, clearing interfaces, flexible charges and comprehensive interest facilities such as floating or tiered interest rates with penalty rates are available for use by all products.
- **Notice Account Savings** – supports numerous features for savings accounts, including notice periods, free withdrawal facilities and penalties for early withdrawal.
- **Lending** – provides support for the whole lending process from loan application through opening and monitoring to delinquency management and reporting.
- **Branch Automation** – which contains components including:
  - *Relationship Manager* – supports the interaction between customers and staff of the bank by providing a customer session-based system with tools to rapidly identify customer relationships, manage contacts, provide workflow management and display bank-definable product information.
  - *Co Sign* – handles the storage and retrieval of signatures and photographs. Signing rules and maintenance, including the scanning of images, can be done either centrally or in each branch.
  - *Cashier System* – supports teller operations, including account opening, transaction posting, enquiries, foreign exchange, commission, interest and tax calculation.

Over 200 banks worldwide, including Alfa Bank, use Misys Equation to support their business every day.

Chordiant® Retail Channel

In spite of the recent emphasis on web and other self-service channels, branches and agencies continue to be a primary customer contact point. Since this is where customers are engaging the organisation, it makes good sense to transform these service outlets into highly effective sales centres as well.

Chordiant® Retail Channel transforms branches and agencies into customer-focused sales-through-service centres. Interactions are driven by real-time customer data and unique business processes, policies and marketing strategies to optimise service efficiency and streamline account opening. More relevant product offers and advisory selling helps channel agents make the most of every customer interaction to increase wallet share[83] and customer retention.

---

83 This is the percentage of the customer's overall revenue and profit potential that an organisation is realising.

Chordiant Retail Channel provides end-to-end work management to drive and track service requests from initial customer inquiry through transaction completion in the back office. Agents gain real-time control of the entire selling and servicing process.

Key features include:

- **Universal, role-based desktop** – integrates Chordiant and non-Chordiant applications for streamlined processing.
- **Process-driven desktop applications** – streamlines servicing and account opening and automatically guides agent through relevant cross-sells.
- **Pre-built components for key servicing tasks, account opening and product advisory** – reduces development effort, speeds implementation, reduces risk and increases ROI.
- **Direct integration with back-end applications and data** – enables a consolidated, real-time customer view, including MultiChannel interaction history.
- **Intelligent work management** – automated hands-off and tracking of work across back-office systems to speed turnarounds.

Users within retail banks that use Chordiant Retail Channel Solution include:

- Relationship managers
- Front desk managers
- Branch managers
- Financial advisors

A host of global banks including HSBC, Barclays and CIBC use Chordiant Retail Channel.

iflex FLEXCUBE®

FLEXCUBE® is a complete banking product suite for retail, consumer, corporate and internet banking. A comprehensive, integrated-yet-modular core banking solution, it can cater for all the needs of a modern financial institution and its multiple business segments.

The unique features of FLEXCUBE include:

- **Customer-centric banking** – affording a single view of customers; analysis of customer needs; creation and modification of new products; and solutions based on accurate, up-to-date customer profiles, which in turn improve customer service levels and generate cross-sell opportunities.
- **Compliance with regulatory requirements like Basel 2 and Anti-Money Laundering** – using highly secure data management features to integrate with third-party solutions, which enable banks to validate compliance with regulatory requirements such as Basel 2 and anti-money laundering.
- **Flexibility through parameterisation** – business rules can be parameterised. Parameters, once defined, are available universally for re-use.

- **Relationship-based pricing** – enabling banks to offer special benefits and facilities in terms of preferential pricing for interest, charges, commissions, fees, brokerage expense and taxes to customers, based on the value of the customer's overall relationship with the bank. This can be performed through the use of user-defined tools.
- **Other features** – such as support for multiple delivery channels to reach new customers and market segments, multicurrency processing and multilingual capabilities, and online validations and automated exception processing.

The modules in FLEXCUBE support the following retail products:

- The current and savings accounts (CASA) module supports the operation of savings and current accounts.
- The deposits module supports complete processing of term deposits.
- The credit module includes credit offered as loans or as overdraft limits on CASA accounts.
- The collections module of FLEXCUBE has comprehensive support for collections and recovery operations.
- The safe deposit box module will help the banks to offer customers a facility for the safekeeping of their valuables.

Services supported by FLEXCUBE include:

- Sweeps, allows linking of customer accounts – thereby offering bank customers a convenient and effective tool for managing funds.
- Standing instructions that automate the periodic processing of customer instructions.
- Direct debits/credits offering a safe, efficient and reliable method for paying utility bills and making credit card payments.
- Payments module for processing all types of incoming and outgoing funds transfers. This module also supports multiparty, multicurrency transfers, including multiple media such as mail, Telex and SWIFT.
- The utility payments module, allowing the bank to offer "across-the-counter" bill payment services to customers/non-customers.

Many banks worldwide, including CitiGroup, use FLEXCUBE to support their business everyday.

Siebel Banking Contact Center

Oracle's Siebel Banking Contact Center transforms a bank's call centre into an integral part of its total sales, marketing and service delivery strategy. The application enables agents to seamlessly handle service, support, and sales interactions across all communication channels. As a result, banks can reduce costs while enhancing service delivery.

Banking call centre agents use Siebel Banking Contact Center to:

- provide call resolution as well as service request routing;
- resolve service issues;
- transfer service requests to another call centre representative or operations expert.

Key features:

- **Complete View of the Customer** – Siebel Banking Contact Center provides the bank with a single view of each customer relationship regardless of what channel is used for interaction. Agents have an uninterrupted view of customer information including contacts, activities, assets, transactions and payment histories.
- **Intelligent Call and Service Request Routing** – Siebel Banking Contact Center intelligently routes requests from multiple communication channels including the telephone, email, and the web. Requests are routed to the call centre's most qualified agent based on skills, customer value, business logic, or availability. In addition, the agent can trigger assignment routing should a customer request additional approvals such as a large cheque request or new account approval.
- **Computer Telephony Interaction (CTI)** – Siebel CTI improves call productivity by identifying the customer before the conversation begins and "screen-popping" the customer record from the Siebel database. Information is captured once so customers do not need to repeat information to each agent.
- **Integrated eMail Management** – Siebel eMail Response lets banks respond to high volumes of email quickly and professionally. This application automatically responds to selected customer enquiries without agent intervention. It provides easy-to-administer routing and queuing rules that send email messages and suggested responses to the most appropriate agent.

A number of banks including Bank of Ireland and Oversea-Chinese Banking Corporation (OCBC) use Siebel Banking Contact Center.

Tenemos T24

Temenos T24 (formerly known as Globus) is an integrated banking package which automates all banking work. It is a modular package that consists of a Core System which provides all common operations between various banking activities, and a series of modules which cover the various different operational requirements of users.

Temenos T24 retail banking functionality includes:

- teller applications;
- savings accounts;
- mortgage processing with Past Due obligations;
- funds transfers and standing orders;

- cheque and card management;
- ATM Interface branch server processing.

Temenos T24 is built on open architecture and is claimed to offer a low cost of ownership and uses established standards such as HTTP, XML and J2EE. The design of Temenos T24 offers multiple application server support, offering horizontal scalability and supporting huge numbers of users with inherent non-stop resilience. Temenos T24 was designed to remove the need to run end-of-day processing.

Temenos' Open Standards allow for the most flexibility in converting legacy systems.

Temenos T24 runs on:

- Open hardware;
- Open database;
- Open J2EE application server;
- Open user interface through browser;
- HTML and XSLT;
- Open connectivity through XML and web services;
- Open C language code;
- Open Java development environment.

The T24 system is based on established industry standards as promoted by independent bodies and not on the particular interpretation of these standards by other vendors.

Temenos T24 operates in 500 banks and financial institutions including Fortis and HSBC.

Aurius

Aurius is a retail banking system from APAK group. With full back- and front-office functionality, Aurius can help banks and building societies increase profitability in today's competitive financial services marketplace. Multicurrency based, with sophisticated customer relationship management (CRM), the system is fully compliant with Bacs, CCA, euro, multicurrency and Data Protection Act regulations.

Aurius can support an extensive range of retail banking products encompassing:

- term deposits;
- secured/unsecured lending;
- personal/commercial loans;
- payment cards.

Developed with Microsoft .NET for maximum system performance, Aurius is highly scalable and configurable to suit a multitude of operational requirements. .NET web deployment compatibility allows for rapid distribution over an intranet. The system is also capable of running across multiple databases and is fully scalable to grow with an organisation's future requirements.

Supported functionality includes:

- full back-office system with integrated front end;
- customer relationship management;
- workflow management;
- online, real-time general ledger;
- 24 x 7 processing;
- N2 money laundering compliant;
- online product designer;
- internet/intranet deployable.

Aurius achieves maximum system interoperability through its advanced .NET design and compatibility with a service oriented architecture (SOA). The system's business rules can be exposed via web services, which allow the system to easily interface with different banking applications and institutions, supporting bank delivery channels as well as workflow and document archiving software.

A number of retail banks, including Unity Trust Bank, use APAK Group's Aurius to support their business.

Infosys Finacle

Finacle, the universal banking solution from Infosys, empowers banks to transform their business leveraging agile, new generation technologies. This modular solution addresses the core banking, CRM, treasury, mobile banking and web-based cash management requirements of retail banks.

The following are some of the key features from the Finacle stable to ensure growth and success in a competitive and demanding environment:

Future-proof infrastructure

The solution is built on open standards with an architecture that is easy to deploy, parameterise and scale. The platform-independent web services in the service oriented architecture (SOA) offer interoperability and reusability of components, 24/7 capabilities for the continuous operation of branches and channels, and single sign-on for a secure and authenticated login.

Customer-centricity

Finacle supports the capture of extensive customer information, which is displayed across the enterprise and back-end systems. The enterprise customer information can be managed from the early stages of prospecting to every stage in the lifecycle of the relationship with the customer. The CRM application enables a relationship-driven approach to customer management with marketing, sales, support, interaction, loan origination and service level management modules.

Innovative product offerings

The core banking solution offers the capability to create and roll out a range of products and services in the fastest time. A few of the new-age products that can be parameterised are top-up loans, off-set products, Shari'a-compliant products, incremental deposits, structured deposits and mortgages. Innovative services can be offered by way of features such as target balancing, notional pooling, securitisation etc. with linkages to bank-definable payment systems. These capabilities empower banks to offer a wide and extensive range of products and services targeted at new customer segments with time-to-market advantages.

Automation capabilities

The enterprise workflow abilities of Finacle enable the linking and chaining of different types of business scenarios to provide a high degree of automation. The BPEL- and BPML-compliant workflow module is based on a graphical user interface and allows business users to define and deploy workflows to suit the bank's own environment. The referral infrastructure enables effective management of exceptions that may occur during financial or non-financial transactions. The infrastructure allows the bank to automate the approval process and to effectively manage the skill sets available within their organisation.

Regulation and compliance

Finacle has extensive data capture and security features built in and along with allied analytical solutions, these enable banks to comply with regulations such as Basel 2, Sarbanes-Oxley, AML, IBAN, KYC, IAS 39, the Patriot Act etc. The solution has been built around a process-driven set-up to help banks manage their operations under ever-increasing compliance and regulatory requirements.

Efficient payment systems support

The core banking solution offers a comprehensive payment systems module to cater for the evolving needs in cross-border and domestic payments. The module addresses the complete transaction lifecycle for inward and outward transactions with settlement and reconciliation processes and is compatible with different payment systems such as SWIFT, ACH, GIRO, Bacs, CHIPS and CHAPS.

Treasury solution

The treasury solution provides end-to-end capabilities for banks to manage their capital and money market business dealings. It supports products in money markets, foreign exchange markets, securities and derivatives with tightly knit front-, middle- and back-office functions from a single application. This provides greater flexibility to the bank, better processing abilities and centralised management of limits, risk and accounting.

Corporate and consumer e-banking solution

The corporate and consumer e-banking solution is a new-generation banking application that enables anywhere, anytime access to bank accounts and transactions for end-customers. The comprehensive set of features range from the simple account inquiry to the complex debit transfer with multicurrency and multilingual support. The solution supports other functions such as bill payments, account aggregation, mutual funds and credit card support for retail customers.

Integrated alerts capabilities
The alerts solution helps banks to disseminate information through multiple channels such as handheld devices, SMS, email, fax or voice. The solution has the capability to deliver multilingual push and pull alerts, two-way alerts, internal and external alerts – internal to branch users and external to customers – and supports an extensive framework for pricing of alerts and report generation on alerts delivered. This solution is an innovative module that delivers convenience which is a powerful and cost-effective way for banks to differentiate in the competitive marketplace.

Departments/divisions in retail banks using Finacle handle the following functionalities:

- Current and Savings Accounts;
- Retail Loans and Deposits;
- Branch Front End – Teller functionalities;
- Payments (Remittances);
- Clearing.

Leading global banks including ABN AMRO, Credit Suisse, DBS Bank, Emirates Bank, ICICI Bank and ANZ use Infosys Finacle.

Other systems

Name	Vendor	Category
System Access Card Pro	Sungard Corporate	Payment Cards
Forpost Cards	FORBIS Ltd	Payment Cards
CBK Chargeback and Dispute Management	Clear2Pay	Payment Cards
Corebank	Fidelity National Information Service	Core Banking[84]
ATM Manager Pro	Profit Stars	ATM Technology
Check 21 Solutions	Profit Stars	Cheque Processing
Bancs Core Banking	TCS Financial Solutions	Core Banking
iMetaBank	iMeta Technologies Limited	Internet Banking

---

84 Core Banking Systems usually consist of modules like Deposits, Loans, General Ledger and Card Management.

SMART	TCS Financial Solutions	Core Banking
Olympic Banking Systems	ERI Bancaire S.A.	Core Banking
Simple Image	Maverick International	Cheque Processing
Spectrum	Profile Systems and Software	Core Banking
Intercept Payments	Aqua Global	Payments Processing
Kyoudo Web Branch Management	Callataÿ & Wouters	Branch Management
AFS Business Banking Origination	Automated Financial Systems, Inc.	Commercial lending
Tallyman	Experian Decisions Analytics	Revenue and collection management
KASTLE Core Banking	3i Infotech	Core Banking
iMAL	Path solutions	Islamic Core Banking

Conclusion

Faced with the array of systems as shown above, banks in all parts of the world are deciding on the future shape of their systems landscape. Armed with an understanding of their building blocks as well as a comprehensive overview of application systems – a functional map and application landscape – decision makers are focusing on application renewal and extension. These will also support application strategy planning and create an essential input for architectural design.

IT Projects in Retail Banking

This chapter lists the types of IT projects in retail banking and describes the adoption of business process automation and screen scraping. A case study on business process automation is also included.

Introduction

IT projects in retail banking, as in other segments of financial services, are instigated as a result of the introduction of new regulations or changes to existing ones and also to keep abreast of the latest technological trends. However, as the retail banking business is focused mostly on personal customers, there are other drivers for embarking on new projects such as:

- the sheer volume of transactions in retail banking given the high number of customers;
- the number of interfaces to external systems such as credit referencing systems, electoral registers, address verification systems and payments systems;
- the high volume of data and hence stricter performance requirements;
- the frequent introduction of unmanned delivery channels such as internet banking and mobile banking;
- the fierce competition for customers in this industry and therefore IT projects are enablers for the delivery of superior customer service and consequently customer retention.

List of Common IT Projects

- Data migration
- Implementation of payment systems
- Implementation of account opening systems
- Rationalisation projects
- Implementation and upgrades of capital adequacy databases
- Implementation and upgrades of adverse trends reporting systems
- Upgrades to the general ledger
- Branch automation
- Implementation of lending systems
- Implementation of card systems
- Implementation of customer relationship management (CRM) systems
- Implementation of enterprise resource planning (ERP) systems
- Desktop integration
- Implementation of online banking systems
- Implementation and upgrades of retail credit decisioning systems
- Implementation and upgrades of regulatory reporting systems
- Integration of legacy systems into the IT environment
- Decommission of legacy systems

Automation of Business Processes

The automation of business processes has been gaining momentum in the financial services sector in recent times. This is because in large organisations like retail banks, most customer-facing and back-office staff are hampered by the number of IT systems they need to do their job. They often need to access and change many systems to complete even simple tasks.

There are a number of systems in the software market that automate business processes, but Blue Prism's Automate (BPA) uses a technique known as robotic integration to rapidly automate business processes in a scalable, secure and controlled environment.

Robotic integration is the practice of replicating the actions of a user without changing the underlying systems in order to automate a currently manual process.

It can include directly interfacing with the graphical user interface (GUI), the calling of web services, and native application programming interfaces (APIs) published by the system author.

In this section, a list of retail banking processes that can be automated with a tool like BPA will be discussed.

Real-time Agent Hand-offs

These processes are initiated by telephone contact or customer visit, where an agent will negotiate with a customer to derive the appropriate action. Once the call is complete, the agent hands off the administrative element of the wrap-up by triggering an automated process and moving on to the next call.

Process	Description	New Bus.	Cust. Serv.	Coll. & Rec.
Charge and Fee Refund	Actioning the refund of a fee or charge when this has been agreed in negotiation with the customer – the operator enters the required details into a shared repository and these are processed by an automated process.	–	√	√
Dial Stop	In a mixed call centre, incoming calls are removed from outgoing call lists by an automated process triggered by agent email request to stop calling.	√	√	√
VISA Card Account Closures	Following customer requests, VISA accounts are closed off and refunds issued where a credit balance is detected.		√	
Direct Debit	Agents in customer service handle calls from customers wishing to cancel various direct debits. Once noted, the cancellation is handed off to a back-office automated process which executes and audits the cancellation.		√	√

Process	Description	New Bus.	Cust. Serv.	Coll. & Rec.
Lost and Stolen Blocks	Cards reported as lost or stolen by a customer are handed off by the operator to a back-office process which stops the cards.		√	
Refund Validation	A customer request for a refund is validated and either actioned or declined depending on account usage criteria/patterns.		√	√

Agent preparation

In order for an agent to deal with a call or request efficiently, the following automated processes take on the administrative, time-consuming preparation work and present this information to the agent to streamline the customer contact experience.

Process	Description	New Bus.	Cust. Serv.	Coll. & Rec.
Account Categorisation	Accounts entering into arrears are categorised according to the debt patterns and moved into agent workflow.		√	√
Fraud Administration	Accounts identified as undergoing fraudulent usage are processed in order to prevent further abuse, to notify the customer and to schedule for further expert analysis by agents.	√	√	√
Decline Queries	Customers who query the reason for declined card transactions speak to an operator and give information such as card number, date and amount. An automated process works in the background to conduct a transaction search using the data and presents the decline reason to the operator to communicate to the customer.		√	

Back-office bulk processing
These processes do the work of back-office administrators who execute repetitive tasks in order to support customer requests and operational requirements.

Process	Description	New Bus.	Cust. Serv.	Coll. & Rec.
Action Customer	Accounts where the customer has "Gone Away" are actioned – cards cancelled, cheque books stopped, mail stopped and accounts are handed off to trace agents electronically.			√
Utility Bill Low Payer	Customers who have paid less than the monthly instalment for their gas/electricity are identified and their monthly instalment adjusted according to business rules.		√	
CHAPS Requests	Customer requests for CHAPS payments are actioned and audited.		√	
Exit to Recoveries	Accounts are moved from Collections to Recoveries cycles and various hand-off operations are completed.			√
Escalating Excess	Accounts with escalating arrears patterns are identified and appropriate action taken.			√
Change of Address	Customers who notify of a change of address have their requests executed and details updated by an automated back-office process.		√	
Account Closures	Dormant savings, current and investment accounts are identified and closed and the customer notified.		√	
Business Account Closures	Corporate customer's account is closed at customer request.		√	
Internet Applications	Applications for new accounts taken over the internet are transformed into proposals on legacy mainframe systems, credit-checked, activated and welcome packs, cards and cheque books issued.	√		
Personal Loan Closures	Settlement quotes are derived and actioned, insurance claw-backs and monies transferred before the loan account is closed and the customer notified.		√	

Process	Description	New Bus.	Cust. Serv.	Coll. & Rec.
Fund Transfer	Opportunistic sweeping of monies between various accounts on a regular basis to minimise arrears situations.			√
CRM Updates	Reports are produced from a dialler and relevant notes regarding the contact status are automatically updated on the CRM.		√	
Corporate Account Opening	Applications for business bank accounts are manually keyed from the paper application into a credit-scoring system. An automated process selects those approved accounts and inputs the data into the account management system.	√		
Exceed Account Limit	Bank accounts that have pending transactions that will take them over the limit are cautioned according to appropriate business rules.		√	
Mortgage Redemption	Mortgage accounts are actioned according to business rules and a redemption letter is printed for issuing to relevant parties.		√	
Mortgage Product Switch	The customer informs the mortgage provider about details of the new product and an automated process closes the existing account and opens a new one, producing all necessary customer letters.	√	√	
Insurance Cancellation	Any building or content insurance taken as part of the mortgage is cancelled by the automated process according to the business rules.		√	
Money Transfer	Requests to withdraw funds from an account are made online by the account holder. The automated process transfers the requested amount from the savings account to the nominated bank account.		√	

Third-party hand-offs

The following processes automate the gathering of information and interaction with external agencies, both outbound and inbound.

Process	Description	New Bus.	Cust. Serv.	Coll. & Rec.
Audit	Commercial accounts are audited for year-end purposes and an audit pack is produced and sent to accountants.		√	
Mortgage Valuation Requests	Requests for property valuations are identified and relevant data collated before transmitting requests to third-party valuers.	√	√	
Mortgage Valuation Results	Incoming valuation results are processed and mortgage application systems updated with the valuation details before the account is moved to the next workflow step.	√	√	
Mortgage Solicitor Packs	A solicitor pack detailing all of the information within a mortgage offer is assembled using an automated process and batched up before being dispatched to the relevant solicitors electronically.	√	√	
Data Cleanse	An incoming file from a bureau with the most recent telephone numbers is received and an automated process updates the CRM systems accordingly.		√	√
Insurance Payments	A file is received from solicitors or claims specialists detailing the claims payments and these are automatically updated on the system.		√	
Monthly Financial Reports	Data is gathered from multiple systems and reports are created to be issued to clients.		√	√

Case study
The following is a case study on the use of Blue Prism's BPA to automate business processes within BizEast, a fictional retail bank.

Project summary
Business Process Automation project to automate a number of highly manual, labour-intensive processes within the customer service centre operation using Blue Prism Automate.

- 10 processes identified and automated within 12 months.
- Rapid ROI (Return on Investment) – project paid for itself in 12 months.
- A significant FTE saving (full-time equivalent salaries) in Year 1.
- Incremental cost savings year on year.

- Improved levels of customer service – more agents now have customer-facing roles.
- Automation results in a consistent, audit-approved approach to each business process.
- Customers benefit from improved service levels.
- Project resulted in improvements in speed, consistency and accuracy of administration processes.
- Intuitive system – processes can be mapped by the business users – low IT involvement in the project.
- Further processes identified for next project stage.

Business case

Excellent customer service is of paramount importance to the BizEast Bank and the organisation regularly reviews its internal processes in order to continually improve the customer experience.

As part of the Bank's drive to further improve customer service levels, the business has focused on a business process automation project in order to reduce the levels of manual administration in the business and to move staff away from time-consuming manual activities and into customer-facing roles. The business case for the project was to save FTE salaries in the first 12 months and to enhance customer service by improving the speed and accuracy of dealing with customer queries.

Jenny Small, Business Systems Manager at the BizEast Bank, explained, *"It was easy for us to identify our most labour-intensive processes, but we'd always struggled to imagine how we might actually automate them. We considered a number of options including bespoke solutions, but these were significantly more expensive and had longer lead times than the Blue Prism solution. Once we'd seen the Blue Prism technology in operation, we conducted a feasibility study to automate one of the most complex processes within the collections and recoveries division. Having successfully automated this first process, we were confident that Blue Prism could automate many of the Bank's processes."*

Business process automation project

The Bank identified 10 processes in total, including direct debit cancellation, account closures, CHAPS payments, foreign payments, audit reports, internet applications and Card and Pin Pulls. The business case for automating these processes was high – all had a high level of manual intervention and a high number of people managing the processes.

Mapping the processes

Having identified the processes to be automated, the next step was to fully understand the steps taken in each process before capturing each of the steps in Blue Prism Automate to enable the automation

Jenny Small commented, *"Blue Prism's role went beyond the automation work. They constantly challenged each process and helped us to refine and improve many of our underlying procedures before automation began. They developed a detailed understanding of our complex processes and added value at each stage of the project."*

Process automation benefits
As each process was automated, the ROI was rapid – with staff released immediately from their manual workload. Each process has resulted in its own unique benefits.

Account closure
This process closes personal accounts when customers either transfer to a new BizEast account or leave the Bank completely. A lengthy and time-consuming process when performed manually, account closure required the manual cancellation of direct debits and standing orders, transfer of interest charges and the transfer of funds from one account to another etc. Customer service agents now complete an electronic form over the phone. The form is sent to a central mailbox where it is picked up by the Blue Prism system which automatically deals with the account closure, with no manual intervention by a member of staff.

On average, using the manual processes, staff could close an average of 12 accounts per hour. The automated process can close around 200 accounts per hour. Furthermore, automation has removed any backlog of accounts waiting to be closed.

Internet applications
Previously when customers applied online for loans, a partially automated system processed the application from the internet to the Bank's mainframe. However, this required a high level of manual intervention before the application could be keyed into the Bank's mainframe. Each form was checked manually and errors corrected – for example, many customers would enter incorrect county details with their address. Application forms are still completed online in the same way, but Blue Prism Automate now validates each form before passing it directly into the mainframe – the Blue Prism system works intelligently to find relevant county details etc.

The Bank now processes 99% of loan applications on the day they are keyed in, resulting in fewer delays for the customer. Decisions on whether to grant the loan are made within the Blue Prism system, which also generates the confirmation letters on the following day.

Audit
The Blue Prism process supports requests by auditors for company audit reports. The system finds the entire set of customers' accounts, year-end balances etc. and returns the audit to the audit clerk in the form of a Word document.

With the previous manual system, an average audit would take several hours to complete and a large audit could take several days.

These now take around 1 minute and 30 minutes respectively.

CHAPS

This process performs CHAPS payment transfers. Manually taking around 10 minutes per request, the automated process takes around 20 seconds to check fund availability, perform the transfer to the point where manual authorisation is required without error, and charge the customer and notepad the account.

The automation of the CHAPS payments ensures that the Bank can easily maintain the bank-wide service-level agreement for the time allowed for CHAPS transfers.

The Bank has quickly seen additional benefits as a result of the BPA project. Blue Prism Automate is intuitive and simple so that business users are able to change and maintain their own processes without IT assistance, thereby reducing IT support costs.

Project benefits summary

The project, which has already paid for itself, will result in savings year on year since these manual processes will never again require staff to manage them.

Jenny Small explained, *"We exceeded our FTE savings target by 25%. So far, we have been able to release staff as each process went live and the project has enabled us to move a significant number of FTEs away from manual roles and into customer-facing positions. Apart from the obvious cost savings from the reduction in FTEs, there are a number of benefits that are more difficult to quantify. We're now able to resolve most customer queries in one phone call, our staff now spend more time dealing directly with customers and our service-level agreements can be maintained and guaranteed. Overall, the project has enabled us to improve the experience that customers have with the BizEast Bank."*

Future projects

The Bank now has a list of additional processes to be automated and, subject to budget approval, the work will commence in the near future.

Use of Screen Scraping for Data Migration[86]

Data migration projects are typical IT projects in retail banking and usually accompany system upgrades and cutovers in complex environments. The complex nature of retail banking means that in a multi-system environment, the simplest customer service processes may make use of a core banking system, a customer relationship system, various fraud prevention and risk management systems, workflow and work scheduling, not to mention the financial ledgers and everyday productivity tools such as Microsoft® Office and Excel.

Furthermore, the mix of these systems may range from COBOL-based legacy "green-screen" systems to internally built client-server and web-based portals. There will also be third-party products based on various technologies.

---

86 Contributed by Blue Prism.

The high risk involved in major migrations normally leads to a phased approach which creates the additional problems of managing processes that span two sets of systems during the transition period. Often the only way of managing the extra workload created is to employ more contract staff.

However, recent advances in technology have offered the chance to use non-invasive "screen scraping" techniques to help overcome the problems of data conversion and migration in a complex systems environment.

Such tactical techniques are now being used by enterprises to address temporary workarounds not only in the fragmented processes highlighted during the transitional period, but also in the technical migration process itself.

The Problems of Data Migration
In a multi-system environment, there is usually no one-to-one mapping of data fields between major software versions making data migrations more difficult. This is even more of a problem when migrating data between different applications.

Moving data from a 5-line to a 4-line address format is an obvious example of a problem that can be encountered. However, simpler problems like field sizes are just as problematic. Frequently there is also a need to transform data during the migration, performing not just format changes, but calculations and decisions prior to importing to the new database.

Furthermore, when data is moving across technologies, for example from a mainframe system to an application sitting on an Oracle database, there are technical formatting considerations to take into account.

All this leads to undue complexity when trying to create a migration or conversion routine to move the data between the various databases. The complexity is multiplied as more systems become involved.

There is not always a one-to-one mapping between the old and the new systems. The diagram below shows an example of data flows during a typical migration.

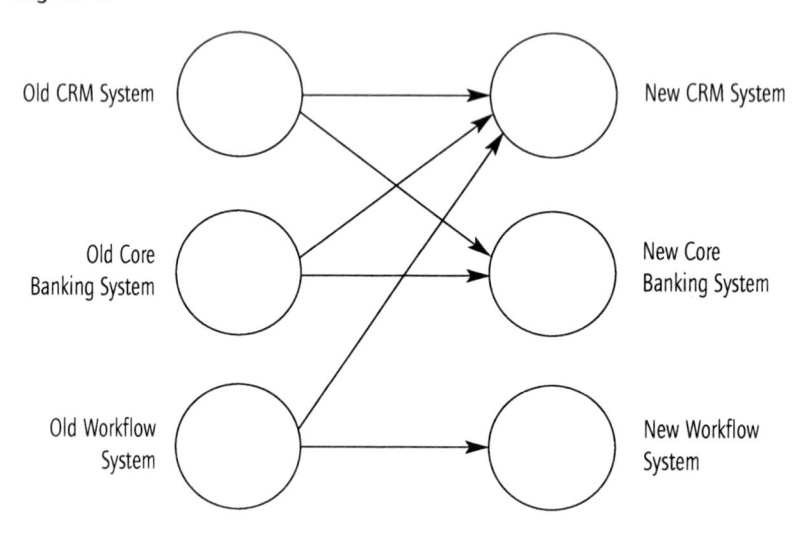

Phased migrations

In retail banking, "big bang" implementation, in which the old systems get switched off on the day the new system springs to life, is rare. The sheer scale of data movement, and the enormous risk this presents to customer service, leads to the sensible conclusion that major migrations should be phased. However, this presents a problem in managing business processes that span two sets of systems during the transitional period.

Business processes fragmented during the transition can be temporarily automated using tactical methods which are likely to be the only cost-effective means, given the disposable short-term nature of the requirement.

The integration of an old system with a new system is pointless unless it can pay for itself before the old system is decommissioned. This often points to a non-invasive "interfacing" solution rather than a back-end integration exercise.

The same tools and techniques used in the technical migration process can be used to address the manual workarounds created by a phased migration.

Traditional technical migration method

If migration processes were straightforward, some simple database scripts would be all that were needed.

More complex scenarios can be handled by common data transformation applications (such as Microsoft DTS).

However, databases are linked to applications and there is an ever-present risk of data corruption which may not actually manifest itself until after migration when users try to access the data through the application. This can affect not only the new systems but also presents risks to those remaining static.

Other options for migration

There is an acknowledged notion that in many cases the use of traditional "direct" data transfer is the quickest, most secure and the most accurate method.

However, accepting that it cannot always solve 100% of the migration requirements, the following are other options:

- Manual transfer of the data is a workaround frequently used for the complex parts of an otherwise simple migration. Additional staff can be hired to monitor the progress and success of the automatic migration and to mop up the bits not done automatically. This can be expensive, inaccurate and risky.
- A recent option enabled by the flexibility now available in most GUIs is the use of screen-scraping techniques.

What is screen scraping?

Screen scraping is programming that translates between legacy application programs (written to communicate with now generally obsolete input/output devices and user interfaces) and new user interfaces so that the logic and data associated with the legacy programs can continue to be used. Screen scraping is sometimes called *advanced terminal emulation*. A program that performs screen scraping must take the data coming from the legacy program that is formatted for the screen of an older type of terminal such as an IBM 3270 display or a Digital Equipment Corporation VT100 and reformat it for a Windows 98 user or someone using a web browser.

Using this method, data can be copied from the old application and keyed into the new one, if necessary using a flat file as a staging post. One of the advantages of using this technique is that data can be transformed, parsed, concatenated, sorted etc. on the way. Any problems with differing technologies are removed since interfacing with the graphical user interface (GUI) is what is being accomplished.

Risk of data corruption is much lower since data entered into the database is being verified by the application on the way. This simultaneously preserves the integrity of the data and the application.

Screen scraping methods
Screen scraping from applications can be broadly split into three categories:

1. "Green Screen" applications where EHLLAPI[87] and other very simple methods can be used to interface with a range of terminal emulators.
2. Standard applications (including web-based GUIs) where it is frequently possible to connect to objects in the GUI or to use APIs published by the application author.
3. Legacy or closed interfaces where it can be necessary to use sophisticated techniques for character recognition, or resort to crude keyboard and mouse control methods.

How to scrape an application is only part of the solution, however. There needs to be some rules-based processing built around it, especially if automating temporary processes created by the use of old and new systems during the transition.

A scalable runtime environment needs to be considered for large-volume migrations. Also to be considered is the feasibility of running multiple instances of applications coexisting on the same machine or deploying the migration process over a number of PCs or servers. If the deployment of the process is done remotely, however, central monitoring must be available to ensure that each process completes successfully and any exceptions are handled.

When deciding on using screen scraping for a migration project, the option of whether to build or buy has to be carefully considered.

An approach to the build/buy decision
The decision to build or buy a screen-scraping tool is not an isolated decision, and is approached the same way any IT investment decision is made.

The early steps include:

---

[87] Emulator High-Level Language Application Programming Interface.

1. **developing a concept proposal** – brief definition of the need, purpose, stakeholders, required functionality, priority, alternatives, anticipated benefits and costs;
2. **getting early buy-in** – ensuring that there is agreement in principle among key decision-makers that they (a) are prepared to implement a new system and make the necessary budget process changes, and (b) will objectively evaluate the build vs buy alternatives;
3. **performance analysis** – requirements refinement and estimate of in-house development requirements;
4. **risks, benefits, and costs evaluation** – comparison of the in-house option to the commercial alternatives and determination of which makes the most sense for the bank.

Choosing a screen-scraping tool for migration

There are different solutions to choose from depending on the requirements of the IT project to be executed. They are as follows:

- Crude EHLLAPI script writers may be "fit for purpose" if the data is to be migrated from one mainframe to another. They are often available from the emulator environment being used within the bank.
- Automated regression test tools can be used to quickly create useful scripts to interface with Windows-based and other applications. However, the deployment and monitoring facilities are geared up for testing not bulk live running so these are only recommended in a low-volume environment.
- A range of rules-based business process automation (BPA) tools have enhanced facilities that allow bulk deployment and include other flexible features such as flowcharting tools to capture and drive the migration process. Usually there will be a rules engine allowing sophisticated data-transformation and exception-handling mechanisms. Audit, change control, security and logging can be important features for running real business processes during the transition, but may not be needed in a secure technical migration environment.

Checklist for choosing a tool

- **Data volumes** – in high-volume environments, deployments and control of routines are critical and so are reviewed thoroughly. In high-volume environments the ability to multi-thread processes is usually critical and so the tool should be proven in enterprise environments.
- **Range of systems** – the more systems in use, the more complex the solution. The tool should have a sophisticated rules engine with data transformation facilities.
- **Range of technologies** – the tool should be able to interface with all types of GUI in use at the bank.
- **Flexibility** – depending on the level of change, a choice between a flowchart interface and script interface should be considered.
- **Reuse** – the tool should allow publishing of subroutines for use in more

than one process if there is an anticipation of reuse of any of the routines in other projects.
- **Web services** – if the migration can make use of web services, these could be more transactionally reliable than screen scraping. Some tools have simple interfaces to web services already built in.
- **Change control and security** – if the tool is used for running live processes (for example the temporary ones controlling old and new systems during the transitional period) then the tool should have features that track changes to the processes and that control which users can create, change or run a process, for example.
- **Audit logging and MI** – consideration should be given to features in a chosen tool that capture each step of the process.
- **Vendor evaluation** – other customers, especially in the banking sector, of the chosen tool's vendor should be contacted for a reference.

Building Mainframe Functionality into the Extended Enterprise[88]

Mainframe systems have been the backbone of most retail banks for decades. Their capability, scalability and dependability are what these banks bet their business on. In fact, Gartner estimates that more than 70% of the world's data still resides on mainframe computers. Most of these systems have been running in a highly tuned state for decades.

At the same time, developments in the IT industry, such as the emergence of service-oriented architecture (SOA) and the enterprise service bus (EBS), offer banks new and more effective ways to build IT environments capable of evolving and adapting to meet changing business requirements in a way that has not been previously possible.

Tapping into the benefits offered by these new approaches to application design, while retaining the mainframe as a key element of these environments, is one of the central challenges facing today's IT managers and CIOs.

In this section, the considerations for an IT project in retail banking that seeks to enable mainframe functionality to be exposed to web services will be discussed.

The Importance of the Mainframe

The mainframe represents existing, working technology. Businesses especially banks, have a wealth of information, not least customer data, and applications deployed. No organisation likes to replace such systems, and many would regard it as foolish to even try. Furthermore, with billions of dollars invested in these systems, it makes sense to reuse existing business functions as much as possible and to avoid incurring the cost of changing them.

Completing and reflecting this reality, recent trends in the integration field have focused on the need to create new business services from existing ones.

---

88 Extracted with permission from "Building Mainframe Functionality to the Extended Enterprise" by PolarLake and GT Software.

SOA applications are based on existing or newly built components that can be reused and combined to form new systems and applications. For an enterprise to attempt an SOA implementation without including the mainframe would be an exercise in futility.

Fortunately, with the advent of new software technologies, mainframe systems will be able to participate as true peers in the SOA environment.

Building a system that incorporates the mainframe within an SOA essentially involves three distinct processes:

- the exposure of mainframe functionality as components or web services;
- the mediation between the diverse data models and technologies used to implement these services;
- the creation of applications handling the routing and management of messages throughout the organisation in order to automate business processes.

In the following section, the challenges associated with each of these processes will be discussed in turn, as will the ways in which successful organisations implement SOA solutions that incorporate the SOA.

Integrating the Mainframe
Just as the mainframe has been in existence for decades, so have attempts to integrate it with the IT environments that have emerged over this period. Over time this has led to a number of mainframe integration options still available today, but with particular drawbacks that make them unsuitable for the integration of mainframe and SOA.

These approaches include the following.

Screen scraping
Screen-scraping technology is probably the oldest option for integrating the mainframe applications. These fragile solutions are based on the geometric positions of data on the screens used in off-host applications. Unfortunately, changing the locations of data elements in the display breaks all dependent applications if they are not notified of the change – and even with notifications, adapting and extending these solutions can be a hugely complex undertaking.

Gateways
Gateways run off the host on a mid-tier processor to communicate with the host systems. Usually a process is running on the mid-tier communicating back to the mainframe over different protocols (TCP/IP, LU 6.2 or a proprietary solution).

Adapters
Adapters run on the host systems and offer connectivity to the underlying systems, but they usually require interfaces that are aware of underlying mainframe systems. Adapters are usually a one-to-one mapping that exposes the existing application or transaction as an interface. Thus each interface is simply

a wrapper for a unique service and does not support composite business functions. Adapters are normally a costly and time-consuming approach to integration, usually requiring a different adapter for each system.

Web services "wrappers"
These solutions interface with the mainframe using their own unique definition of web services. Most use only HTTP and wrap an XML payload without conforming to web services' definitions or standards. In most cases these solutions are actually based on older technologies, with a few front-end functions that attempt to simulate a true web service.

Rewriting
The most expensive of all solutions is to rewrite existing mainframe systems to meet new requirements. This solution is both time-consuming and costly, and may result in no new functionality and reduced return on investment (ROI).

Mainframe Web Services
Fortunately, there is now a genuine and workable alternative to the above approaches that retail banks can implement. Banks can extend mainframe functionality within a truly standard-based environment by implementing a web services solution that conforms to widely adopted standards such as WSDL,[89] SOAP,[90] UDDI[91] and XML.

As noted earlier, most mainframe application designers do not want an intrusive approach that affects existing applications. A true mainframe web service will interface to the underlying applications or systems and present the result without interfering with the existing system. Similarly, applications based on service-oriented architectures do not want or need to be concerned with the mainframe implementation details; they just need the ability to request services via the WSDL standard.

Mainframe web services offer the capability of accessing previously hard-to-get information quickly, easily and securely using industry standards. WSDL provides a clean, fast and easy-to-use mechanism to describe the mainframe process for consumption by other web service clients: the specifics of the transactional nature of the systems, the data formats and the locations for processes can be hidden from the requesting web service. Furthermore, the security that is used by the mainframe system is now bypassed or compromised. The WSDL should follow standards as specified by WS-I (Web Services Interoperability Organisation) and can be used by clients with no vendor extensions or client modifications required.

---

89 WSDL is an XML-based language that provides a model for describing web services.
90 SOAP is a protocol for exchanging XML-based messages over computer networks, normally using HTTP/HTTPS.
91 Universal Description, Discovery and Integration (UDDI) is a platform-independent, XML-based registry for businesses worldwide to list themselves on the internet.

Exposing Business Services

If the mainframe is to enable functionality to be exposed as web services, a decision must first be made concerning the exact method by which functionality will be mapped to services as defined within the SOA. There are two basic approaches – "bottom up" and "top down" – but before these approaches are discussed, the concept of Enterprise Service Bus (ESB) will be explained.

What is ESB?

An enterprise service bus (ESB) refers to a software architecture construct, implemented by technologies found in a category of middleware infrastructure products usually based on standards, that provides foundational services for more complex architectures via an event-driven and standards-based messaging engine (the bus).

An ESB generally provides an abstraction layer on top of an implementation of an enterprise messaging system, which allows integration architects to exploit the value of messaging without writing code. Contrary to the more classical enterprise application integration (EAI) approach of a monolithic stack in a hub and spoke architecture, the foundation of an ESB is built of base functions broken up into their constituent parts, with distributed deployment where needed, working in harmony as necessary.

ESB does not implement a service-oriented architecture (SOA) but provides the features with which one may be implemented.

Key benefits of ESB

- Faster and cheaper accommodation of existing systems.
- Increased flexibility; easier to change as requirements change.
- Standards-based.
- Scales from point solutions to enterprise-wide deployment (distributed bus).
- Predefined ready-for-use service types.
- More configuration rather than integration coding.
- No central rules engine, no central broker.

The "bottom-up" approach

While it is technically possible to expose mainframe applications through an application program interface (API), exposed on a one-for-one basis, the net result is usually a very limited and granular solution.

For example, retrieving customer information within a mainframe application may currently involve traversing a series of CICS transactions to obtain the relevant information unit of work. To invoke each of the transactions as a separate web service would result in an extremely fine-grained and consequently insufficient solution.

The "bottom-up" approach first looks at the available transactions and data, and creates services based upon these by wrapping the entire transaction or data source with an interface to the clients. This is a one-to-one mapping of the transaction to a web service interface, with no inherent combination of functions.

This would expose all the data to clients, possibly using WSDL, but combining these services into meaningful processes would be left to web service consumers using technologies such as ESB. Using this approach, the chosen integration solution would be responsible for the co-ordination of all data and control flow between these individual web services, and therefore the bus could become a performance bottleneck. All data and messages are routed through the ESB rather than being transferred directly from the point of consumption.

This leads to unnecessary traffic on the network. In addition, it is possible that a web service will generate data that is irrelevant to the composite service; yet this data will be transferred through the bus, where it is discarded, thereby again putting unnecessary load on the network. These factors can lead to poor scalability and performance degradation at high loads. In this approach, the existing functionality is only refaced – it is not retooled as a new business function (service), and cannot impose business rules on the data because it does not know about the functions being defined in the other transactions.

The "top-down" approach
The alternative is a "top-down" approach that first defines the business service that is specified or requested, and only then looks at the inputs and outputs required to satisfy this service. Usually a business analyst would be involved in this definition of services and once these were agreed upon, the designer would then look to see if there were any existing business components within the mainframe that could be used to help support the implementation of these services.

Of course there may be more than one business component (transaction or data source) necessary to complete the request, and after these business components have been identified and specified, they would be included into one definition with any required business flow also specified within that definition. Then the underlying components would be mapped into a flow of required logic to complete the request.

The composite business service definition would be published as a single WSDL document that could then be called by clients as part of the SOA solution. The requesting clients would make one request for one result. The co-ordination of these business components would be performed on the host system and would not require end-user knowledge or a mid-tier assembly step. There is no centralised co-ordinator that could be a potential bottleneck. Distributing the data also reduces traffic and improves transfer time. In the case of the mainframe being the composite business service provider, there is only one invocation, reducing network latency, TCP/IP stack time and session creation time, and saving time by marshalling the data only once on request instead of every request.

Leveraging Mainframe Services within the SOA Infrastructure
The approach detailed above enables organisations to expose mainframe functionality as web services in an efficient manner, and ensures that integration has as little effect on the performance of the existing infrastructure as possible.

However, exposing these web services is only half the battle in delivering truly seamless access to mainframe functionality within the context of an SOA environment. There remain two central challenges, namely:

- integration with other technologies, applications, transport protocols and data models;
- creating business applications using these services.

Given the benefits of ESB listed above, managers in IT now understand the benefits associated with handling these challenges using ESB technology that combines the strong features of both message-oriented middleware (MOM) and web services standards.

However, even using these approaches, integration is not necessarily a simple proposition, particularly given the continued presence of incompatible complex data and message formats likely to be in use in the various technologies and departments of the bank. Simply exposing web services does not necessarily address these issues; the services themselves will remain incompatible if they output messages in formats unreadable elsewhere in the bank. Without addressing these issues, a simple web services approach is liable to fail.

Building working applications from the individual web services, and in particular those that rely upon new and existing technologies, depends on two related but different activities – orchestration and is what is known as *mediation*. The former is the activity by which calls to various web services are managed over an extended period of time in order to model and automate a business process. The latter can be thought of as everything that lower-level integration activities require to get the right message into the right place in the right format, and is a challenge of particular significance in this context. Assuming the infrastructure handling delivery of messages throughout the bank is already in place, these are two core functions of any ESB.

The following is a discussion of orchestration and mediation:

- **Orchestration** – this involves the sequencing or "stitching together" of web service calls, with simple decision logic and some data transformation occurring between calls, in order to complete a business process. The Business Process Execution Language (BPEL) standard is rapidly becoming accepted as the appropriate method to orchestrate web services in this manner, and provides a standard way of defining these orchestrations to enable them to be dropped into diverse implementations if necessary.

    However, orchestration as supported by BPEL is limited to situations where there are web services and definitions available, and those definitions are in each case appropriate for the process being orchestrated. As discussed above, experience tells us that in many cases neither is true, which is why mediation is essential.

- **Mediation** – involves the transformation, routing, validation and enrichment of messages, which in turn enables differences in data models between web services providers and users to be accounted for and overcome when creating applications. Mediation can be viewed as a process of "breaking up" and reconfiguring data as it is passed from one web service to another, a process that is absolutely essential when integrating newly defined web services with existing infrastructure.

As shown above, orchestration is typically handled by defining processes in BPEL. Mediation, on the other hand, is often regarded as something of an afterthought and as a consequence translations are often hard-coded in order to ensure multiple services are able to work together. This introduces a number of problems, most specifically those associated with adapting and extending such solutions when they inevitably must adapt to meet changing business requirements. Each time services are reconfigured in order to create or adapt applications, the organisation must delve back into this code and rewrite it according to these changing requirements. This process negates all the supposed benefits of the web services "loosely coupled" approach to integration.

Thus, in order to support flexible and adaptable mainframe integration, the ESB must configure both orchestration and mediation, requiring as little new code as possible in order to enable the creation of composite applications incorporating mainframe functionality.

More on the ESB

ESBs not only handle the orchestration and mediation of web services, they can also be used to integrate seamlessly with existing enterprise infrastructure. ESB servers can work alongside messaging systems, J2EE application servers, enterprise applications such as SAP and PeopleSoft, relational databases and SNMP management platforms. As a result, they provide seamless and guaranteed integration with the existing infrastructure – meaning that an investment in SOA and web services need not involve replacing working systems, and that mainframe functionality can form composite applications with all these technologies and more in an entirely seamless manner.

Combining this "out of the box" ability to integrate across existing systems with orchestration and mediation capabilities enables exposed mainframe web services to take their place alongside the rest of the enterprise in truly scalable, flexible and adaptable integration solutions.

Conclusion

Adopting modern architectural standards – and in particular SOA and ESB – can often be a challenge for banks with existing working solutions. Realising the benefits of SOA whilst minimising the costs of disruption requires a sophisticated approach to both the exposing of web services based on mainframe functionality, and the orchestration and mediation of those services across the enterprise.

IT projects that involve the adoption of these standards will not only improve efficiencies in the infrastructure, but provide a sustainable competitive advantage.

10
Common Terminology used in Retail Banking

This chapter lists the terminology commonly used in the industry that IT professionals will come across in the course of the business day in the retail banks.

Introduction

As IT is increasingly aligned with business and reliance on IT is impacting on business performance, the dichotomy caused by the knowledge gap between IT and business can no longer be overlooked. In the multidisciplinary project teams that are ubiquitous in the banking environment, miscommunication can be the difference between success and failure for the projects being undertaken and could have other dire consequences for the profitability and reputation of the banks.

Some of the terms used in the industry are discussed below, but these are by no means exhaustive. Further searches can be carried out on the internet (**www.Bizle.biz**)[92] or in textbooks and journals for other terms not covered in this section.

List of Terms

Acquirer* – A bank having a business relationship with merchants, retailers and other service providers to process their plastic card transactions. Acquirers obtain financial settlement from the card issuers, typically via the card schemes which maintain the clearing systems, and pay the proceeds to the merchant, charging a fee.

Agency arrangement* – A facility extended by a Settlement Member to a non-settlement institution, allowing the latter to obtain clearance of items on behalf of themselves and their customers.

Assets – Tangible or intangible possessions such as buildings (tangible) or bank loans (intangible assets of bankers).

ATM (automated teller machine)* – Also known as a cash machine or cash dispenser.

Barter – Direct exchange of goods for goods, without the need for money.

Base rate (UK-specific)[†] – The lowest rate at which a bank will charge interest. Banks usually charge at a stipulated figure "above base rate", and the figure will depend on all sorts of circumstances to do with the loan and the borrower.

Bill of exchange[†] – An order in writing by one person to another to pay a specified sum to a specified person or bearer on a particular date.

Branch ATM* – Refers to the location of ATMs at the premises of banks or building societies; includes all ATMs, whether inside the premises or installed in the exterior wall.

Broad money – The total amount of money in an economy at a given time.

---

92 Online portal for the alignment of IT and Business.

Card-not-present (CNP)* – A transaction where the merchant, retailer or other service provider does not have physical access to the payment card; examples are transactions by telephone, mail order or the internet.

Capital† – The overall assets of an individual less liabilities.

CBT – Collecting bank truncation.

Cheque clearing* – An operational clearing for presenting and exchanging cheques between Settlement Members and their branches in order to transfer funds to named accounts.

Conversion – A legal tort (a wrong) whereby rightful owners are denied their goods. With respect to cheques this means the payment of a cheque to somebody other than the rightful owner.

Deposit account – A savings account with a bank, normally demanding seven days notice for withdrawals. It earns interest normally proportional to and below current base rates. The notice period for withdrawal will also affect the interest rate. No cheque book is issued with a deposit account.

Direct credit* – An electronic credit to a customer's account initiated directly by the payer. Direct credits consist primarily of business-to-individual payments for wages, salaries, pensions, state benefits and tax credits, and payments initiated by businesses to pay their trading partners or by individuals to pay bills.

Direct debit* – A pre-authorised debit on the payer's account initiated by the payee (known as an originator). Direct debits are typically used to make regular payments for debts such as utility bills and insurance payments, and amounts may be variable.

Direct payment* – The payment by direct credit of state benefits and pensions into an account nominated by the recipient. The account could be a current or basic bank account with a bank or building society or a post-office card account.

Domestic Cheque Guarantee Card Scheme* – A UK scheme whose members issue cheque guarantee cards to personal customers to guarantee the holder's cheques up to a specified amount, and providing common, easily identifiable design features to simplify acceptance procedures at the point-of-sale.

Dynamic currency conversion (DCC) – Dynamic currency conversion is a service which some merchants offer to foreign cardholders, whereby a currency conversion to the cardholder's currency of domicile is conducted at the point-of-sale.

Electronic banking* – A service enabling users to access banking facilities over the internet or other computer network.

Equitable mortgage – Created by the deposit of title deeds with the intention that they are treated as security. Weaker than a full legal mortgage, the security provider also agrees to create a legal mortgage should the bank call upon on them to do so.

Equity – This has two relevant meanings: ordinary shares in a company; the difference between the value of property and the loan outstanding on it.

Equity release scheme† – A scheme designed to allow homeowners to "release" cash from the value of their property.

Euro-denominated bulk debit clearing (euro debit clearing)* – An operational clearing for presenting and exchanging euro-denominated cheques drawn on a UK account between Settlement Members and their branches in order to transfer funds to named accounts.

Euro† – The successor to the European Currency Unit (ECU) as the European currency. The euro was introduced in 11 member states on 1 January 1999. These were Austria, Belgium, Finland, France, Germany, Ireland, Italy, Luxembourg, Netherlands, Portugal and Spain.

Eurocheque* – A Europay scheme, withdrawn on 1 January 2002, which allowed cash withdrawals by plastic card and retail payments by uniform cheques (eurocheques) drawn against the customer's current account in the currency of the country where the transaction took place.

Exchange rate – The price of one country's money in terms of another country's money.

Exchange rate mechanism – The mechanism by which members of the EC formerly operated their currency exchange rates within given upper and lower limits. In January 1999 certain members of the EC adopted the euro for their currency.

Financial intermediary – An organisation or person (usually a salesperson) who intermediates between ultimate lenders and ultimate borrowers.

Fiscal policy† – The use of spending and taxation by the government in order to achieve its economic objectives. Put simply, higher taxation reduces people's disposable income and suppresses spending, which is supposed to make inflation less likely.

Floor limit* – A limit on the value of each transaction, agreed between the merchant and acquiring bank, above which authorisation must be obtained by the merchant from the card issuer.

General lien – The legal right for a creditor to seize an asset of a debtor to satisfy an outstanding debt.

Giro – A centralised payment system, used widely in Europe and operated by the clearing banks in which a paper slip/document instructs a bank branch to credit a sum of money to a specified account at that branch.

Guarantee – A written agreement for one person (the guarantor) to be answerable for the debts or liabilities of another.

IBDE – Inter Bank Data Exchange (UK banking system).

Inflation† – The increase of prices in an economy over a period of time; usually annualised for comparative purposes.

In-house payment* – A payment between different accounts held at the same branch of a financial institution.

Interchange – A fee which may be paid between two banks each time a card is used.

Insolvency – The inability of a person or company to settle debts when they become payable.

Inter-bank clearing* – The process of clearing payments between two Settlement Members.

Inter-branch clearing* – Also known as intra-bank clearing. The process of clearing payments between branches or agencies of the same Settlement Member.

Inter-bank routing and switching – A term used in connection with the processing of card transactions. Using the information within a card account number, processing systems of a card company such as Visa will automatically send authorisation requests and clearing and settlement messages to the cardholder's issuing bank.

Legacy currency* – The former national currencies of the states in the Economic and Monetary Union (EMU). These states have now adopted the euro as their national currency.

Leisure* – Refers to the location of ATMs, comprising sports and leisure centres, hotels, campsites, gambling casinos, cinemas, stadiums, zoos, etc.

LINK* – LINK Interchange Network Ltd is a company limited by shares that is wholly owned by 22 of the UK's largest banks and building societies. LINK has two constituent parts: the Operating Company provides the services (including settlement) that make ATM sharing possible throughout the UK; the Card Scheme determines the operating rules that define the terms of trade between members. LINK-enabled cards are issued by all UK card issuers, and the cards can be used in virtually all ATMs in the UK except for a very small number of privately owned cash dispensers.

Loyalty card* – A card issued typically by a retailer or group of retailers that earns rewards or discounts.

Laundering† – The manipulation of money obtained in a wrongful manner, for example theft, so that it seems to have originated from a lawful source. An example is to pay the unlawful money into an overseas bank and subsequently transfer it back to the country of origin.

Law – A system of dispute settlement between society and individuals (criminal law) and between individuals (civil law).

Legal charge/mortgage – A contract between a lender and a borrower (or security provider) giving the lender rights (including sale) over an asset following the default of the borrower.

Merchant – Retailer or service provider that accepts card payments.

Merger[†] – The process by which two companies become one. If the companies are listed, the merger may be by agreement, or hostile. A hostile bid is one in which the directors of the target company reject the approach, but it is still possible for the predator company to obtain control if enough of the target's shareholders accept its offer.

Mobile ATM* – Refers to the locations of ATMs regularly moved between locations, e.g. at exhibitions, shows, circuses.

Mobile payment* – A payment involving the use of a mobile phone. The phone network can be used solely as the channel to authenticate the customer, or the payment can involve a debit to an account held by the customer with the mobile operator or other service provider.

MO/TO* – An acronym for mail order/telephone order that refers to card-not-present transactions.

Monetary policy[†] – The control of the money supply and interest rates by a government in order to achieve its economic objectives, in particular the restraining of inflation.

Money mule* – A "money mule", or "money transfer agent" as they are sometimes called, is someone recruited by fraudsters needing to launder the funds obtained as a result of phishing and Trojan scams.

Mortgage[†] – A loan in which the borrower (the mortgagor) offers a property and land as security to the lender (the mortgagee) until the loan is repaid. Repayments of the loan are usually made on a monthly basis over a long period of time, typically 25 years. In the UK, the most common forms of mortgage are the repayment mortgage and the interest-only mortgage.

Multifunction card* – A payment card fulfilling two or more roles, typically a debit card also providing ATM and/or cheque guarantee functions.

Narrow money – The total of money used in a country as a means of payment. Normally includes only notes and coins but sometimes includes current accounts.

National Savings (UK-specific) – A variety of savings schemes, backed by the government, in which the public can participate.

Non-bank financial intermediary (NBFI) – A mixed bag of institutions, ranging from leasing to factoring. The common characteristic of these institutions is that they mobilise savings and facilitate the financing of different activities, but they do not accept deposits from the public. NBFIs play an important dual role in the financial system. They complement the role of commercial banks by filling gaps in their range of services.

Not-on-us transaction* – A transaction where a card used at an ATM is issued by a different institution from that which owns the ATM.

Other financial intermediary (OFI) – A European Union term for insurance company or pension fund.

Overdraft – A facility, usually at a bank, enabling an account holder to borrow up to an agreed amount and often at an agreed rate.

On-site/off-site* – The description on-site is used to refer to ATMs that are located at or within the premises of banks or building societies.

On-us transaction* – A transaction where a card used at an ATM is issued by the financial institution owning the ATM.

Other retail ATM* – Refers to the location of ATMs, comprising department stores, national chains, shopping centres, retail parks, etc.

PIN (personal identification number)* – A set of characters, usually a four-digit sequence, used by cardholders to verify their identity at a point-of-sale or at a customer-activated device such as an ATM.

Phishing* – Phishing is the name given to the practice of sending emails at random purporting to come from a genuine company operating on the internet, in an attempt to trick customers of that company into disclosing information at a bogus website operated by fraudsters.

Plus* – A Visa brand signifying global ATM acceptance.

POS (point-of-sale)* – A physical location where a customer makes a purchase.

POS terminal* – An electronic device used to process card payments at a point-of-sale.

POS transaction* – A transaction taking place at a point-of-sale.

Post Office card account* – A service available in the UK from April 2003. The account can receive state benefit, pension and tax credit payments only

Prepayment card* – Also known as an electronic purse. A stored-value payment card used to pay for goods and services. It is an alternative to cash.

Principal – The original (capital) amount on a loan, later reduced by repayment capital or increased by non-payment of interest. The term also refers to a person or company for whom an agent acts.

Recurring transaction* – An authority to charge a transaction to a credit or charge card at regular intervals (typically monthly), granted by the cardholder to a merchant, retailer or other service provider.

Reference – A reference sought from a bank by a company or individual regarding the creditworthiness of another company or individual in order to assess whether or not credit trading terms should be offered. Also known as a status enquiry.

Risk – The statistical chance of a deal not being completed or a loan not being repaid.

Retail prices index (RPI) – An index of the prices of a basket of consumer goods and services used to measure the rate of inflation. Also called headline inflation.

RPIX – Retail prices index excluding interest paid on mortgages. Also called underlying inflation.

Secrecy – One of the major factors that characterise the customer–banker relationship. It is the duty of a bank to maintain secrecy regarding the customer's dealings with the bank.

Security – An asset which is offered by a borrower to a lender to safeguard a loan. It is also sometimes referred to as "collateral".

Settlement Member* – A member of an operational clearing able to make and receive payment for the value of its clearings over its account at the Bank of England.

Set off – This is a process whereby a bank nets or combines accounts held in the same name and same capacity, provided the sums in each account are certain (no contingent liabilities).

Solo* – A debit card. All Solo purchases are subject to electronic authorisation.

Stand-alone card* – A plastic card having a single function. The term is normally used in the context of ATM-only cards to describe cards issued by banks and building societies (e.g. cards related to savings products) to withdraw cash from ATMs but not to be used for purchases.

Standing order* – An instruction from customers to their bank or building society to make regular automated payments of a specified amount to a named creditor. The term is also used to refer to individual payments arising from the instruction.

SWIFT – Society for Worldwide Interbank Financial Telecommunications, which is an international messages system for payments in different countries.

Switch* – A UK debit card scheme rebranded as Maestro with effect from 1 July 2004.

TARGET (Trans-European Automated Real-time Gross Settlement Express Transfer System)* – A system which interlinks the national real-time gross settlement systems of EU Member States through a central message switch.

Town clearing* – A largely manual, low-volume, same-day value paper clearing for high-value cheques and other debit items, which operated between branches within a designated area corresponding roughly to the City of London. The Town clearing ceased operation on 24 February 1995.

Trojans* – Trojans take their name from the term "Trojan Horse" and are a type of computer virus which can be installed on your computer without you realising. Trojans are sometimes capable of installing a "keystroke logger" which captures all of the keystrokes entered into a computer keyboard.

Truncation – The abridgment of the cheque clearing process before the clearing cycle is complete. Truncation allows electronic transaction messages to supersede the physical presentation of cheques.

Telegraphic transfer (TT) – A method of transferring money abroad from one bank to another.

US dollar clearing* – The US dollar clearing is the only remaining operational currency clearing under the auspices of the Currency Clearing Committee. It handles paper items drawn on, or payable at, UK branches of members and those with agency arrangements.

VADD – Variable Amount Direct Debit. A direct debit authority with no set amount. This enables originating users, such as mortgage lenders, to vary repayment levels without the debtor needing to take action.

Visa Intelligent Scoring Of Risk (VISOR) – This is a sophisticated fraud detection system developed by Visa Europe and provided to member banks.

Web-based payment terminal – Web-based payment terminal is a secure, browser-based interface that enables businesses to process credit card transactions.

---

* Sourced from Association of Payment Clearing Services.

† Sourced from Finance Glossary at www.finance-glossary.com/pages/glossary.htm.

Methodology, Skills and Tools

This chapter covers the methodologies, methods used and skills required to work in retail banking.

Introduction

The methodologies, skills and tools used in the retail banking industry will be discussed in this section to ensure that readers focus on what is required. As retail banks have historically adopted mainframe technologies to support the business, a section will be dedicated to skills required to work with mainframes.

The array of tools on the market presents opportunities for banks to put structures in place for their IT projects and, as a consequence, the choice of tools is increasingly a strategic decision. To this end, the tools on the market will be discussed.

An overview of mainframe technologies will be discussed to give readers an insight into the benefits of acquiring mainframe skills.

Overview of Mainframe Technologies

Mainframe technologies have been well known for decades and in recent times have been combined with distributed architectures to provide massive storage and to improve system security, flexibility, scalability, and reusability in the client/server design. Mainframes are used intensively in retail banking organisations because they excel at simple transaction-oriented data processing to automate repetitive business tasks such as accounts receivable, accounts payable, general ledger, credit account management and so on.

In comparing mainframes with client/server systems, it could be noted that while client/server systems are suited for rapid application deployment and distributed processing, mainframes are efficient at online transactional processing, mass storage, centralised software distribution and data warehousing.[93]

As retail banks have a relatively large number of customers and product lines, they prefer mainframes for big batch jobs and storing massive amounts of vital data. They also use the tools in mainframes for monitoring the performance of their entire system, including networks, and for applications not available today on UNIX servers.

Methodologies

In software engineering and project management, "methodology" is often used to refer to a codified set of recommended practices, sometimes accompanied by training materials, formal educational programmes, worksheets and diagramming tools. In retail banking, the best methodologies are employed to ensure that business-critical systems are built to a sufficient level of quality as required by the activities carried out in the industry.

---

93 Data warehousing and data mining provide executive decision makers with data analysis information to make informed business decisions.

International Technology Infrastructure Library (ITIL®)
ITIL is essentially a series of documents that are used to aid the implementation of a life-cycle framework for IT service management. This customisable framework defines how service management is applied within an organisation. It is also aligned with the international standard, ISO 20000.

How is ITIL organised?
ITIL is organised into a series of five volumes (the books): Service Strategy, Service Design, Service Transition, Service Operation and Continual Service Improvement. These in turn describe a closed-loop feedback system that provides feedback throughout all areas of the life cycle. The volumes continue to provide a framework of best practice disciplines that enable IT services to be provided effectively (IT Service Management Zone).

RUP
The Rational Unified Process (RUP) is an iterative software development process created by the Rational Software Corporation, now a division of IBM. RUP is not a single concrete prescriptive process but rather an adaptable process framework. As such, RUP describes how to develop software effectively using proven techniques. While RUP encompasses a large number of different activities, it is also intended to be tailored, in the sense of selecting the development processes appropriate to a particular software project or development organisation. RUP is recognised as being particularly applicable to larger software development teams working on large projects.

Figure 11.1 RUP

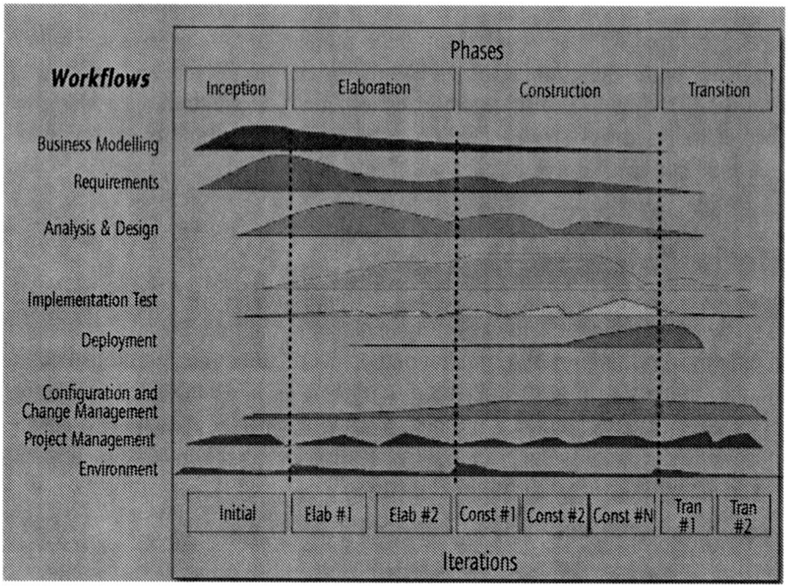

Source: Rational Software

Capability Maturity Model (CMM)
The Capability Maturity Model (CMM) is a way to develop and refine an organisation's processes. It was developed by the Software Engineering Institute at Carnegie Mellon University in Pittsburgh. The first CMM was for the purpose of developing and refining software development processes. The latest version (1.2) of Capability Maturity Model Integration (CMMI) contains 22 key process areas indicating the aspects of product development that are to be covered by company processes. The method by which a company chooses to adopt CMMI is called a representation. Both the staged representation and the continuous representation contain all 22 process areas. The previous version of CMMI (1.1) had 25 process areas.

A maturity model is a structured collection of elements that describe characteristics of effective processes. It is a layered framework providing a progression to the discipline needed to engage in continuous improvement, while the key processes mentioned above identify a cluster of related activities that, when performed collectively, achieve a set of goals considered important. The goals of a key process area summarise the states that must exist for that key process area to have been implemented in an effective and lasting way. The extent to which the goals have been accomplished is an indicator of how much capability the organisation has established at that maturity level. The goals signify the scope, boundaries and intent of each key process area.

There are five levels of CMM that an organisation can achieve and they are as follows:

- Level 1 – Initial: at this level processes are usually ad hoc and the organisation usually does not provide a stable environment. Success in these organisations depends on the competence and heroics of the people in the organisation and not on the use of proven processes.
- Level 2 – Repeatable: at this level software development successes are repeatable. The processes may not repeat for all the projects in the organisation.
- Level 3 – Defined: the organisation's set of standard processes, which are the basis for level 3, are established and improved over time. These standard processes are used to establish consistency across the organisation. Projects establish their defined processes by the organisation's set of standard processes according to tailoring guidelines.
- Level 4 – Quantitatively managed: using precise measurements, management can effectively control the software development effort. In particular, management can identify ways to adjust and adapt the process for particular projects without measurable losses of quality or deviations from specifications. Organisations at this level set quantitative quality goals for both software processes and software maintenance.
- Level 5 – Optimising: maturity level 5 focuses on continually improving process performance through both incremental and innovative technological improvements. Quantitative process improvement objectives for the organisation are established, continually revised to reflect changing business objectives, and used as criteria in managing process improvement.

PRINCE2

Prince stands for Projects in Controlled Environments. Prince2 is the latest version of Prince, released in 1996, and is a project management methodology for the organisation, management and control of projects.

Figure 11.2 Prince2

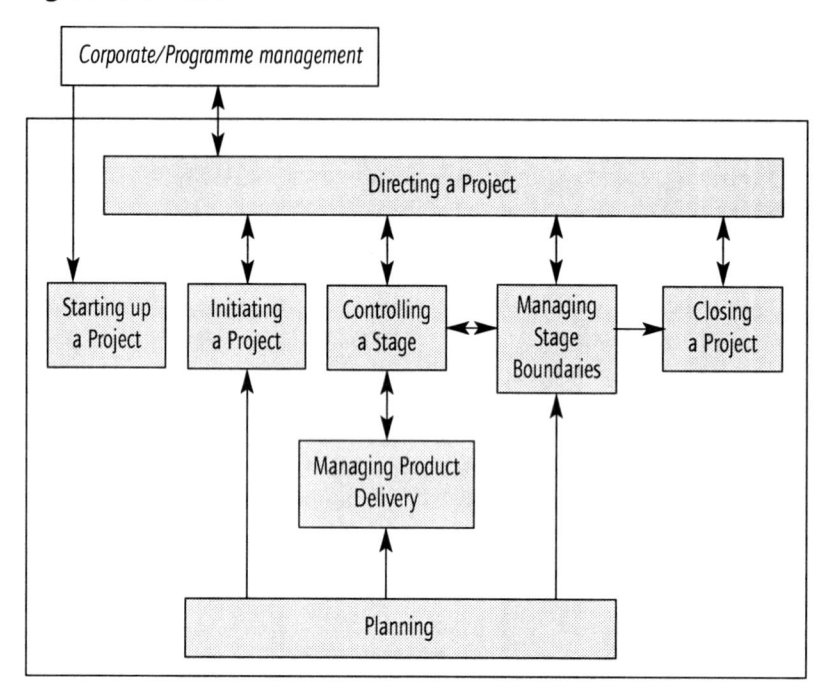

Source: Wikipedia

Figure 11.2 shows Prince2 processes. The arrows symbolise flows of information.

Prince2 offers a process-based approach to key areas of project management. It is made up of eight high-level processes:

- directing a project (DP);
- planning (PL);
- starting up a project (SU);
- initiating a project (IP);
- controlling a stage (CS);
- managing product delivery (MP);
- managing stage boundaries (SB);
- closing a project (CP).

UML

The Unified Modelling Language (UML) is a non-proprietary, object modelling and specification language used in software engineering. The UML model can be used to showcase the functionality of a system, the structure and substructure, and the internal behaviour. The following are artefacts that can be created using UML:

- use cases;
- class diagrams'
- sequence diagrams;
- state activity diagrams.

Figure 11.3 An example of a Use Case Diagram

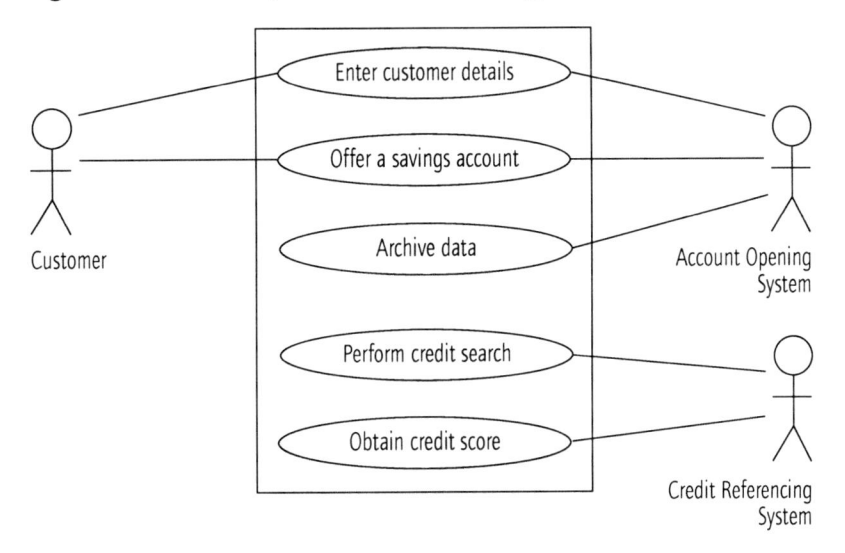

V-Model

The V-model is a graphical representation of the system development life cycle. It summarises the main steps to be taken in conjunction with the corresponding deliverables during the life cycle.

The left side of the V shows the specification stream where the system specifications are defined, while the right side of the V represents the testing stream where the systems are being tested (against the specifications defined on the left side). The base of the V, where the sides meet, represents the development stream.

RAD

Rapid Application Development (RAD) is a software development process that involves iterative development and the construction of prototypes.

Figure 11.4 V-Model

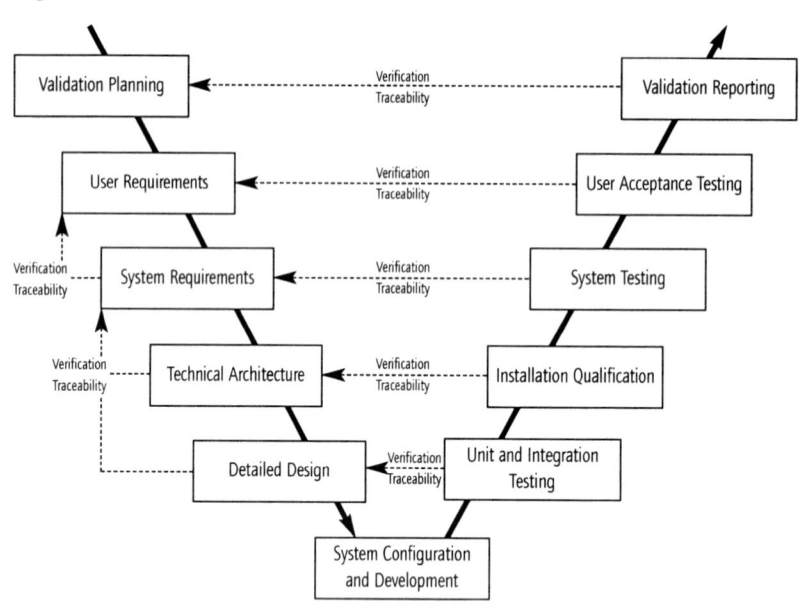

[V-Model diagram showing: Validation Planning → User Requirements → System Requirements → Technical Architecture → Detailed Design → System Configuration and Development → Unit and Integration Testing → Installation Qualification → System Testing → User Acceptance Testing → Validation Reporting, with Verification Traceability arrows between corresponding left and right sides]

Source: Wikipedia

Core elements of RAD

RAD has six core elements:

- prototyping;
- iterative development;
- timeboxing;
- team members;
- management approach;
- RAD tools.

Agile

Agile software development is a conceptual framework for undertaking software engineering projects. Agile methods attempt to minimise risk by developing software in short timeboxes, called iterations, which typically last one to four weeks. Each iteration is like a miniature software project on its own and includes all of the tasks necessary to release the mini-increment of new functionality: planning, requirements analysis, design, coding, testing and documentation. While iteration may not add enough functionality to warrant releasing the product, an agile software project intends to be capable of releasing new software at the end of every iteration. At the end of each iteration, the team re-evaluates project priorities.

Extreme Programming

Extreme Programming (XP) is a software engineering methodology for the development of software projects. It prescribes a set of day-to-day practices for developers and managers; the practices are meant to embody and encourage particular values and:

- involve new or prototype technology, where the requirements change rapidly, or some development is required to discover unforeseen implementation problems;
- are small and more easily managed through informal methods.

Pair Programming

Pair programming involves having two programmers working side by side, collaborating on the same design, algorithm, code or test. One programmer, the driver, has control of the keyboard/mouse and actively implements the program. The other programmer, the observer, continuously observes the work of the driver to identify tactical (syntactic, spelling, etc.) defects and also thinks strategically about the direction of the work. On demand, the two programmers can brainstorm any challenging problem. Because the two programmers periodically switch roles, they work together as equals to develop software.

Business and Systems Analysis Methods

Business and systems analysis methods adopted in the development of software in the retail banking industry are vast and varied but the following are the most commonly used.

Business Rules Approach

The business rules approach is a development methodology where rules are in a form that is used by but not embedded in business process management systems.

The business rules approach formalises an enterprise's critical business rules in a language the manager and technologist can understand. Business rules create an unambiguous statement of what a business does, with information to decide on a proposition. The formal specification becomes information for process and rules engines to run.

Entity Relationship Diagrams

The entity relationship model or entity relationship diagram (ERD) is a data model or diagram for high-level descriptions of conceptual data models and it provides a graphical notation for representing such data models in the form of entity relationship diagrams. Such models are typically used in the first stage of information system design; they are used, for example, to describe information needs and/or the type of information that is to be stored in the database during the requirements analysis.

Prototyping

The prototyping model is a software development process that begins with requirements collection, followed by prototyping and user evaluation. Often the end-users may not be able to provide a complete set of application objectives, detailed input, processing or output requirements, in the initial stage. After the user evaluation, another prototype will be built based on feedback from users and again the cycle returns to customer evaluation. The cycle starts by listening to the user, followed by building or revising a mock-up and letting the user test the mock-up, then it goes back to the beginning again.

Testing Methods

The following are common testing methods adopted in systems development in retail banking.

Equivalence Partitioning

Equivalence partitioning is a systematic process that identifies, on the basis of whatever information is available, a set of classes of input conditions to be tested. Each class is a representative of a large set of other possible tests.

Boundary Value Analysis

Boundary value analysis is a variant and refinement of equivalence partitioning with two major differences. First, rather than selecting any element in an equivalence class as being representative, elements are selected such that each edge of the equivalence class is the subject of a test.

Second, rather than focusing exclusively on input conditions, output conditions are also explored by defining output equivalent classes.

Error Guessing

Error guessing is an ad hoc approach, based on intuition and experience, to identifying tests that are considered likely to expose errors. The basic approach is to make a list of possible errors or error-prone situations and then develop tests based on the list.

Tools

Some of the most popular tools used in the retail banking industry for software development, project management, test management and defect tracking are listed below.

IBM Rational Rose

Rational Rose is an object-oriented, Unified Modelling Language (UML) software design tool intended for the visual modelling and component construction of enterprise-level software applications.

IBM Rational ClearCase
ClearCase provides life-cycle management and control of software development assets. It is used in the banks for change management and control of source code and artefacts.

Mercury QTP
This Mercury interactive test automation tool is used mainly in the banks for the automation of regression tests and data-driven tests.

IBM Rational ClearQuest
ClearQuest helps to automate and enforce development processes, manage issues throughout the project life cycle and facilitate communication between all stakeholders across the enterprise software. It is used in the banks for defect management and change tracking.

Mercury Test Director (Quality Centre)
This Mercury interactive test management tool is used in the banks for storing requirements, test cases and scripts. Test Director is fast becoming the industry standard for test management.

Oracle Designer
Oracle Designer offers a toolset to model, generate and capture the requirements and design of web-based applications quickly, accurately and efficiently, and also to assess the impact of changing those designs and applications.

PowerDesigner
PowerDesigner is a business process modelling approach to align business and IT, is an enterprise data modelling and database design solution that helps implement effective Enterprise Architecture, and brings a powerful conceptual data model to the application development life cycle.

PowerDesigner uniquely combines several standard data modelling techniques (UML, Business Process Modelling and market-leading data modelling) together with leading development environments such as .NET, Workspace, PowerBuilder, Java, Eclipse, etc. to bring business analysis and formal database design solutions to the traditional software development life cycle. Also, it works with all modern RDBMSs.

Common IT Skills Required

IT professionals usually update their skills in line with technological advancements but to compete in the skills market in retail banking some specific skills are required in various capacities. These are some of the skills that employers in the industry demand:

- **JAVA** – experience and knowledge of Java Collections Classes, threads, swing development, design patterns, messaging middleware concepts.
- **C++** – experience and knowledge of C++ multithreading, STL, design patterns, messaging middleware concepts.
- **BizTalk** – good knowledge of Microsoft BizTalk.
- **ControlM** – knowledge and experience of ControlM – a system that provides advanced production-scheduling capabilities across the enterprise from a single point of control – is desirable.
- **.NET** – experience and understanding of web services – small, reusable applications that help computers from many different operating-system platforms work together by exchanging messages – from technical and business perspectives.
- **J2EE** (Java 2 Platform, Enterprise Edition) – appreciation and experience of this platform is essential.
- **Junit** – knowledge of Junit – a regression-testing framework used by the developer who implements unit tests in Java – is desirable.
- **XP** – proficiency in Microsoft XP is important and also Microsoft Vista.
- **Microsoft Excel** – it is essential to be proficient in Microsoft Excel. It is also desirable to have good skills in VBA.
- **Business Objects** – knowledge of Business Objects and the ability to manipulate data for reports in Business Objects is an essential skill to have.
- **UNIX** – it is essential to have knowledge and experience of UNIX and Linux and associated scripting languages.
- **SQL** – proficiency in writing SQL queries. Most banks use Sybase and Oracle databases, therefore it is vital to have a good command of PL/SQL and also TransactSQL, and tools such as TOAD and Oracle Discoverer.
- **IBM Websphere** – the ability to perform administrative tasks such as starting and stopping processes and deploying builds in IBM Websphere is essential.
- **Messaging platforms** – knowledge of IBM's MQ series, MINT and Tuxedo is essential.
- **Cruise Control** – knowledge of Cruise Control is desirable. Cruise Control is usually used for deploying software builds.
- **FIX protocol** – at least a basic knowledge of FIX (Financial Information Exchange) protocol is desirable.
- **XML** – a rudimentary knowledge of XML is required to work successfully in IT in retail banking.
- **SWIFT** – understanding the format and categories of SWIFT messages.
- **TIBCO** – good knowledge of TIBCO business process and optimisation software is desirable.
- **ISO 15022** – knowledge of ISO1 5022 – principles necessary to provide the different communities of users with the tools to design message types to support their specific information flows – is important. It is necessary to understand the set of syntax and message design rules and the dictionary of data fields.

Mainframe Skills

As stated above mainframe skills are invaluable for a career in retail banking IT. In this section a discussion of the popular mainframe skills and levels of proficiency will be carried out.

Skill	Requirements	Level of Proficiency[94] (on a scale of 1-10)
COBOL	• Understanding of the structure of COBOL programs • Ability to declare data in COBOL • Ability to use XPEDITER to interactively test, debug, and analyse COBOL programs • Ability to utilise and navigate Time Sharing Option (TSO) and its facilities	9
MVS ABEND	• Ability to use Abend-AID to debug COBOL programs • Understanding of Hex arithmetic • Understanding of Job Entry System (JES) job log information • Ability to read COBOL compiler outputs (Maps, Clists, Xref)	7
CICS (Customer Information Control System)	• Understanding of the origin of online systems • Ability to navigate the CICS environment • Ability to create fields • Ability to design and format the "screen presentation" with BMS • Ability to use COBOL to access files and communicate with other CICS application programs • Ability to execute tasks with CICS commands • Understanding of asynchronous processing • Ability to create Virtual Storage Access Method (VSAM) files	8
COBOL II and OS 390	• Ability to develop batch programs • Understanding of code for Working Storage entries using standard picture clauses, 88 levels and redefine clauses • Understanding of code for Procedure Division logic including Moves, If, Perform • Understanding of coding procedures and Data Division entries to handle sequential files • Understanding of code and manipulation of COBOL data stored in Occurs clauses • Ability to use a mainframe text editor such as Interactive System Productivity Facility (ISPF)	9

---

94 This is our assessment of the levels of proficiency required.

Skill	Requirements	Level of Proficiency (on a scale of 1-10)
EasyTrieve Plus	• Understanding of the use of EasyTrieve to create reports • Ability to code EasyTrieve programs to read data and create reports using QSAM and VSAM data • Ability to update, add and delete VSAM data • Ability to create Queued Sequential Access Method (QSAM) and VSAM files • Ability to use DB2 data and Information Management System (IMS) data to create reports	7
Endevor	• Ability to recognise the Endevor life cycle and logical structure • Understanding of the information displayed about system, subsystems, environment types, and processors • Ability to recognise panel layout and navigate in Endevor • Understanding and the ability to use foreground and batch processing techniques • The ability to display/browse an element and to retrieve an element from Endevor	7
FILE-AID	• Appreciation of the features and functions of the File-Aid product in a batch environment • Ability to use File-AID with a focus on the features and capabilities as they pertain to DB2	8
IMS	• Understanding of IMS database concepts and design • Ability to write application programs that access and update DL/I databases • Appreciation of the program specification block and the program communication block • Ability to identify DL/I call function use • Understanding of update call design considerations • Appreciation of command codes and Boolean SSAs • Appreciation of the major components of the IMS/DC environment including receiving and sending messages • Understanding of conversational and non-conversational transaction processing and Message Format Services (MFS) • Ability to test and debug with BTS utility	8
Job Control Language (JCL)	• Understanding of the concepts and principles of MVS JCL and how it relates to JES and the operating system (O/S) • Ability to execute basic JCL statements • Ability to use JCL to submit batch jobs • Ability to use Debug and fix JCL errors • Ability to interpret and understand JES output • Ability to use standard MVS utilities	9

Skill	Requirements	Level of Proficiency (on a scale of 1-10)
REXX Scripting	• Ability to code REXX programs in an OS/390 environment • Understanding of the structure of REXX syntax • Ability to develop constructs in REXX scripts • Ability to browse an application with REXX • Ability to manage data set and file I/O services EXECIO	7

Soft Skills

- **Numeracy** – having numerical skills is important if readers want to work on banking projects as there are usually complex calculations involved in developing and verifying the functionality of some applications.
- **Business acumen** – a solid business acumen and awareness is required to perform well in the retail banking sector. Readers should make a habit of reading news in the financial pages of the broadsheets or periodicals such as *The Economist*.
- **Good communication skills** – it is essential to be able to explain concepts in banking and finance from both a technical and business standpoint in order to gain the confidence of the business users.
- **Business analysis skills** – the ability to understand business requirements and be able to document them is a nice skill to have. Readers should learn the art of extracting vital information from workshops and meetings with business users.
- **Inductive thinking** – the ability to think inductively will stand readers in good stead.
- **Good writing skills** – good writing skills are important in order to produce high-quality documentation.
- **Ability to withstand pressure** – the work environment in the banking sector is highly pressurised and as such requires the ability to withstand pressure.
- **Ability to see the "big picture"** – ability to see the bigger picture in order to understand the wider implications of the work tasks for the profitability of organisations.
- **Basic understanding of economics** – a basic understanding of economics is required to work in the sector if readers want a fulfilling career in retail banking.
- **Proficiency in different languages** – a proficiency in different languages would be beneficial as some of the projects could span different continents. The discerning IT professional should be able to communicate with business users and other IT professionals in another language.

- **Negotiation skills** – good negotiation skills are important because of the aggressive deadlines to which projects are executed.
- **Time management skills** – IT professionals in retail banking should have good time management skills to be able to prioritise work tasks to meet aggressive project deadlines.
- **Leadership skills** – leadership, a critical management skill, is required to motivate other people towards a common project or organisational goal.
- **Project management skills** – these, include scheduling skills such as the use of Gantt charts and Critical Path Analysis, are essential for the type of project work undertaken in retail banks.

12 The Future

This chapter covers the future trends that might shape the business and IT in retail banking.

The Future

What does it hold for Retail Banks in Business and IT?

The business model of retail banking has been illustrated over the last 11 chapters: the market segments, the competitive landscape, different products on offer and technology adopted amongst other issues. However, of all the traditional factors that shape the business environment in the retail banking sector, globalisation and adoption of technology appear to be the most significant. With the advent of the arrival of new entrants and the lower barriers to entry, the playing field is being flattened and the old rules no longer apply.

Against this backdrop, what does the future hold for both the established and the new players: the virtual, the real, the standalone, and the banks that are part of a universal banking group?

The following are some of the factors that will shape the future of retail banking.

Adopting Globalisation Strategies for Growth

Retail banks have been innovating by creating new products and services to circumvent commoditisation, which is endemic in this sector of the financial services industry. Despite the wave of innovation and given the fact that financial services firms have enjoyed double-digit revenue growth in the last decade – in spite of the downturn at the turn of the century – the growth opportunities appear to be dwindling, at least in the mature markets. The principal markets for most of the global retail banks, i.e. the USA, Japan and the United Kingdom, present limited growth opportunities, amidst intense competition, for the banks. As a consequence, banks have to seek out new markets that offer opportunities for significant future expansion.

IBM Global Business Services recently carried out an analysis in collaboration with the Economist Intelligence Unit, which involved developing a model and using it to trace the effect of globalisation across 35 of the world's largest economies and also to survey 848 financial market executives from around the globe and 107 of their corporate clients. Accordingly, the analysis results in some unexpected lessons for financial markets:

- *The worldwide opportunity is large – but it won't necessarily be found in the same old places.* Worldwide investable assets are expected to double by 2015 to almost US$300 trillion. By 2025, the opportunity quintuples to nearly US$700 trillion. However, 60% of this future growth is coming from non-traditional places that are called prospect markets – this is more than twice that of the veteran markets. While veteran markets will remain large, these new markets could soon have asset bases that rival those of their longstanding peers.

- *Firms are not prepared to capture this emerging opportunity.* Many financial markets firms are not in a position to capitalise on this more geographically dispersed industry opportunity.
- *What the business model executives generally believe is best may actually be the wrong bet.* Among industry executives, the general gut reaction was that large diversified universal banks are the firms best positioned to compete globally. However, when reflecting more deeply about the capabilities required, executives actually rated specialists higher than universals on some critically important global capabilities. This self-contradiction reinforces the point that being the best in every niche of the industry is increasingly difficult and costly.
- *The people side of financial markets firms may be getting short shrift.* Many financial markets firms may be neglecting the people-related implications of running a global business.

Together, these lessons reinforce the opinion amongst industry watchers who believe there is a rocky road ahead for banks in their bid to effectively globalise their operations. An interesting view from IBM on how globalisation is playing out in the financial markets categorises a number of factors that are dictating the pace of globalisation as follows:

- the socio-political environment within a given country (such as government stability, regulatory environment and legal system);
- the ability to connect with the rest of the world (transportation, infrastructure, use of global standards, technology adoption and so forth).

Our view on the approach to globalisation involves doing away with a "cookie cutter" approach and replacing it with IT and business strategies that encompass intimate knowledge of each market that is deemed a candidate for direct investment. Retail banks need to deal with globalisation by carving out localised strategies that enable them to compete effectively with a cross-section of local and regional players. Banks will therefore need to balance a global strategy with a local face. One trend that has been observed in implementing such a strategy is alliances and collaborations. HSBC's tagline "World's Local Bank" represents their approach to globalisation, while Citibank's approach to establishing a local presence in mainland China by acquiring a minor stake in financial institutions is another example of a feasible approach to globalisation.

Introduction of a New Technology Paradigm

With the opening of the world's financial markets to financial services firms seeking to increase their global presence, the use of technology will be pivotal in their quest to achieve these goals. However, the role technology will play will be different to what is customary in the current business environment as business models will continually evolve.

The principal driver for change is the shifting of the balance of power from the financial services providers (FSPs) such as banks towards the consumer. Consumers will have access to most of the technology, data and analytics used by FSPs and will use it to play firms against each other in real time (Infosys, 2007).

The role of the IT function will undergo dramatic reform. Enterprise IT systems will be componentised and sourced from external suppliers. These components will be assembled automatically to allow the focus to shift from technology to business and processes.

As products and services become commoditised and barriers to entry lowered, banks will be looking to gain competitive advantage by becoming adept at assembling and deploying compelling products from internal and external components and retooling them rapidly and flexibly on demand, and not by depending on proprietary systems.

Another significant factor in the quest for the new technology paradigm is the growing population of a demanding and growing middle class in today's lagging economies that could be well developed by 2015. The middle class in these countries is expected to expand as prosperity becomes widespread, especially in growth countries like China, India and Brazil. The burgeoning middle class will expect and demand sophisticated financial products tailored to their local tastes and requirements. Banks will be responding to these requirements by building products and providing front-ends with interfaces that satisfy varied demands for features, channels, media and pricing. In addition, they will be using a core set of product components, built in-house or purchased from external vendors, to automatically build and customise products to support a number of regional preferences at a much lower cost than they would be otherwise.

Grid computing[95] could also play a defining role in the introduction of a new technology paradigm as banks will be looking to harness the computing power from the resulting infrastructure to support complex algorithms and calculations that are hitherto difficult to complete. In the future, computing power will be at the disposal of consumers via utility computing,[96] enabling them to easily run complex applications. Banks and their customers will able to benefit from using these technologies in ways that are unimaginable at the moment.

Banks will also be using the internet in a totally radical way in the future. At present, the internet is mainly a medium for document retrieval and basic transactions. Customers can view documents, but they are incongruent and connections are difficult to make. Service-Oriented Architecture (SOA) is being used to build bridges that allow applications to better share information and at the

---

95 The creation of a "virtual supercomputer" by using spare computing resources within an organisation or by using a network of geographically dispersed computers.
96 Also known as "On Demand" computing. It is the packaging of computing resources, such as computation and storage, as a metered service.

same time function independently. In the future, the Semantic Web[97] will extend this capability and provide a universal medium for sharing data and reusing data across applications, enterprises and community boundaries.

This medium will encompass light-weight, autonomous software programs that reside on a variety of devices, making and executing decisions on behalf of their owners. These programs will run continuously and have the capability to learn and become trusted agents. This will allow their owners to delegate decision making with confidence. They will become ubiquitous by their integration into the environment as opposed to being perceived as distinct objects. There will be improved decision making as agents can do what their owners cannot easily do for themselves, for instance gathering and analysing vast amounts of information in short periods of time. This will result in consumer empowerment as the agents play banks against each other in real time to get the best deal for their owners. At present, information management occurs largely within the boundaries of an organisation, where most of the information resides. In future, the capability for evaluating soft, qualitative information will improve and as a consequence use of public information will soar.

An example of the application of the Semantic Web in retail banking is as follows.

Mr Biggs walks in to an apartment complex in the year 2020 to buy a condominium. Via the Semantic Web, the intelligent agent on his mobile phone talks to agents of several banks about a mortgage loan. The banks proffer deals to his agent, which analyses them by getting information, analytic models and computer power over the Web and negotiates with them to get the best deal. Mr Biggs' agent has more leverage than he does because it can do all of this in real time. His agent closes the mortgage loan with a bank, the completion process for the condominium with the property developer, obtains home insurance, submits the deed to the land registry and so on. Mr Biggs moves into his brand-new condominium without signing a piece of paper or touching a keyboard.

Rethinking the Business Model

The traditional retail banking business model can be considered in three dimensions: products offered, markets served and established infrastructure, which covers the people, processes and technology required to support these products and includes the agent bank services currently in use. In order to adapt to the identified changes in the business environment, banks are rethinking their business models in the following ways:

97 This is an evolving extension of the World Wide Web in which web content can be expressed not only in a natural language, but also in a format that can be read and used by software agents, thus permitting them to find, share and integrate information more easily. The semantic web is a vision of information that is understandable by computers, so that they can perform more of the tedious work involved in finding, sharing and combining information on the web.

- Expansion of their geographical footprint and establishing a presence in each region to provide services to meet the exacting demands of their clients. This will increase demand from the business customers for efficiency in the financial supply chain, ensuring that working capital is maximised through effective international transfer and deposit of funds.
- Expansion of their product set to counter diminishing revenue from commoditised services as corporates and individuals are consistently targeted by competing banks for their custom and these banks can exploit a gap in one institution's product range.
- Consideration of the option of buying off-the-shelf packages from specialist providers to reduce product time-to-market. Although this might prove to be cheaper in the short-term than developing an entire new product from the ground up, as a longer-term investment the benefits are more debatable.
- Formulation of new strategies for compliance in the face of increasing demands for transparency and supervisory pressure from regulators. This will include expanding their due diligence and audit programmes for external suppliers and enforcing stricter performance reliability and disaster recovery measures.
- Forming partnerships and collaborations as a result of an examination of services on offer to establish whether they are truly core to the organisation's ongoing operations, and investigating whether value can be derived from leveraging other businesses' core capabilities instead. This could result in individual banking functions being migrated to niche specialists.
- Exploitation of cross-border mergers and acquisition opportunities, especially among global banks, with a view to scaling up in light of other regional banks' rapid and comprehensive consolidation into a number of giants in market capitalisation terms. This can ensure that they can compete effectively with them for banking assets in emerging markets.

Outsourcing and Offshoring

Retail banks, like many other industries, consider outsourcing and offshoring as key ways to transform their operating models. Outsourcing is a practice that involves transferring or sharing the management control and decision making of business functions, while offshoring concerns the relocation of business processes from one country to another. Several objectives are at stake, including cost savings, customer service improvements, economies of scale, access to skills, and business responsiveness (Cap Gemini, 2007).

According to the 2007 World Retail Banking Report by Cap Gemini, ING and EFMA, their survey results show that retail banks appear unwilling to change their current outsourcing practices and those that are currently outsourcing are unlikely to change their practices in the next five years. Nevertheless, support function outsourcing practices will grow rapidly by 13% over the next five years.

In the retail banks that were surveyed, approximately one-third of the IT and support function staff is outsourced. Over the next five years, this proportion for IT will jump to 52% and the rate for support functions will also increase, but more slowly. Outsourcing growth will come mainly from retail banks that already outsource, by enlarging the proportion of their outsourced staff.

The findings from the report also indicate that payments, mortgages and life insurance, which are the most frequently outsourced today, will remain so over the next few years until about 2012. As for IT functions such as development, maintenance, and operations, they are usually the primary concern as regards outsourcing at the moment and will remain so until around 2012.

In the future, retail banks expect to have a substantial portion (approximately one-third) of their IT and support function staff offshored. Offshoring is expected to grow rapidly, especially in IT, which is expected to grow by 10% over a five-year period from 2007 to 2012.

Reverse Offshoring
The rise of the Indian software industry as a dominant force in the global software outsourcing market has been one of the most remarkable success stories of the past 15 years. The industry has been able to achieve this market dominance in large measure by relying on India's large pool of low-cost, highly qualified, technically proficient workers.

However, in recent times it seems things are going back to square one as the rising cost of paying engineers in Bangalore in India has prompted at least one Silicon Valley start-up to save money by closing its Indian engineering centre and moving the jobs back to the USA.

While this "reverse offshoring" remains unusual, it points to a broader belief in the retail banking industry that the savings that drove software engineering jobs to India's technology capital are quickly eroding.

This trend is expected to continue in the future as companies will be questioning the viability of offshoring their IT functions to labour markets that are deemed to be competitively priced. It is not only the rising costs that could be the problem, but also the shifting demands of the business on IT which could not be fulfilled by IT workers in these labour markets that lack the requisite business knowledge.

Adoption of Customer Retention Strategies

Customer-centricity is a buzzword now commonplace in the retail banking landscape as customer loyalty is on the wane. It is perhaps the most common business concept in an industry where customer service is a major differentiator.

Customer-centricity is about leveraging the knowledge of clients' needs to not only cross-sell and up-sell opportunities, but also to better segment customers and create packages designed to anticipate the needs of target populations.

Retail banking customers are becoming knowledgeable and more demanding and as a result they are increasingly intolerant of poor responses from their banks. This is already redefining the rules of the game as customers are shopping around for the best products/services and reliable advice and are no longer blindly loyal but easily move around frequently in search of better deals. Traditional banks and other new organisations offering financial services are the beneficiaries of this phenomenon as these customers are unwilling to put up with inefficient organisations and complex, difficult-to-understand products and fees.

In the coming years, it is anticipated that customers will become more fickle and more knowledgeable about technology and will not hesitate to move to other organisations that are more competent in anticipating and servicing individual needs. They will demand greater transparency in their dealings with their bank as opposed to complicated fee structures or contracts with vague terms and conditions. People will pay more for personal value but demand low prices for basic goods.

According to IBM, by 2015 technology will make it even easier for customers to research, compare, form and break relationships with financial institutions while demanding greater advocacy and control over their transactions.

Industry experts are united in their opinion that faith in banks is faltering: in the USA for example, around 31% of customers at the top American institutions believe companies act more in the interest of their own profitability than that of their customers, leading to defection rates at some banks of 30% (IBM, 2007).

Based on the conventional wisdom that it is cheaper to retain existing customers than acquire new ones, intimate knowledge of the client base and continual improvement of personal experience are some of the vital elements for maintaining a competitive edge in the future. Whilst it is crucial to offer a greater choice, and tailored products and services, as well as attractive loyalty schemes, the key to profitability for the banks in future will be focused on identifying and cultivating their most profitable customers. Banks will adopt techniques for mining data and drilling down into their existing databases in real time with a view to anticipating and being proactive in recommending banking solutions that fit exacting lifestyle requirements. This functionality is essential to a bank's capability in foreseeing and accommodating indecisive and unpredictable customers.

Growth of Bank Retailing

Banks are realising the increasing difficulty in achieving differentiation through product, service, reach or price as legalisation is driving financial management to an ever-increasing level of standardisation. In the past, the introduction of a unique product provided a long-term business opportunity and banks, in recent times, have realised that no matter how quickly they bring products to market, it is virtually impossible for product differentiation to be sustained as competitors can copy concepts within a short space of time. For established banks, the edge they have left is competitive pricing and it would appear that the preferred long-term source of competitive differentiation for a bank can only be in its ability to better serve customers and prospects.

In light of this, industry experts have been alerting banks to a noticeable atmosphere of change in the banking industry that suggests that customer loyalty is shifting and banks that take this for granted do so at their peril. According to ATOS Origin: *"There is a subtle but significant indication that the sector now refers to itself generically as 'retail' banking. Today's banks see themselves as part of industry, in contrast to the old perception of being a 'profession'."*

Retail banks have become more like modern retail businesses in recent times in the sense that they appear to be able to react to customer behaviour in any given branch or channel in a timely manner. Modern retail businesses spot buying trends in real time and react accordingly. They understand how to present their offerings in the best way possible, not just in terms of product portfolio, but also by location, customer segments and time of year.

Most banks are not yet in a position to achieve such levels of sophistication, but the technology to enable such commercial agility has been emerging recently and it is only a matter of time before it becomes commonplace.

Recent innovations in retail banking clearly demonstrate this trend and the desire to rebuild personal relationships lost as a result of the advent of banking through the telephone, internet and ATMs. An example of the innovative initiatives undertaken by retail banks to enhance their retailing capabilities is HSBC's decision to hire hundreds of extra staff from the retail industry to work in its branches and also the retail-style "January sale" promotion. RaboBank is another bank that a took a giant stride towards adopting a retail-style sales strategy when it commissioned designers from the retail industry to redesign branches to be more like shops than banks, including packaging banking and insurance products in boxes to be displayed on shelves for customers to browse through and select.

Technology is also playing an increasingly pivotal role in the pursuit of better service in the drive to achieve effective bank retailing by providing:

- better information in order to make smarter, quicker decisions, which allows banks to create new product propositions for customers where they need it, when they need it and how they need it;
- easy access to serve the customer in the most convenient way possible and with the maximum flexibility, night or day, local or remote.

Intensification of KYC Initiatives

In the face of an increasing number of cases of identity fraud, banks are introducing a number of Know Your Customer (KYC) initiatives to minimise losses and have a more accurate view of their customers. In a country like the UK for example, it costs the British economy more than £1.7 billion a year[98] and

---

98 Source: APACS.

because of consumer loss limits, much of that burden is borne by the banking industry.

Total card (credit and debit) fraud resulting in losses in the UK reached £439.4m in 2005, a figure that shows a reduction of 13% when compared to 2004, while over a period of ten years from 1995 to 2005, overall losses from card fraud rose by 530%.

When a customer's ID gets into the wrong hands, it could spell the beginning of a raft of fairly predictable activities. The customer's details are used to apply for fraudulent credit cards and loans from unsuspecting banks and other financial institutions and even to launder money for criminals and terrorists, which could cause untold distress for the customer. As for the banks, losses traced to identity theft will not only lead to monetary consequences but also costly loss of reputation.

Most banks still utilise low-tech methods to identify new and existing customers, giving them an inaccurate view of their customers. The current process for identification inadvertently adds up to a losing proposition, especially in a high-stakes business environment under pressure from customers, a widening competitive field and governmental regulatory agencies.

The justification for the adoption of improved identity resolution technology by banks is two-fold: to address the significant monetary and public relations risks associated with fraud and to ensure regulatory compliance.

Global banks, in a bid to comply with the demands of recent regulations such as Basel 2 and the USA Patriot Act, implement time-consuming compliance projects. Regulations such as these either recommend or mandate that banks put procedures in place to enable them to have a more intimate knowledge of their customers than they did in the past.

The following are three minimum elements that the regulators of the Patriot Act, for instance, stipulate as a practicable customer identification programme:

- documentary verification of the identity of any person seeking to open an account;
- a system for maintaining customer information for at least five years after closing an account;
- cross-checking of customer identification against lists of known or suspected criminals and terrorists.

As for Basel 2 and other KYC regulations, the guidelines mainly advocate credit and operational risk assessment in relation to a single enterprise-wide view of the customer that encompasses information about associations that they may have with other bank customers (individuals or legal entities), external groups, bank employees or associations with people on government watch lists.

In the future, technology-based KYC strategies will be the norm. A veritable technology-based KYC strategy can help banks reduce account-opening and management costs as customer data is harmonised across the enterprise. It can also help reduce operational risk as customer information is updated and managed from a central source. In addition, capital can be increasingly diverted to worthy customer segments with a view to cutting credit risk, and customer data can be used as a competitive differentiator, providing the opportunity to offer bespoke financial products and increase customer loyalty.

Entity analytics is an example of a KYC technology that will be used extensively in the future.

Conclusion

The retail banking landscape is set for dramatic reforms over the years as the factors discussed above show. However, retail banks will be restructuring in response to market changes and will be seeking to optimise employee productivity and retain/recruit superior expertise to drive the new strategies to ensure competitiveness. Business-aligned IT professionals will have a key role to play as the line between IT and business blurs.

Appendix

A Sample Summary Box using Bizle Business Credit Card as illustration is shown below.

Bizle Business Credit Card Summary Box

APR	Typical **18.20% APR** variable	
Other rates	Annual rate	Monthly rate
Purchasess	13.30%	1.109%
Cash advances	13.30%	1.109%
Interest-free period	Up to 45 days on purchases if the total balance is paid off in full by the due date on both the previous and latest Statement	
Interest charging information	With the exception of Purchases (please see above), you'll have to pay interest on all Transactions from the Transaction date even if you pay your full balance by the due date	
	Your due date is 14 days after the statement date (or the next working day should the payment date fall on a weekend or a Bank Holiday in England and Wales)	
Allocation of payments	If you make a payment that isn't enough to pay everything you owe us in a statement, we'll use it to reduce your payment in this order: • Anything overdue or above your Business Limit • The minimum payment as shown on your Statement • Interest • Fees and charges (including annual card fees andother charges including charges for exceeding the Business Limit and late payment charges • Cash Withdrawals • All other amounts on the Business Account	

Minimum payment	You must pay at least the minimum payment every month of 5% of the balance shown on the statement (minimum £5 or the full alance if less than £5)
Amount of credit	Minimum credit of £500 Maximum credit of £10,000
Fees	£28 annual fee per cardholder

Charges

Cash withdrawals	2% of amount or minimum £2
Cash withdrawals abroad	2% of amount or minimum £2 plus 2.75% foreign exchange fee
Foreign currency card transactions	2.75% foreign exchange fee
Copy of statements	£6 for a copy of a non-current statement
Copy of sales vouchers	£5 per item There will be no charge if your query reveals an error has been made
Copy of report	£15

Default Charges

Late payments	£12
Limit exceeded	£12
Returned payment	£12
Arrears letter notification	£12

Calculation of Simple and Compound Interest Rates

Simple Interest

Simple Interest is the product of the principal, the interest rate (per period), and the number of time periods. If the following symbols are used:

P = Principal i.e. the sum of money borrowed
t = Term i.e. the time over which the money is borrowed
r = The interest rate expressed as a percentage
I = Simple interest

Then, simple interest can be calculated using the following formula:

I = S*r*t

For example: Bob Bixby borrows £23,000 to buy a new car, and the rate is 5.5% over five years. The resulting simple interest is:

£23,000 * 5.5% * 5 = £6,325

The simple interest on Bob's auto loan is £6,325. If Bob repays his debt in full, he will repay the principal plus the interest, or £29,325.

To calculate the simple interest rate I, interest paid or payable is added together in a period. The result is divided by the principal at the beginning of the period. This result is the simple interest rate.

Compound Interest

Compound Interest is very similar to Simple Interest. The difference is that the principal changes with every time period, unlike simple interest where the principal remains the same. The new principal at the end of every time period is essentially the simple interest on the principal at the beginning of the time period added to the principal.

For example, suppose P is the principal, and r and t have the same meanings as above. The principal at the end of the first period will be P*r (for t=1 period). Similarly, the principal at the end of the second period will be (P*r)*r. Thus we can land upon a general formula:

$C = p * (r)^t$
$A = p * (1 + r)^t$

Where:

C is equal to compound interest which is the product of the principal (p), and the rate (r) in decimal form raised to the power of the number of terms (t);

A is equal to the compound amount which is the product of rate (r) and the quantity of the rate (r) plus one, raised to the power of the number of terms (t).

APR
Loans often include various non-interest charges and fees and as a result lenders are regularly required to provide information on the "true" cost of finance, often expressed as an annual percentage rate (APR). The APR attempts to express the total cost of a loan as an interest rate after including the additional fees and expenses, although details may vary by jurisdiction.

EU Directive 98/7/EC is the legislation that applies to all EU member states and is usually incorporated into each country's consumer legislation. A similar method is used in the USA and other countries.

Useful Websites

American Bankers' Association	www.aba.com
Australian Bankers' Association	www.bankers.asn.au
Association of Certified Fraud Examiners	www.acfe.com
Association of Payment Clearing Services (APACS)	www.apacs.org.uk
Bacs	www.bacs.co.uk
Bank of International Settlements	www.bis.org
British Bankers' Association	www.bba.org.uk
Business Money	www.business-money.com
Callcredit	www.callcredit.co.uk
Canadian Bankers' Association	www.cba.ca
CIFAS	www.cifas.org.uk
Council of Mortgage Lenders	www.cml.org.uk
Credit Action	www.creditaction.org.uk
Dun and Bradstreet	www.dnb.com
Equifax	www.equifax.com
Experian	www.experian.com
Euromoney Publications	www.euromoney.com
European Bank for Reconstruction and Development	www.ebrd.com
European Central Bank	www.ecb.int
Financial Ombudsman Service	www.financial-ombudsman.org.uk
Financial Services Authority	www.fsa.gov.uk
Financial Services Practitioner Panel	www.fs-pp.org.uk
Financial Times	www.ft.com
HM Treasury	www.hm-treasury.gov.uk
MasterCard	www.mastercard.com
Intelligence in Finance	www.intelfasterfs.com/newsletter
International Banking Federation	www.ibfed.org
International Monetary Fund	www.imf.org
Joint Money Laundering Steering Group	www.jmlsg.org.uk
LINK	www.link.co.uk
London Stock Exchange	www.londonstockexchange.com
Money Advice Trust	www.moneyadvicetrust.org

Royal Mail	www.royalmail.com
SWIFT	www.swift.com
TransUnion	www.transunion.com
The Bank of England	www.bankofengland.com
The Guild of International Bankers	www.internationalbankers.co.uk
The Economist	www.economist.com
VISA	www.visa.com
Voca	www.vocalink.com
Windows in Financial Services	www.windowsfs.com
World Bank	www.worldbank.com

Useful Job Boards

Banking Technology Jobs	www.bankingtechnologyjobs.com
Career Center	http://jobs.careerzone.banktechnews.com
Career Center	www.finextra.com/finjobLIST.asp
Computer Weekly	www.computerweekly.com/Jobs
Cv Library	www.cv-library.co.uk
efinancialcareers	www.efinancialcareers.com
IT Job Feed	www.ciquery.com
Job Databases	www.jobdatabases.co.uk
Job Crawler	www.jobcrawler.co.uk
Jobserve	www.jobserve.com
Jobsite	www.jobsite.co.uk
Monster	www.monster.co.uk
Online Job Match	www.onlinejobmatch.co.uk
Planet Recruit	www.planetrecruit.com
The IT Job Board	www.theitjobboard.co.uk
Total Jobs	www.totaljobs.com

Specialist Recruitment Agencies

Abraxas	www.abraxas.com
Alexander Mann Solutions	www.alexandermannsolutions.com
Allegis Group	www.allegisgroup.com
Astbury Marsden	www.astburymarsden.com
Aston Carter	www.astoncarter.co.uk
Anson McCade	www.ansonmccade.com
Badenoch and Clark	www.badenochandclark.com
Cititec	www.cititec.com
Computer People	www.computerpeople.co.uk
Elan	www.elanit.com
E-Synergy Solutions	www.esynergy-solutions.co.uk
Hudson	www.hudson.com
Huxley Associates	www.huxleyassociates.com
iKas International	www.ikasinternational.com
James Harvard Financial	www.jamesharvard.com
JM Contracts	www.jmpeople.com
Lorien	www.lorien.co.uk
Madison Black	www.madisonblack.com
Madison Maclean Technology	www.madisonmaclean.com
McGregor Boyall	www.mcgregor-boyall.com
Michael Page	www.michaelpage.com
Modis	www.modisintl.com
Morgan Hutchins Associates	www.morganhutchins.com
Mortimer Spinks	www.mortimerspinks.com
OTC	www.otc-computing.co.uk
Parity Resourcing Solutions	www.parity.net
Penta Consulting	www.pentaconsulting.com
Project Partners	www.projpartners.com
Real Resourcing	www.realresourcing.com
Robert Half	www.roberthalf.co.uk
Robert Walters	www.robertwalters.com
Rullion Computer Personnel	www.rullion.co.uk
Templeton and Partners	www.templeton-recruitment.com
The Kaizen Partnership	http://kaizenpartnership.com
Xchanging	www.xchanging.com

Bibliography

About American Express. Available on http://home3.americanexpress.com/corp/default.asp?us_nu=footer

About Barclays. Available on www.aboutbarclays.com

About BBA. Available on www.bba.org.uk/bba/jsp/polopoly.jsp?d=103&a=1559

About CallCredit. Available on www.callcredit.co.uk/business/about-us

About Citi. Available on www.citigroup.com/citigroup/about/index.htm

About Diner's Club .Available on http://www.dinersclubus.com/dce_content/aboutdinersclub/companyhistory

About EMVCo. Available on www.emvco.com/about.asp

About Equifax. Available on www.equifax.co.uk/our_company/about_efx/index.html

About Fair Isaac. Available on www.fairisaac.com

About HSBC. Available on www.hsbc.com/1/2/about-hsbc

About LINK. Available on www.link.co.uk/company/mn_company.html

About RBS. Available on www.rbs.com/about01.asp?id=ABOUT_US

About VISA. Available on www.visaeurope.com/aboutvisa/

About the Bank. Available on www.bankofengland.co.uk/about/index.htm

Abramson, F., Croxford, H. and Jablownoski, A. (2004). *The Art of Better Retail Banking: Supportable Predictions on the Future of Retail Banking.* John Wiley and Sons Ltd.

APACS: *Cheque and Credit Clearing.* Available on www.apacs.org.uk/uk_payment_scheme/cheque_credit_clearing.html

APACS: *Standing Orders.* Available on www.apacs.org.uk/payment_options/automated_payments.html

APACS: *Issuer Identification Number.* Available on www.apacs.org.uk/industry_standards-2.html

ATOS Origin. *Power to the Customer Creating Convenience, Trust and Value in Retail Banking.* Available on www.atosorigin.com

Bathgate, A. (2006). *The Use of Screen Scraping Techniques to Solve Data Migration Problems in Enterprise Upgrade Systems.* Blue Prism.

Becker, K. (Feb. 2007). *Mobile Phone: The New Way to Pay?.* Emerging Payments Industry Briefing. pp1-2.

British Computer Society: *The International IT Professional Practice Programme* (2007). Available on www.bcs.org

Bonnet, F., Jobanputra, P. and Mangat, B. (2006). *Getting to Know You. How Know Your Customer Programs can Improve Banks' Business Health.* Available on www.ibm.com

Buckle, M. (2004). *The UK Financial System Theory and Practice.* Manchester University Press.

Capgemini, EFMA and ING (2007). *World Retail Banking Report.*

Casu, B., Girardone, C. and Molyneux, P. (2006). *Introduction to Banking.* FT Prentice Hall.

Caves, R., Frankel, J. and Jones, R. (2006). *World Trade and Payments: An Introduction.* Addison Wesley.

Chip and PIN. Available on www.apacs.org.uk/payment_options/plastic_cards_5_1.html

Clear2Pay: *Accelerated Faster Payments.* Available on www.clear2pay.com

Dence, S., Fellee, W. and Latimore, D. (2006). *Get Global. Get Specialized. Or Get Out. Unexpected Lessons in Global Financial Markets.* IBM Global Business Services.

DiVanna, J. (2003). *The Future of Retail Banking.* Palgrave Macmillan.

Evans, D. and Schmalensee, R. (2005). *Paying with Plastic: The Digital Revolution in Buying and Borrowing.* The MIT Press.

Eiger Systems Limited. (1 April 2007). *SWIFTNet for Corporate Treasurers: Exploring the Business Case.* Available on www.eiger.co.uk

European Banking Association. (1, October 2006). *Banks Preparing for SEPA-Issues to be Addressed to Achieve SEPA Compliance.*

Finlay, S. (2005). *Consumer Credit Fundamentals.* Palgrave Macmillan.

Future Trends in Cards and Payments. (2005). Business Insights Limited.

Grealish, A. (2006). *Customer Analytics Triathlon: Data, Knowledge, and Wisdom.* Available on www.iflexsolutions.com

Hefferman, S. (2004). *Modern Banking.* John Wiley and Sons Ltd.

Hock, D. (2005). *One On Many: VISA and the Rise of the Chaordic Organization.* Berrett-Koehler.

Hoppermann, J. (30 April 2007). *Topic Overview: Banking Platforms.* Forrester.

Hulme, M. and Wright, C. (Oct. 2006). *Internet Based Social Lending: Past, Present and Future.* Available on www.zopa.com

Keasey, K. and Mcdonald, O. (2002). *The Future of Retail Banking in Europe: A View on the Top.* John Wiley and Sons Ltd.

Khan, Z. (2000). *Islamic Banking and its Operations.* Institute of Islamic Banking and Insurance.

Lipscombe, G. and Pond, K. (2002). *The Business of Banking.* Financial World Publishing.

Mann, R. (2006). *Charging Ahead: The Growth and Regulation of Payment Card Markets Around the World.* Cambridge University Press.

Mastercard Corporate Overview. Available on www.mastercard.com/us/company/en/corporate/index.html

Misys: *Future of Retail banking.* Available on www.misys.com/banking

Misys. (2007). *Islamic Banking: A Growing Force in the World of Finance.* Available on Misys.com/banking

Moore, S. (3 October 2006). *Which Service Provider Can Help Retail Banks?.* Forrester Research.

Niche Specialists and Customer Empowerment Mean a Devolving Role For Financial Institutions in Their Own Industry. Banking Technology News. April 2006 Vol. 19 No. 4 pp1.

Paper Statements: Expensive and Less Secure. Available on www.bai.org/nl/v1/articles/paperless.asp

Petit, Cirmac. (2006). *The Future of Banking.* IBM.

Pirker, A. (2006). *Islamic Finance – A Market Overview.* Available on www.iflexsolutions.com

Polar Lake and GT Software. *Building Mainframe Functionality To the Extended Enterprise.* Available on www.polarlake.com

Purchia, R. (2006). *The Unbanked Score.* Available on www.iflexsolutions.com

Reavley, N. (2007). *Boosting Customer's Confidence in Online Banking.* Xiring.

Ricci, M. (March 2007). *A Look at How Globalisation and Technology Will Radically Change Financial Services Over the Next Decade.* Banking Technology News Vol. 20 No. 3 pp1-2

Rouse, C. (2004). *Bankers' Lending Techniques.* Financial World Publishing.

SunTec: CRM and Beyond. A New Dimension to Pricing Retail-Banking Customers. Available on www.suntec.com

Thomas, R. (09 Sept 2006). *The Growth of Buy-To-Let.* CML Housing Finance.

White, V. (June 2007). *Technology to Meet Burgeoning KYC Requirements.* Complinet.

Index

References to figures or tables appear in italics

A

Abbey National Group 9, *12*, 14, 47, 50
ABN Amro 50, 73
account management 93-4
account opening
account closing 92-3
    account cycles 94
    account opening process 79-81
    account opening requirements 82-3
    account opening systems 79, 86-94
    address checking process 83, 88-9
    customer data entry process 86-8
    Electronic identification and verification (EID&V) 84, 90-1
    events during life of customer 92-3
    product offering process 89-90
accounts
    account sections 126-7
    account types 16-25
    auditing 79
    business accounts 21-3
    current accounts 16-21
    guaranteed investment accounts 25
    individual savings accounts (ISA) 25-6
    Islamic accounts 23
    joint accounts 84, 86, 92
    savings accounts 24-5, 172
    tax-free savings accounts 25-6
ADDACS service *130*, 131
Alliance and Leicester *12*, 14, 50
allied organisations 40-51
American Express 14, 31, 43, 69, 121, 214
AML *see* anti-money laundering
anti-money laundering (AML) 48, 58-9, 81-2, 89, 141, 145, 146, 174, 210
    see also know your customer
APACS 33, 46, 62, 65, 210, 214
APR 28, 100, 209
    fixed APR 100
    introductory rates 100
    variable APR 100
    see also interest rates
ARUCS services *130*, 131
ARUDD services *130*, 131
ATM fees 115, 116
ATM transactions 175, 176
ATMs 5, 10, 16, 27, 49, 65, 115, 171
    independent ATM deployers (IAD) 115-16
    types of 174, 175, 176
auditing
    audit programmes 199
    audit trails 82
    auditing controls 56
automated payments 51, 55, 177
automation of business processes 150-8
AWACS service *130*, 131

B

Bacs 46, 50-1, 122, 123-31, 210
    euro credit transactions 126
    processing cycle 128-9
    sterling credit transactions 126
    sterling debit transactions 126
    transaction types *125*
bank accounts *see* accounts
bank codes 31-3
Bank Identification Code (BIC) 31-2
Bank of England 11, 24, 41, 47, 49, 50, 116, 117, 177, 211, 214
Bank of Scotland 9, *12*
bank retailing 201-2
bank statements 17, 75-6, 94, 216
banker's drafts 5, 21, 117, 134
banker-customer relationship 2, 6, 7
Banking Code 4-5
banking platforms 138-48
bankruptcy 92, 106, 111, 113
Barclaycard 63-4
Barclays 9, *9*, *12*, 14, 39-40, 63-4, 214
Basel 2 Accord 8, 56-8, 141, 203
Blue Prism Automate 151, 155-8
    see also BPA
BPA
    agent preparation process 152

Index

back-office bulk processing 153–4
    case study 155–8
    migration process 162
    process mapping 156–7
    real-time agent hand-offs 151–2
    robotic integration 151
    third-party hand-offs 154–5
branch networks 5
brands
    brand loyalties 11
    brand stretching 2
    branding reputation 82
    branding strategy 43
British Bankers' Association (BBA) 34, 48–9, 210
British Computer Society (BCS) x
building societies 3, 11
Building Societies Association (BSA) 48
business and systems analysis methods 186–7
    brainstorming 186
    business rules approach 186
    entity relationship diagram (ERD) 186
    prototyping 184, 185, 187
    timeboxing 185
business environment 36–51, 195, 196, 198, 203
business process automation (BPA) 150–8, 162
Business Process Execution Language (BPEL) 168, 169
business process modelling 188
buy-to-let 73–4

C

Callcredit 44, 45, 106, 210, 214
CAMPARI 96–7
Capital One 14, 64
card companies 42–3
card industry initiatives 66–8
    chip and PIN 27, 41–2, 63, 66–7, 121, 215
    contactless payment 68–9
    Industry Hot Card File (IHCF) 67
    person-to-person payments (P2P) 68
    remittances 67–8
    summary box 67, 206–7
cards 26–8
    charge cards 43, 98, 100, 121
    cheque guarantee cards 116, 172
    contactless cards 68
    credit card sector 11

    credit cards 26–7, 121
    debit cards 27, 119
    gift cards 27
    loyalty cards 174
    pay later cards 121, 122
    payment cards 119, *120*
    prepaid cards 27, 122, 176
    store cards 122
cash machines *see* ATMs
CHAPS 46, 49–50, 158
Cheque and Clearing Company 50
cheques
    cheque processing 75
    cheque truncation 74–5
    clearing cycle 116–17, *118*, 172
    clearing organisations 49–51
    payments 116–17, 134
chip and PIN 27, 41–2, 63, 66–7, 121, 215
CIFAS 47–8, 107, 210
Citigroup 8, 9, *12*, 14, 39, 69, 142, 214
clearing organisations 49–51
clearing systems 116–17, 171
client/server systems 158, 180
collateral 96, 97
collateralisation 98–9
commercial banks 3
compliance with regulations 53–4, 56–9, 69–71, 85, 199, 203
computer systems *see* systems
corporate electronic banking 6
Council of Mortgage Lenders (CML) 47, 48
credit 99–113
    address information 107–8, 109, 111, 113
    applicant matching 108
    applications for credit 102–4
    bureau scorecards 108
    bureau scores 108
    cost of credit 99–100
    county court judgments (CCJs) 106
    credit bureaus 44
    credit checking process 89
    credit histories 109
    credit life cycle 111, *112*
    credit limits 121
    credit management 111–13
    credit reference data 108

credit referencing 105-6
credit reports 109
credit scoring 103-5
credit searches 107, 109
creditworthiness 44, 101, 102, 103
   definition 101
   Five Cs of Credit 101, 103
   information sources 106-11
   judgemental decision making 102, 105
   linked addresses 109
   No Trace 109
   notice of correction 108
   repossessions 106
   scoring technology systems 104-5
credit referencing agencies 44-5, 105-6, 108
CRM *see* customer relationship management
cross-selling 14, 64, 65, 79, 86, 97, 200
currency exchange *see* foreign exchange
Customer Due Diligence for Banks 80
customer relationship management (CRM) 138
customer service representatives (CSR) 79
customers
   consumer empowerment 198
   customer analytics 64-5
   customer data 64
   customer ID 83
   customer identification number (CIN) 91
   customer loyalty 121, 200, 201, 202
   customer retention strategies 200-1
   customer-centricity 200
   customers' view of banks 201
   definition 6

D

data
   address information 107-8, 109, 111, 113
   credit reference 108
   customer 64, 107
   demographic 64, 108
   electoral roll 106
   public information 198
   shared customer account 107
   socio-economic 108
   third-party 109-11
data migration
   data conversion 159

data corruption 160
data flows 159
data mapping 159
data transformation applications 160
Green Screen applications 158, 161
mainframe integration 164-9
phased migrations 160
problems 159
scalable runtime environment 161
data mining 64, 180, 201
data models 168, 186, 188
data warehousing 180
debt
   arrears 112
   bad debt 96
   collections 112-13
   debt recovery 113
   debt statistics 98
   debtors, definition 6
   defaulters on loans 108
   legal action 113
   write offs 113
deconstruction of banking services 61-2
demographics
   changes 16, 37-8
   data 64, 108
development methodologies 186
digital TV banking 6
Diners Club 43, 121
direct debits 123, 172
   automated direct debit instruction service
      (AUDDIS) 124, *130*, 131
   direct debit guarantee 123
   direct debit instructions (DDI) 124, 125, 129,
      130, 131
due diligence 58, 80-1, 199

E

e-banking 62, 75, 146
electronic banking *see* internet banking
EMV 41-2, 62, 121, 214
enterprise service bus (ESB) 163, 165-9
Equifax 44, 105, 107
ESB *see* enterprise service bus
ethical standing of banks 60
euro 41, 53-4, 133, 173

European Central Bank (ECB) 41, 53, 210
European Committee for Banking Standards 32
eurozone 53-4
exchange rates 37, 133, 173
exotics 132
Experian 44, 45, 105, 107

F
Fair Isaac 47, 103
Faster Payments clearing and settlement system 54-5
fees
    annual 17, 121
    arrangement 29, 30, 97, 100
    business tariffs 23
    charge card 8
    current account 21
    Islamic account 21
    loan 8
    transaction 8, 13
FICO scores 47, 103
Financial Services Authority (FSA) 5, 11, 40-1, 49, 210
financial supermarkets 61
Financial Times, The 46
foreign exchange 37, 132, 133, 173
fraud
    AML/KYC 58-9, 202-3
    card fraud 62-3, 203
    cheques 117
    cloning of cards 66
    corruption 84-5
    electronic 55
    fraud prevention 47-8, 62, 66-7
    hacking 55
    identity theft 203
    key logging 63
    phishing 55, 63, 175, 176
    screen-scraper programs 63
    skimming (cards) 66
    Trojans 175, 177
FSA *see* Financial Services Authority
future trends 195-204

G
global banks 40, 141, 147, 195, 199, 203
globalisation 195-6

Government
    borrowing and debt repayment 36
    fiscal policy 37, 173
    monetary policy 11, 41, 175
grid computing 197
growth opportunities 8, 195, 197

H
Halifax 9, *12*
HBOS 9, 14
high-street retail banks 2
HSBC 9, *12*, 14, 40, 50, 69, 196, 202, 214
HTTP 144, 165

I
IBAN 32-3
IBM 181, 187, 188, 195, 196, 201
ICE 96, 97
IHCF 67
inflation
    hyperinflation 37
    inflation rates 37, 173
Infosys 86, 145
ING 10, 73, 199
insurance 5, 8, 16, 30, 31, 61, 202
insurance companies 10, 11, 38, 61
intangible assets 171
integrated circuit cards (IC) *see* chip and PIN
integration of mainframes 164-9
Intelligent Finance 10, *12*
interest charges 99
interest rates 11, 29, 34, 36
    Bank of England Base Rate 24, 29, 30
    base rates 24, 171
    cash advances 100
    compound interest 208-9
    different rates for different transactions 100
    simple interest 208
    standard variable rate (SVR) 29
    see also APR
international funds transfers 122, 132, 133-5
International Monetary Fund (IMF) 58
internet 2, 45, 66, 197
internet banking 6, 11, 65-6, 150
internet banks 2, 10, 11-12, *12*
internet, role of 197

investment accounts 25-6
Isaac, Earl 47
Islamic accounts 23, 38
Islamic banks 3, 69, 215, 216
Islamic systems *148*
Issuer Identification Number (IIN) 33
IT
    challenges for IT managers 163, 168
    investment in 137, 138, 161-2, 199
    IT service management 181
    outsourcing of 199-200
    projects 150-69
    role of/use of 137-8
    skills 188-92
    spend *137*
    strategy 196
    tools 187-8

J

J2EE 144, 169, 189
Japan Credit Bureau (JCB) 41, 43
Java development environment 144, 188, 189
job boards and websites 212

K

Know Your Customer (KYC) 58, 80-1, 89, 146, 202-4

L

legacy systems 79, 137, 144, 150, 160-1, 161
legislation
    Anti-Terrorism, Crime & Security Act 2001 85
    Bills of Exchange Act 1882 116
    Cheque Acts of 1957 and 1992 116
    Consumer Credit Act 1974 44, 108
    Data Protection Act 1998 44, 108
    EU Directive 98/7/EC 209
    Housing Act 1988 74
    Insolvency and Bankrupt Acts 92
    Proceeds of Crime Act (POCA) 81
    Sarbanes-Oxley Act of 2002 (Sox) 56
lending 96-113
    activities 8
    bridging loans 29
    collateral 96, 97
    Gone Away Information Network (GAIN) 107-8
    personal loans 28-9, 96
    principles of 96-7
    secured lending 96
    types of 96
    underwriters 102-3
    unsecured loans 28, 96
LINK 49, 55, 116, 120, 174, 214
Lloyds TSB 4, *9*, 11, 12, 14, 50, 65, 69
loans *see* lending
London Interbank Offered Rate (LIBOR) 30, 34

M

m-payments *see* mobile payments
MA-CUG 71
Maestro 42, 119, 122, 177
mainframe integration 164-9
    adapters 164-5
    bottom-up approach 166-7
    gateways 164
    mainframe web services 165-9
    mediation 168-9
    orchestration 168, 169
    top-down approach 167
    Web Services Interoperability Organisation (WS-I) 165
    web services standards 168
    web services wrappers 165
    WSDL standard 165, 166, 167
mainframe skills 190-2
mainframe systems 163-9
mainframe technologies 180
markets
    emerging markets 72, 199
    global markets 49, 132
    Islamic market 69
    market changes 204
    new markets 37, 195
    prospect markets 195
    unbanked retail market 72
    veteran markets 195
MAST 98-9
MasterCard 28, 41, 42, 43, 68, 69, 121, 122, 210, 215
MBNA 2, 11, 14
merchant services 28, 119, *120*, 121, 174
mergers and acquisitions 11, 175, 199
messaging services 46, 47, 70, 129-30

methodologies 180-6
    agile software development 185
    Capability Maturity Model (CMM) 182
    Extreme Programming (XP) 186
    International Technology Infrastructure Library (ITIL) 181
    iterative software development processes 181, 184-5
    maturity models 182
    pair programming 186
    Prince2 183
    project management methodologies 183
    prototyping 184, 185, 186
    Rapid Application Development (RAD) 184-5
    Rational Unified Process (RUP) 181, *181*
    UML 184, *184*, 187, 188
    V-model 184, *185*
Microsoft .NET 144, 145, 188, 189
mobile (phone) banking 6, 49, 77, 145, 150
mobile payments 51, 68, 76-7, 175
Monetary policy 175
Monetary Policy Committee 41
money 3-4
money laundering 48, 58, 81-2, 174, 203
mortgage banks 3, 11
mortgages 29-30, 175
    buy-to-let 73-4
    fixed-rate mortgages 29-30
    mortgagor and mortgagee relationship 7
    tracker mortgages 30
multidisciplinary project teams 171

N
NatWest 9, *12*, 39
news agencies 45-6

O
Official List 41
offshore banks 3
offshoring 5, 199-200
online banks *see* internet banks
online communities 60
Oracle Designer 188
originations *see* account opening
outsourcing 5, 62, 138, 199-200
    Indian software industry 200

overdrafts 16, 17, 18, 19, 23, 68, 176
overseas funds 36

P
partnerships 10, 199
payment files (Bacs) 126
Payment gateways 28
payment instructions (Bacs) 124-5, *130*
payments 115-35
    adjustment items 127
    cash cycle 115
    cash payments 115-16
    contactless payment 68-9
    contras 126-7
    destination accounts (Bacs) 125-6
    direct credits 123, 172
    direct payments 172
    electronic payment methods 119-35
    mail payment orders 134
    manual payment methods 115-19
    money orders 134
    person-to-person payments (P2P) 68
    standing orders 122, 177
peer-to-peer banks 12-14, 59
people-related implications 196
PeopleSoft 169
Personal Identification Number (PIN) 121, 176
politically exposed persons (PEPs) 81, 84-5
Post Office banking 5, 6, 49, 176
postal saving banks 3
PowerDesigner 188
private banks 3
product offer 195, 198, 199, 201, 202
Professionalism in IT programme x
Prosper 13, 59

R
Rational ClearCase 188
Rational ClearQuest 188
Rational Rose 187
recruitment agencies 213
regulations 49, 53-4, 56-9, 57, 85, 92, 100, 199, 203
regulators 40-2
Remote Card Authentication 62-3
retail banking

business model 198-9
challenges 56, 64
distribution channels 5-6
global industry 8-9
non-bank firms 10
players 38-51
services 2, 5
systems 137-48
trends 53-77, 195-204
UK retail banking sector 9-11
retail banks
definition 2
list 14
restructuring of 204
revenue generation 7-8
types of 2-3
reverse offshoring 200
see also offshoring
risk 176
acceptable risk 101-2, 103
AML/KYC 58, 59
credit risk 14, 45, 47, 72, 101-11, 204
migration projects 159, 160, 161
risk assessment (credit) 61, 102, 203
risk controls 13
risk management 55, 56-7, 58, 81, 105
risk profiles 97, 103
Royal Bank of Scotland Group 4, 9, *9, 12*, 39, 50

S

sanctions 85
Santander Central Hispano 9
SAP 169
Sarbanes-Oxley Act of 2002 (Sox) 56
SCORE 70-1
screen scraping 158, 159, 160-3, 164
Second Life 73
security issues 55, 63, 66, 68, 69, 70, 180
Semantic Web 198
SEPA 53-4
service oriented architecture (SOA) 145, 163, 164, 166, 167-8, 169, 197-8
settlements 50, 55, 116, 133, 134
Shari'a law 23, 69, 146
see also Islamic accounts
Single Euro Payments Area (SEPA) 53-4

skills
IT 188-92
mainframe 190-2
soft 192-3
SOA *see* service oriented architecture
social lending 59-60
socio-political environments 196
soft skills 192-3
software *see* systems
sort code 33
specialist banks, future 196, 199
SPUDRAD 4
summary box, credit card 67, 206-7
SUMS 3-4
supermarket banks 2, 10, 11
SWIFT 31, 32, 46-7, 69-70, 71, 134, 177, 189, 211
system development life cycle 181, 184, 188
systems 137-48
Aurius 144-5
call centre systems 142-3
Chordiant Retail Channel 140-1
core banking systems *139*, 147-8
Finacle 145
FLEXCUBE *139*, 141-2
Misys Equation 139-40
Siebel Banking Contact Center 142-3
Temenos T24 143-4
systems analysis methods *see* business and systems analysis methods
systems architectural design 148

T

takeovers 9, 39, 40
TARGET 54, 177
technology
new technology paradigm 196-8
role in retail banking 38, 63-4, 137-8, 195
trends 150
telemoney 77
telephone banking 6
terminology 171-8
terrorism 58, 81, 85, 138, 203
testing methods and tools 187
boundary value analysis 187
equivalence partitioning 187
error guessing 187

    Mercury QTP 188
    Mercury Test Director (Quality Centre) 188
    test automation tools 188
    test management tools 188
    user evaluation 187
third-party data 109–11
third-party debt collector 113
third-party solutions, integration with 141
tier one capital 8, *9*
tools 187–8
trade associations 46–9
travel services 30–1
traveller's cheques 30–1, 119
trends in retail banking
    current 53–77
    future 195–204

U

UK Listing Authority (UKLA) 41
unbanked retail market 72
Unity Trust Bank 145
universal banks 8–9, *9*, 38, 195, 196
UNIX 180, 189
up-selling 200
US dollar clearing 178

USA banks 8
USA Patriot Act 203
utility computing 197

V

virtual worlds 73
Visa 28, 41, 42, 67, 68, 69, 121, 122, 178, 211, 214, 215
Voca 51, 55, 211

W

Wall Street Journal, The 46
Web 2.0 13, 60
websites
    financial 210–11
    jobs 212
    recruitment agencies 213
wire services *see* news agencies
wire transfers 133–4

X

XML 47, 144, 165, 189

Z

Zopa 13, 59, 60

Index compiled by Amanda Jones

About the Bizle Professional Series

Bizle is the first of its kind that seeks to bridge the knowledge gap between IT professionals and the business community. Any professional that has worked in IT can attest to the disparity which is plaguing the workplace in terms of the gulf in business knowledge.

IT has to be more business aligned and this is more evident with the increasing dependence by the "business" on it. Application vendors, in investment banking for instance, are surpassing themselves in getting business-critical systems into the market for trading, compliance and risk management only to realise that the in-house IT staff and contractors are not adequately skilled to deploy and maintain these systems.

This situation has to change and quickly too; technology is shaping the operations and reliance on it will be even greater in the longer term.

Bizle publications aim to be at the forefront of these radical changes and there is ongoing effort and research at Essvale Corporation Limited to achieve these goals.

Introducing Bizle.biz

Bizle.biz is the first online portal dedicated to the alignment of IT and business. When fully operational, Bizle will be the reference point for IT students and professionals that want to keep abreast of issues concerning IT and the alignment with the business community. It will also provide answers to "on-the-job" queries that professionals might have during the course of their everyday tasks.

Bizle.biz will have the following features:

- IT jobs adverts partitioned into the industry sectors to allow both candidates and advertisers to tailor their job requirements
- Recommended Books
- Industry News
- 'Ask' support service
- Glossary of Terms
- Forum
- Content in different languages.

Other Titles in the Bizle Professional Series

**Business Knowledge for IT
in Global Investment Banking**

**Business Knowledge for IT
in Private Equity**

**Business Knowledge for IT
in Hedge Funds**

**Business Knowledge for IT
in Prime Brokerage**

**Business Knowledge for IT
in Insurance**

**Business Knowledge for IT
in Private Wealth Management**

These and other exciting titles can be pre-ordered from Amazon sites worldwide or from www.essvale.com

Printed in the United Kingdom
by Lightning Source UK Ltd.
124844UK00001B/65-98/A